PRIMORDIAL MODERNISM

Edinburgh Critical Studies in Modernist Culture
Series Editors: Tim Armstrong and Rebecca Beasley

Available

Modernism and Magic: Experiments with Spiritualism, Theosophy and the Occult
Leigh Wilson

Sonic Modernity: Representing Sound in Literature, Culture and the Arts
Sam Halliday

Modernism and the Frankfurt School
Tyrus Miller

Lesbian Modernism: Censorship, Sexuality and Genre Fiction
Elizabeth English

Modern Print Artefacts: Textual Materiality and Literary Value in British Print Culture, 1890–1930s
Patrick Collier

Cheap Modernism: Expanding Markets, Publishers' Series and the Avant-Garde
Lise Jaillant

Portable Modernisms: The Art of Travelling Light
Emily Ridge

Hieroglyphic Modernisms: Writing and New Media in the Twentieth Century
Jesse Schotter

Modernism, Fiction and Mathematics
Nina Engelhardt

Modernist Life Histories: Biological Theory and the Experimental Bildungsroman
Daniel Aureliano Newman

Modernism, Space and the City: Outsiders and Affect in Paris, Vienna, Berlin, and London
Andrew Thacker

Modernism Edited: Marianne Moore and the Dial *Magazine*
Victoria Bazin

Modernism and Time Machines
Charles Tung

Primordial Modernism: Animals, Ideas, transition *(1927–1938)*
Cathryn Setz

Forthcoming

Slow Modernism
Laura Salisbury

Modernism and the Idea of Everyday Life
Leena Kore-Schröder

Novel Sensations: Modernist Fiction and the Problem of Qualia
Jon Day

Hotel Modernity: Literary Encounters with Corporate Space
Robbie Moore

The Modernist Exoskeleton: Insects, War and Literary Form
Rachel Murray

Modernism and Still Life
Claudia Tobin

www.edinburghuniversitypress.com/series/ecsmc

PRIMORDIAL MODERNISM

Animals, Ideas, *transition* (1927–1938)

Cathryn Setz

EDINBURGH
University Press

Edinburgh University Press is one of the leading university presses in
the UK. We publish academic books and journals in our selected subject
areas across the humanities and social sciences, combining cutting-edge
scholarship with high editorial and production values to produce academic
works of lasting importance. For more information visit our website:
edinburghuniversitypress.com

© Cathryn Setz, 2019, 2021

Edinburgh University Press Ltd
The Tun – Holyrood Road, 12(2f) Jackson's Entry, Edinburgh EH8 8PJ

First published in hardback by Edinburgh University Press 2019

Typeset in 10/12.5 Adobe Sabon by
IDSUK (DataConnection) Ltd

A CIP record for this book is available from the British Library

ISBN 978 0 7486 9217 0 (hardback)
ISBN 978 0 4744 8425 1 (paperback)
ISBN 978 0 7486 9218 7 (webready PDF)
ISBN 978 0 7486 9219 4 (epub)

The right of Cathryn Setz to be identified as the author of this work
has been asserted in accordance with the Copyright, Designs and Patents
Act 1988, and the Copyright and Related Rights Regulations 2003
(SI No. 2498).

CONTENTS

List of Figures vii
Acknowledgements ix
Series Editors' Preface xii

Introduction 1
1 Amoeba: Figures of Abstraction, Surrealist Influence and
   the Revolution of the Word 23
2 Fish: Evolving the Artwork in James Joyce's
   'Shem the Penman' (1927) 55
3 Lizard: Gottfried Benn, 'the "Dark" Side of Modernism'
   and *transition*'s 'Pineal Eye' 92
4 Bird: Editorial Flights with Eugene Jolas 130
Conclusion 167

Bibliography 175
Index 205

How happy are those tiny creatures who
continue in the womb which gave them life.
Happy the gnat: even its nuptial dance
is danced within the womb. Womb is all things.
Look at the birds, at their half-certainty,
who seem to fly with one wing in each world
as if they were the souls escaping from
Etruscan dead . . . from one who shares a box
with his own effigy, at liberty,
reposing on the lid.

[. . .]

And we, we stay spectators; turned towards
all things and still transcending none.
All overwhelms us. We set all in order.
All falls apart. We order it once more
and fall, collapse, disintegrate ourselves.

      Rainer Maria Rilke, 'The eighth elegy' (1923)

FIGURES

I.1 Eugene Jolas et al, 'The Revolution of the Word, PROCLAMATION'. Frontispiece to *transition*, 16/17, July 1929. Reproduced by permission of Betsy Jolas. 4
I.2 Grace Pailthorpe, *Ancestors II, 1935*, ink. Printed in *transition*, 26, 1937. 14
1.1 MoMA exhibition catalogue cover. Alfred Hamilton Barr Jr, *Cubism and Abstract Art*, 1936. Digital image © Museum of Modern Art/Scala Florence, 2014. 24
1.2 *Amoeba proteus*. Illustration of organism before and after reproduction by binary fission, 1924. From Joseph Levy, 'Studies on Reproduction in *Amoeba Proteus*' (1924), 147. © Genetics Society of America. 29
1.3 Yves Tanguy, *Painting* (1928). Reproduced in *transition*, 11, February 1928. © ARS, NY and DACS, London 2018. 32
1.4 Wassily Kandinsky, *Composition, 1937*. Reproduced in *transition*, 27, April–May 1938. 50
2.1 Paul Klee, *Fish-Man; Man-Eater* (1920). Reproduced in *transition*, 18, November 1929. 61
2.2 R. W. Miner, 'The tree of life'. Diagram hanging in the Darwin Hall of the American Museum of Natural History, August 1927. Photograph by H. S. Rice and Irving Dutcher. © Image No. 312029, American Museum of Natural History Library. 65

2.3	Helen Ziska, 'Man's debt to the lower vertebrates'. From William K. Gregory, 'The origin, rise, and decline of *Homo sapiens*', *Scientific Monthly* (1934), 482. © American Association for the Advancement of Science.	67
2.4	Helen Ziska, 'Our face from fish to Man'. Frontispiece to William K. Gregory, *Our Face from Fish to Man*, 1929. © Image No. LS262–16, American Museum of Natural History Library.	68
2.5	'Our face from fish to Man'. Installation in the Biology Hall of the American Museum of Natural History, c. 1932. © Image No. 314251, American Museum of Natural History Library.	69
2.6	'The face from fish to Man'. Installation in the Biology Hall of the American Museum of Natural History, 1949. Photograph by Thane L. Bierwert, August 1949. © Image No. 320564, American Museum of Natural History Library.	69
3.1	'Twilight of the horizontal age'. Editorial in *transition*, 22, February 1933. Reproduced by permission of Betsy Jolas.	106
3.2	F. K. Studnička, 'Schematization of the pineal region in Sphenodon' (1905). Reproduced in Frederick Tilney and Luther Fiske Warren, *The Morphology and Evolutionary Significance of the Pineal Body*, 1919.	110
3.3	Nobumichi Tamura, 'Tuatara skull' (2007). Illustration. © Nobumichi Tamura.	116
3.4	Tuatara (*Sphenodon*; *Hatteria punctata*). Photograph by Andrew McMillan (undated). Reproduced under Creative Commons Licence CC0 1.0 Universal.	117
4.1	André Masson, *Portrait d'Eugene Jolas* (1942). Reproduced by permission. © ADAGP, Paris and DACS, London 2018.	162

ACKNOWLEDGEMENTS

I would first like to thank the various organisations that have funded and facilitated this project: Birkbeck College at the University of London, the Arts and Humanities Research Council, the Royal Merchant Navy Education Foundation, the Arts and Humanities Research Institute at King's College London, the Andrew W. Mellon Foundation, the Oxford Research Centre in the Humanities and the Rothermere American Institute at the University of Oxford. For their invaluable editorship and support, I offer special thanks to Tim Armstrong and Rebecca Beasley; and to my readers at Edinburgh University Press, whose suggestions for revisions greatly improved the book; to Merl Storr for her meticulous copy-editing; and to the publication team, with whom it was a pleasure to work. For reading portions of the drafts, I send heartfelt thanks to James Emmott, Andrew Frayn, Len Gutkin, Orsolya Kiss, Lynn McAlpine, Céline Sabiron, Glyn Salton-Cox, Bernard Vere and Jamie Wood. For their mentorship and guidance, I am hugely grateful to Richard Kirkland, Francis Leneghan, Tyrus Miller, Tara Stubbs and Michael Whitworth.

The composer Betsy Jolas – Maria and Eugene Jolas's daughter – was kind enough to grant me permission to reproduce portions of *transition*'s editorial content. Every effort has been made to contact rights holders and acquire permission to publish quotations. For allowing me to quote passages of prose and verse that appeared in the magazine, I also thank Ian von Franckenstein for a work by Kay Boyle; J. M. Dent & Sons for a poem by Dylan Thomas; New Directions for works by Winifred Bryher and Gottfried Benn; Houghton

ACKNOWLEDGEMENTS

Mifflin Harcourt Publishing Company and the Archibald MacLeish Estate for a poem by Archibald MacLeish; Bob Arnold and the University of California Press for a poem by Lorine Niedecker; Jacques Fraenkel and Editions Gallimard for a poem by Robert Desnos, François Chapon and Flammarion for a poem by Pierre Reverdy; and Wesleyan University Press for a portion of a letter from William Carlos Williams to Louis Zukofsky. Thanks too to the Design and Artists Copyright Society for granting me permission to reproduce works by André Masson and Yves Tanguy, and to Northwestern University Press for kindly supplying a digital scan of Masson's 'Portrait d'Eugene Jolas' (1942). For various biological images I thank the American Association for the Advancement of Science, the Genetics Society of America and the American Museum of Natural History. For granting me the rights to reproduce Grace Pailthorpe's untitled painting for the cover of this book, I send special thanks to James Birch. Thanks too to Stephen Joyce for allowing me to quote a 1933 limerick by James Joyce, written in Versailles.

I have been fortunate to conduct research with the aid of supportive librarians and generous scholars. Thanks especially go to Jay Barksdale at the New York Public Library for granting me access to the Wertheim Study; Alice Weiss and John Moryl at the Hedi Steinberg Library at Yeshiva University, New York; Jane Rawson at the Vere Harmsworth Library in Oxford; Katharine Chandler at the Free Library of Philadelphia for helping me track down a copy of *Rhythmus*; the reading room staff at both the Bodleian and the British Library for allowing me to photograph pages from *transition*; and the librarians at the Beinecke Library at Yale University for their help during my time working with the Maria and Eugene Jolas Papers in 2010. I am especially grateful to Craig Monk for sharing an electronic version of *transition* with me, and to Jason Parks for related material: such a collaborative approach is most encouraging. For their advice and expertise on evolutionary biology, I thank Armand Marie Leroi and Adrian de Froment. For assisting me with some of the German translations, I thank Jason Bryslawskyj of the City University of New York.

This book began in 2008 as my doctoral thesis. I wish to thank the staff at Birkbeck's Department of English and Humanities, and its thriving research community. Special thanks to Joseph Brooker, Steven Connor, Lynne Segal, Susan Wiseman and especially Joanne Winning for her guidance during the study's formative stages. For their input and camaraderie, I thank my fellow Birkbeckians: Mark Blacklock, Dennis Duncan, David Gillott, Sophie Jones, Robert Kiely, Caroline Knighton, Terri Mullholland and Isabelle Zahar. Colleagues in the wider academic community have also contributed to this book through informal discussions at various stages of its development. Special thanks to Iain Bailey, Niamh Campbell, Robin Evans, Gareth Farmer, Matthew Feldman, Peter Fifield, Finn Fordham, Kristin Grogan, Christos Hadjiyiannis, Cleo Hanaway-Oakley, Ben Hickman, J. Matthew Huculak,

Thomas Karshan, Céline Mansanti, Henry Mead, Steven Methven, Sophie Oliver, Elizabeth Pender, Allan Pero, Anna Ross, Brooke Simmons, Matthew Taunton, Erik Tonning, Will Viney, J. T. Welsch and Adam Winstanley.

Numerous friends and relatives have also offered brilliant questions and comments, for which I am forever grateful. In particular I thank Talitha Burgess, Robert Cheshire, Octavia Cox, Victoria Hall, James Hollis, Mark Kanner, Robert Setz, Orly Siow, Sophie Winckel, and especially my mother, Susan Rees. Above all I wish to thank my PhD supervisor, Laura Salisbury, with whom it was an honour to work. The sparks of ignition Laura offered over the years remain an inspiration. It is my overriding hope that this book might extend that energy and focus, as more students and scholars alight upon *transition*'s riches.

SERIES EDITORS' PREFACE

This series of monographs on selected topics in modernism is designed to reflect and extend the range of new work in modernist studies. The studies in the series aim for a breadth of scope and for an expanded sense of the canon of modernism, rather than focusing on individual authors. Literary texts will be considered in terms of contexts including recent cultural histories (modernism and magic; sonic modernity; media studies) and topics of theoretical interest (the everyday; postmodernism; the Frankfurt School); but the series will also reconsider more familiar routes into modernism (modernism and gender; sexuality; politics). The works published will be attentive to the various cultural, intellectual and historical contexts of British, American and European modernisms, and to interdisciplinary possibilities within modernism, including performance and the visual and plastic arts.

Tim Armstrong and Rebecca Beasley

INTRODUCTION

> Perhaps we are seeking God. Perhaps not. It matters little one way or the other. What really matters is that we are on the quest.
>
> Eugene Jolas and Elliot Paul, 'Suggestions for a new magic', June 1927

> The hunger for evasion, which is the symbol of our generation, can find expression in certain definite ways.
>
> Eugene Jolas, 'On the quest', December 1927

In 1917, Eugene Jolas was stationed at Camp Lee, Virginia, having been drafted into the US Medical Corps during the First World War. An unpublished manuscript from this period survives. A discarded draft, it is a short prose poem entitled 'Dementia praecox', a nineteenth-century term for a degenerative cognitive disorder that predates the definition of schizophrenia, or 'schizo-affective disorder' in today's psychiatric discourse. The fragment is telling. Its narrator beholds the 'ascetic' face of Christianity, a visage seen in 'old books' with 'pictures of halo[ed] saints' that now seem flimsy and cheap. Where piety's 'thin lips quiver' with talk of 'Heaven, as if it were a place for old maids and eunuchs', fear and trembling arise elsewhere. In a metaphorical flourish, Jolas turns to an animal. Tiny but powerful, it is a creature that signifies the depths of faith, Western animal totemism, and Jolas's own aesthetic vision. 'I am haunted by dreams of scorpions and ashes', he writes. 'But God,

I think, is deaf, and this frenetic stammering will echo through his lighted halls like a bugle out of tune.'[1]

With this image of scorpions and ashes, Jolas alludes to a unique moment in the Bible: the 'mission of the seventy-two disciples' in the Gospel of Luke. Christ's followers are sent out into the world and warned of the folly of erring from God through vanity. Ashes mark a scene of repentance, of 'sitting in sackcloth and ashes', of turning one's face to God (Luke 10: 13). Five verses on, and with the seventy-two returned, Christ bestows upon his disciples the power to resist evil – to 'tread on serpents and scorpions' (Luke 10: 19), those biblical creatures of Satan. The disciples' scorpion appears as a sign of renounced evil: that which is close to, but unscathed by, the darkness. For Jolas's poetic narrator, though, it is more ambivalent: an animalised image of repentance and faith, uttered in the absence of either. Despite the Catholicism that was close to Jolas's heart for much of his life, these are not lines of piety. The venomous and armoured animal is an emblem of that which steps in when belief has fled. It 'haunts', it is the stuff of dreams – it is a crisis of faith. But even as this arachnid (and the threat of its sting) stands in for a break with God, it is no less readable as a sign of the author's faith in other kinds of ideas. As Jolas would later write in his memoir *Man from Babel*, he was born under Scorpio, the astrological sign of the scorpion, a 'symbol of restless migrations, with its contradictions of geographical, linguistic and psychical change', an animal that has never 'ceased to make itself felt in my life'.[2] Jolas's scorpion offers an imaginative space for a man who is both harrowed by his lost Christian faith, and drawn to magical thinking.[3]

The 'Dementia praecox' fragment also signals Jolas's early exposure to severe mental trauma during the war. Camp Lee was a cantonment for soldiers stationed for training, and during Jolas's time there its population more than quadrupled, from around 14,000 to over 60,000 by the armistice. The experience was a 'searing one' for the young reporter, who contributed to the camp newspaper, *The Bayonet*. America had only recently entered the European conflict, and Jolas observed the periphery of war in the specifically 'linguistic and psychical' terms he applied to the scorpion. Appointed secretary to the chief psychiatrist at the base hospital, he spent his days typing up notes and listening to what he later described as 'fantasies and hallucinations', 'frantic screams' and the 'incessant weeping' of the soldier inpatients. These insights on the 'neuropathic ward' even inspired a series of poems Jolas sent to Louis Untermeyer for appraisal, as the eager poet set about establishing himself in the literary world.[4] Possibly included in that early bundle – and rejected, it seems – these haunting dreams of scorpions and ashes appear at a time of war, and at the beginning of what was to become Jolas's career as one of the most important figures of early twentieth-century Anglo-European literary history. For, a decade after this creaturely gesture, Jolas – an Alsace-Lorrainian, trilingual, French-American

INTRODUCTION

journalist-poet – became the main editor of *transition* (1927–38). His scorpion offers a clue.

'CRUDE WORDS, VOLUPTUOUS WORDS, OCCULT WORDS'

For many years, *transition* remained oddly overlooked, languishing in obscurity in spite of its major significance in modernist culture. This was largely because some of modernism's 'high priests' had offered less than supportive commentary. Ezra Pound called it 'amateur', T. S. Eliot liked to tease it for its earnest protestations and Gertrude Stein once claimed to have effectively started it – a falsehood that was later exposed.[5] But with its wilfully lower-case 't' and its smart visual resemblance to contemporary French journals such as *Commerce* and Georges Bataille's *Documents*, *transition* was more than the sum of its modernist parts. Based in Paris (and later in The Hague and New York), the expatriate American title was founded in the wake of Ford Madox Ford's *transatlantic review*, and it continued after the final issues of both Scofield Thayer's *The Dial* (edited, at its end, by Marianne Moore) and Margaret Anderson and Jane Heap's *The Little Review*. Jolas was the driving force, with an editorial cabal that included *inter alia* Elliot Paul, Stuart Gilbert, Robert Sage and James Johnson Sweeney, as well as the silent partnership and paramount editorial support of Maria Jolas, whose brilliant translations were often unsigned and whose name, at her request, was absent from the masthead. Its mission was partly to house James Joyce's ongoing post-*Ulysses* work, which became the seriatim publication of the 'Work in progress' that was eventually *Finnegans Wake* (1939). It was also founded on the principle of translating Surrealist, Expressionist, Dadaist and other experimental European texts into English for its primarily American readership, often for the first (and sometimes only) time.

Throughout its life, *transition* also became the vehicle for Jolas's quest to seek the 'Revolution of the Word' alluded to in the title of its most famous (and widely anthologised) manifesto (Figure I.1), which somewhat snootily declared: 'THE PLAIN READER BE DAMNED'.[6] Buoyed by his formative friendship with Henri Solveen and the *Arc* circle, Jolas believed passionately in the idea of a cultural 'bridge' between Europe and America; he heralded an international, multilingual future in which language itself would become what he and a group of *transition* authors, in a second manifesto entitled 'Poetry is vertical', came to call a 'mantic instrument'.[7] As well as new material from Joyce, Stein, Hart Crane, Samuel Beckett, Djuna Barnes, Kay Boyle and many other anglophone authors, *transition* introduced its readers to exclusive translations and reproductions of works by European figures such as Antonin Artaud, Alfred Döblin, Max Ernst, Franz Kafka, Yves Tanguy and many more.[8] With its small run, limited circulation and private funding, *transition* nonetheless managed to become the largest and one of the longest-running of the 'little magazines' of

PROCLAMATION

TIRED OF THE SPECTACLE OF SHORT STORIES, NOVELS, POEMS AND PLAYS STILL UNDER THE HEGEMONY OF THE BANAL WORD, MONOTONOUS SYNTAX, STATIC PSYCHOLOGY, DESCRIPTIVE NATURALISM, AND DESIROUS OF CRYSTALLIZING A VIEWPOINT...

WE HEREBY DECLARE THAT:

1. THE REVOLUTION IN THE ENGLISH LANGUAGE IS AN ACCOMPLISHED FACT.

2. THE IMAGINATION IN SEARCH OF A FABULOUS WORLD IS AUTONOMOUS AND UNCONFINED.
   (*Prudence is a rich, ugly old maid courted by Incapacity*... Blake)

3. PURE POETRY IS A LYRICAL ABSOLUTE THAT SEEKS AN A PRIORI REALITY WITHIN OURSELVES ALONE.
   (*Bring out number, weight and measure in a year of dearth*... Blake)

4. NARRATIVE IS NOT MERE ANECDOTE, BUT THE PROJECTION OF A METAMORPHOSIS OF REALITY.
   (*Enough! Or Too Much!*... Blake)

5. THE EXPRESSION OF THESE CONCEPTS CAN BE ACHIEVED ONLY THROUGH THE RHYTHMIC " HALLUCINATION OF THE WORD ". (Rimbaud).

6. THE LITERARY CREATOR HAS THE RIGHT TO DISINTEGRATE THE PRIMAL MATTER OF WORDS IMPOSED ON HIM BY TEXT-BOOKS AND DICTIONARIES.
   (*The road of excess leads to the palace of Wisdom*... Blake)

7. HE HAS THE RIGHT TO USE WORDS OF HIS OWN FASHIONING AND TO DISREGARD EXISTING GRAMMATICAL AND SYNTACTICAL LAWS.
   (*The tigers of wrath are wiser than the horses of instruction*... Blake)

8. THE " LITANY OF WORDS " IS ADMITTED AS AN INDEPENDENT UNIT.

9. WE ARE NOT CONCERNED WITH THE PROPAGATION OF SOCIOLOGICAL IDEAS, EXCEPT TO EMANCIPATE THE CREATIVE ELEMENTS FROM THE PRESENT IDEOLOGY.

10. TIME IS A TYRANNY TO BE ABOLISHED.

11. THE WRITER EXPRESSES. HE DOES NOT COMMUNICATE.

12. THE PLAIN READER BE DAMNED.
    (*Damn braces! Bless relaxes!*... Blake)

— Signed: KAY BOYLE, WHIT BURNETT, HART CRANE, CARESSE CROSBY, HARRY CROSBY, MARTHA FOLEY, STUART GILBERT, A. L. GILLESPIE, LEIGH HOFFMAN, EUGENE JOLAS, ELLIOT PAUL, DOUGLAS RIGBY, THEO RUTRA, ROBERT SAGE, HAROLD J. SALEMSON, LAURENCE VAIL.

Figure 1.1 Eugene Jolas et al., 'The Revolution of the Word, PROCLAMATION'. Frontispiece to *transition*, 16/17, July 1929. Reproduced by permission of Betsy Jolas

the interwar period. During its eleven years it produced twenty-seven issues, gathered around 450 contributors and printed over 4,000 pages. The 'man from Babel' at the helm believed for longer than most in the lasting power of 'the Word' to overcome the perceived 'malady of language' and its utilitarian forms – whether soulless reportage, the machine age or desiccated realism – with the power of new and inventive language.[9] 'What interested me most was the variety of American speech that I heard about me', Jolas recollects of his immigration to America from his native Alsace-Lorraine. 'Words form the workers' universe' or 'that of small towns'. 'Profane words, crude words, voluptuous words, occult words, concrete words': 'a scintillating assemblage of phonetic novelties that enlarged my vision'.[10]

But beyond describing *transition*'s roll call of names and programmatic intent, how can we actually read it? The study of modernist magazines has made significant inroads into what might at first appear an unwieldy undertaking. Recent scholarship has shown not only the importance and range of print culture as integral to our understanding of literary modernism, but also the ways in which students and scholars might access, search and understand periodicals directly. Thanks to expanded coverage by resources such as ProQuest, and to extensive projects designed to establish and disseminate the magazine archive – such as the Modernist Journals Project at Brown University and the University of Tulsa, the Blue Mountain Project at Princeton University, and the online repository Monoskop – it is now possible to read a growing number of journals online, from a two-issue title such as Wyndham Lewis's 1914–15 *BLAST* to *The Listener*, a generalist periodical designed as a companion to BBC radio broadcasts.[11] A burgeoning field of research has begun work on the economic understanding of journals as commodity culture, for instance, or on bibliographic and biographical questions pertaining to a title's editorial formation. Magazine studies has a more globalised, transnational scope than ever before, with a hopeful future as the digital humanities continue to develop interactive, open-access reading experiences. Between 2009 and 2012, Peter Brooker and Andrew Thacker's *Oxford Critical and Cultural History of Modernist Magazines* gathered invaluable essays on a wide range of little magazines from the late nineteenth and early twentieth centuries, and Penn State University Press's *Journal of Modern Periodical Studies*, founded in 2010, continues to widen the field.[12]

Accounts of *transition*'s unique contribution to literary culture have been slower to emerge than studies of its more compact cousins, such as Joseph Kling's *The Pagan* or Harold Loeb and Alfred Kreymborg's *Broom*. Apart from Dougald McMillan's groundbreaking monograph in the mid-1970s, the posthumous publication of *Man from Babel* by editors Andreas Kramer and Rainer Rumold in 1998, and the release of Maria Jolas's memoir by Mary Ann Caws in 2004, for many years most mentions of *transition* were limited to gossipy

Left Bank nostalgia, or a Joycean's footnote.[13] Developments in the late 1990s and into the 2000s made fresh strides in bringing the journal to the attention of a new generation of readers, however. Pioneering work from several scholars has identified significant aspects of the magazine: Marjorie Perloff, Jean-Michel Rabaté, Michael North and Craig Monk respectively discuss its multilingual poetics inspired by Joyce, Jolas's 'Babelist' idealism, *transition*'s presentation of cinema and other visual media, and its engagement with a mode of modernist autobiography.[14]

In 2009 a team of scholars led by Klaus H. Kiefer and Rainer Rumold released an edition of Jolas's 1924–51 critical writings, offering new insight into the editor's earlier career as a journalist, as well as his work with the Office of War Information from 1942 onwards. The year 2009 also saw the publication of Céline Mansanti's *La revue transition, 1927–1938, le modernisme historique en devenir*, only the second *transition* monograph, and a useful accompaniment to McMillan's more biographical account. Mansanti locates *transition* as a cultural object 'between modernisms': between the historical modernism of its predecessors (such as Eliot's *The Criterion* and Pound's *The Exile*) and the political avant-gardism of its successors (such as the *New Masses* and the *Partisan Review*).[15] Along with two doctoral theses (by Lori Cole in 2012 and Jason Parks in 2016) that both put Jolas's project centre stage, the 2010s saw a new wave of scholarship bring *transition* firmly into wider modernist studies. Juliette Taylor-Batty has explored the creolisation of language as an aesthetic vision, with a special focus on Jolas; Leigh Wilson has offered an account of magic and occult thinking during the period, in which *transition* was prominent; Eugenia Kelbert has produced insightful readings of Jolas's unpublished archival poetry; David Allen Hatch has contributed a useful overview of the magazine's distinct phases; and Delphine Grass has mobilised philosophical and political contexts via Jacques Derrida and Hannah Arendt, uncovering further nuances in Jolas's multilingualism.[16]

Jolas's journal has also informed new studies of European avant-garde culture, specifically in Rumold's major 2015 study, *Archaeologies of Modernity: Avant-Garde Bildung*. Rumold locates *transition* in a constellation of French and German artistic movements, specifically in its extreme divergence from *Documents* and in the multifaceted writings of Carl Einstein, who appeared in both publications. Although he rightly underlines the oddly conservative nature of the magazine's universalist vision as a Eurocentric, even colonialist venture, Rumold identifies Jolas's 'starry-eyed idealism' as central to our understanding of the intellectual and artistic climate of the crisis years of the late 1920s and early 1930s, and he explores *transition*'s 'heavy load' of philosophical and mythological claims for modernity. His theoretical account is an essential approach to Jolas's ultimately anti-fascist endeavours, albeit via the editor's frequently esoteric articulations of the 'mantic instrument' of 'the Word'. Situated between Mansanti's 'high' or 'historical' modernism and Tyrus Miller's framing of 'late' modernist formations, *transition* has started to gain critical traction in this new wave of research as absolutely essential to our understanding of modernist culture: as the title that is, in Jane Goldman's words, 'possibly the most important and influential little magazine of the period'.[17] Indeed, so capacious was *transition* as a document of modernist culture that we need to find ways of reading that can make space for its cacophony of divergent voices. It is 'like random shooting', as William Carlos Williams once described it: 'perhaps that's the way it should be, loose, unconfined'.[18]

In light of such research, this book begins with a thought experiment inspired by Jolas's wartime dream of the scorpion. What if we were to read a modernist journal as if it were a novel, or even a person? Reviewing the scholarly field, Evan Kindley asserts that 'it makes sense to think of magazines as characters: like people, they have friends, enemies, social characteristics and guiding motivations (however quixotic)'.[19] Few titles are more quixotic than *transition*: Jolas's faith in the metaphysical power of 'the Word' was often so idealistic that it jarred with the contents. Such idealism even led to a certain suspicion of the journal among its detractors. In 1978, Michael Finney judged the Revolution of the Word to have been no more than a 'frivolity' – mere 'silliness' and 'shrill voices'.[20] Finney inherited this critique from *transition*'s more politicised contemporary opponents. Writing in the *New Masses* in 1932, for instance, Philip Rahv rejected *transition* as a fashionable indulgence of the expatriate literati, 'the proper end-phenomena of a dying class'. This was a slur Michael Gold, the *New Masses*' editor, had pre-empted in an earlier piece denouncing *transition* authors as 'silly snobs' who 'believe in nothing but the empiric sensation, or the undisciplined chaos of the subconscious'.[21] Although Rahv and Gold were right to identify *transition*'s apolitical ethos, they missed something crucial. When one reads *transition* as if it were a person, certain patterns emerge. As Mansanti, Rumold and others have shown, the magazine was recognisably preoccupied with journalistic and populist versions of Carl Gustav Jung's theory of the collective unconscious: archetypes that form the 'primal matter' of the psyche, to echo the words of the 'Proclamation'. Other recurring themes included Christian mysticism and liturgical forms of secular verse and poetry, reflections on the night, psychiatric disturbance, the 'malady of language' and a neo-romantic notion of poetry as 'vertical'. But one theme in particular remains unaccounted for, an extension of what Mansanti identifies as a definitive characteristic of *transition*'s modernism as 'the "soft", and organic': *transition* is full of animals.[22]

From the unspecified *Ungeziefer* or 'unclean animal' (the word denotes both insect and vermin) of Kafka's *Die Verwandlung* ('Metamorphosis') to the shells, fighting fish and trapped birds of André Masson's canvases, an enormity of symbolic creatures can be found across *transition*'s pages.[23] Sometimes these figural animals reveal lines of influence between authors and artists. Sometimes a particular instance throws a series of works into relief. But one thing seems clear: these are not farmyard animals or 'man's best friends'. One does not find a preponderance of dogs or cats or pigs or horses or other mammalian beasts. One finds jellyfish and spiders, praying mantises and vermin, amphibians and fossils.[24] They are the creatures furthest from us: so many *Ungeziefer* that appear to say something about the process by which language might make meaning within a national – and international – modernity. To begin this exploration, I refer to three authors published early in *transition*'s 1927–38 run.[25] All are Europeans, published belatedly in translation. All employ animal gestures in the form or content of their work, and all are representatives of Surrealism, Expressionism or Dada – the three foremost art movements of the early twentieth century, which *transition* was committed to transmitting across the Atlantic. Three creatures, then: an insect, an iguana, and a rasping tick. I begin this study with each.

In June 1927, Jolas and Paul printed the Dadaist artist Kurt Schwitters's poem 'priimiitittiii'. The opening eight lines are like a metronome and a list:

> priimiitittiii   tisch
> tesch
> priimiitittiii   tesch
> tusch
> priimiitittiii   tischa
> tescho
> priimiitittiii   tescho
> tuschi[26]

Schwitters's sound poem plays with the word 'primitive', elongated yet staccato and repeated through the text. Alongside it are 'ticks' or 'tisch' – an Old German root word for a table or plate – and 'tusch', which brings in a Swedish word meaning 'marker' as well as two German meanings: India ink or 'to flourish'. On the poem goes, its metre splicing that 'priimiitittiii' into so many dots on the page, with so many 't's and 'shhh's in the air. If this is a grammar exercise, the implicit perfect verb 'to tick' is split between the sound of 'primitive' and the sound of 'ticks', both metronomical and creaturely. Words are like stridulation, the rasping or singing of a cricket. The form also creates a space between languages, an interstitial, percussive play of words that are as animal and organic as they are 'inky' and written.

In the previous month's issue, the editors included an extract from *Les dessous d'une vie, ou la pyramide humaine* (The Underside of Life, or the Human Pyramid), a 1926 novel by the Surrealist Paul Éluard. Here the reader encounters an explicitly entomological image. Appearing under the title 'In company

(Surrealist text)', Éluard's animal is more figural than formal – indicative of an alienated narrative voice:

> All this lives: this patient insect body, this loving bird body, this loyal mammiferous body, and this lean and vain body of the beast of my childhood, all this lives. Only its head has died. I had to kill it. My face understands me no longer. And there are no others.[27]

Éluard's narrative culminates in this image of four living animal bodies capped by a moribund, ex-rational head, reversing the anthropocentric order of the human thinking subject. Despite their status as outposts of corporeality, the text internalises 'insect', 'bird' and 'beast'. These creatures are at a figurative distance from the 'mammiferous' or breasted bodies of viviparous and milk-producing animals, including humans. On the other side of this taxonomical border are all the 'lower' vertebrates: the animals furthest from humans in an evolutionary sense. They evoke earlier stages in the tree of life, or even the origins of life itself. In this text the living body is brain dead, or deadheaded, in a way that signals psychical trauma and would certainly belong to a parallel history of Surrealism's engagement with psychoanalysis. But I begin with these outposts of corporeality for their markedly animal shapes – a wider thematic that is worthy of its own focus.[28]

In June 1929, *transition* printed another textual animal. Although Carl Einstein's novel *Bebuquin* was published in 1912 in Germany and the extract is dated 1905–8, the translation of this Expressionist writer is significant. In this bar scene in particular, a broad reflection on modernity and the idea of the 'alogical' includes reference to a chameleon:

> 'Who is the father?' the barman yelled [. . .]
> 'Nobody', Euphemia looked with circularly expanded eyes.
> 'I had him in a dream.' [. . .]
> 'But didn't your embryo write a philosophic work and make his doctorate in obstetrics? Isn't the story entitled: the cutting of the navel-cord or the *principium individuationis*?' 'Yes,' Euphemia whispered, 'he has renounced the world, he is becoming spiritual, without desires, unclean and silent. Besides, he has a sensitive skin which constantly changes color. Isn't it possible to use him as a transparent advertising sign? We would save colored lamps.'
> 'The a-logical grows, the a-logical is victorious, he will not be led astray.'
> Bebuquin was balancing himself on the rickety bar-chair.
> 'That, dear ladies, is the reason so many are going crazy. We lack fictions, positivism is ruining us.'

The bar-maid was kneeling in rapture between the champagne coolers.
'We conceive too materially, sir.' [. . .]
Bebuquin threw himself at Euphemia's nose and embraced her passionately at the same time. [. . .]
'We need a deluge.'[29]

Einstein parodies the 'alogical' as another version of religion by echoing the liturgical sounds of the *Missale Romanum*: Christ has died, Christ has risen, Christ will come again, following the language of medicine and birth. This invokes what became better known as the Jungian concept of individuation, the *principum individuationis* or emergence of a personality.[30] The characters talk not of a singular life, but of a cultural desire for the exotic – for everything that is outside the ruin of the exclusively positivist understanding of the world, but which is nonetheless 'unclean and silent', fundamentally animal. Euphemia refers to her child's sensitivity as if he were a chameleon. The iguana that changes colour is often used to describe a social wallflower, a follower – a person who blends in, rather than stands out. But soon after Euphemia's call for change in how we 'conceive', along with her joke about capitalism, Einstein's protagonist becomes incensed. '"We no longer sacrifice," Bebuquin screamed into the street, "the sublime is being lost. You criticise the miracle, the miracle has sense only when it is real, but you have destroyed all the forces which go beyond the human element."'[31] Widely regarded as the first piece of Expressionist prose, *Bebuquin* contains powerful imagery that hovers around an animal figure – an animal figure similar to Éluard's in that it expresses a commentary upon a modern affliction of consciousness. The alternative imperative in the barmaid's line confirms this. 'We conceive too materially' implies a mode of thought that is somehow different, somehow more alive. 'We need a deluge' also anticipates a feature of Jolas's mission: a 'mots-déluge' of words capable of aesthetic renewal.[32]

These examples are significant not only for their distinctive features, but also for their influence on the magazine itself. Where Schwitters's formal and aurally experimental work plays with an interlinguistic space (and a potentially entomological effect), Éluard's concern is to convey a consciousness split into the constituent parts of mammal, bird and insect. Einstein's Expressionist prose touches upon a chameleon that has been cast amid excessive drinking and loquacious demands to 'let us kill reason', as Bebuquin finally declares.[33] The present study begins by suggesting that we follow the shared quality among these early examples: the primordial, animal gesture.

'Word and image-less'

The word 'primordial' has several resonances: Jungian psychoanalysis, nationalism theory and biocentric primitivism. The *Oxford English Dictionary* defines it as 'of, relating to, or existing from the very beginning of time; earliest in time; primeval, primitive; (more generally) ancient' and 'distant in time'. Borrowing from Swiss historian Jacob Christoph Burckhardt's term *Urbild* or 'archetype' – which in turn is derived from the morphological idealism of *Naturphilosophie* (and from Goethe) – Jung developed his theory of archetypes in 1919, revising it throughout the rest of his career. Jung's emphasis on the 'primordial image' – a loose translation of *Urbild* – indicates mythic structures or form-finding instincts in human experiences and relationships. It is also part of his wider and well-documented break with Sigmund Freud over the nature of infantile sexuality and incest.[34] Jolas was clearly influenced by aspects of Jung's thought. In 1930, he secured exclusive English publication of 'Psychology and poetry', an essay in which Jung theorises a 'visionary' (as opposed to 'psychological') mode of art via the 'primordial' (as R. F. C. Hull translates it) or 'primal experience' (as Jolas translates it).[35]

> The primal experience is word and image-less, for it is a vision in 'the dark mirror'. [. . .] It is like a whirlwind carrying everything upward and thus gaining visible form. [. . .] The poet needs a refractory and contradictory form of expression to conjure the terrific paradoxicalness of this vision with approximate validity.[36]

First and foremost, Jolas was a journalist, skilled at synthesising a wide range of intellectual fields. The reader will find not only various invocations of the collective unconscious, but also sound bites and epigraphs from, among others, Henri Bergson, Friedrich Nietzsche and the anthropologist Lucien Lévy-Bruhl. Jung's appearance in *transition* is important, but it is also part of a wider editorial fascination with 'primal experience' in relation to the shapes and sounds of words, and with what Rumold describes as a 'cerebral expression of man and the primordial image'.[37]

A more recent use of the term 'primordialism' can be found in history and the social sciences. In his study of the political history of fascism in the early twentieth century, Roger Griffin conceptualises an imagined and regenerated 'nomos' – an aspired-to and cohesive cosmology and community – in the face of supposed corruption after the First World War.[38] Drawing on Andrew D. Smith's landmark study *Theories of Nationalism*, Griffin analyses this 'nomos' as a 'primordialist' urge traceable in the fantasy of cultural rebirth that was integral to Nazi ideology.[39] Jolas would not have known it, but the earliest histories to explore this 'primordialist' nationalism appeared during his lifetime, in 1931 and 1944, from C. Hayes and Hans Kohn respectively.[40] These early historians paved the way for a distinction between 'primordialist' and 'modernist' nationalism – a belief in 'natural' or ineffable identity versus definitions cognisant of post-industrial factors and economic, social and cultural transformation. Griffin goes a step further, combining the terms to refer to a fascism that emerged from 'liminoidality' and that desired 'mazeway' leaders for a better future for the state – a fantasy of cultural and national transition. For Griffin, this historical modernism saw primordialism as a 'behavioural syndrome' – a phenomenon in which the 'nomic drought' was 'slaked'.[41] Since the term 'primordialist' (as opposed to 'modernist') nationalism was not explicitly defined until 1957, I will register the discursive context only indirectly.[42] Informed by Griffin's work, I nevertheless depart from it somewhat by allowing *transition*'s animal representations to guide my analysis, rather than by simply applying the socio-economic concept of primordialist nationalism per se. After all, *transition* requires a prior engagement with what I wish to highlight as primordialist aesthetics *qua* linguistic and formal innovation – although, as Chapter 3 will reveal, the magazine did participate in a problematic 'nomos' through its persistent search for a new mythos.

Another iteration of the term 'primordial' appears in the magazine's particular fascination with primitivism. Artists and writers often engaged with such objects as African masks and prehistoric stones, and with what Jolas termed the 'metanthropological crisis' in 1932, along with ethnographic content from such figures as Leo Frobenius and Carola Giedion-Welcker, frequent quotations from Lévy-Bruhl, and contributions from Michel Leiris that Rumold reads as staging 'primordial battles'.[43] Jolas's project was therefore a major player in modernist appropriations – and disavowals – of what David Richards calls the 'imperialist discursive construct' of the primitive. Early twentieth-century excitement over the exotic 'other' stripped non-Western subjects of their history and agency completely, in the service of self-perpetuating claims to affinity between imagined paradisal or mystical societies and Eurocentric breaks from the urban capitalist world view. Such fetishism, as Richards explains, goes to the heart of much modernist myth-making in both art and literature – from Pablo Picasso's rendering of Iberian stone heads to Roger Fry's art criticism in *Vision and Design* (1920) – which was nigh on social Darwinist in its colonial attitude, with a wide array of writers including Eliot and D. H. Lawrence perpetuating the imperial utilisation of the homogenised subaltern. Yet the picture is more complex. The Surrealists were acutely aware of colonialist endeavours, and they mounted resistant exhibitions and parodies of contemporary anthropology.[44] Given the sheer scale and heterogeneity of *transition*'s content, a committed study of its ethnographic material (whether as appropriation or refutation) exceeds the scope of the present study. Instead, I am interested in the primordial gesture as a tributary of broader primitivist culture, specifically in animal writing.

As such, the primitivism I am exploring in this study is closer to the 'organic' theme Mansanti identifies in her reading, and it prompts attention to contemporary scientific discourse, which will inform my methodological approach in the middle chapters of this book.⁴⁵ The 1920s saw seismic shifts in biological understandings of the origins of life on earth. In 1924, the Russian biochemist Alexander Oparin established his 'primordial soup' theory, with a similar hypothesis appearing independently towards the end of the decade from the British geneticist J. B. S. Haldane. Developed and revisited later in the century, Oparin's theory postulated that the conditions for the origin of life on earth began as a slowly evolving, 'soupy' chemical environment within the ocean, leading eventually to polymers and other structures essential to the earliest forms of algae.⁴⁶

The primordial soup or 'ooze' is a traceable entity in *transition*, inviting further thought. 'From the baking and caking ooze', reads a line from a Charles Recht poem, subtitled 'Reconciling evolution',

> pebble and mire,
> To build bigger and better hard mud empire.

Descriptions of art as submerged and in need of excavation also invoked the 'primordial'. In 'The road through the word', Friedrich Marcus Huebner writes of the 'primordial purpose' of poetry to 'suggest' not the 'manifest element in man', but 'the hidden one'. Writing about the Hindu faith and the nature of language, Raja Rao describes words as 'aggregate electrons of Primordial Force, for force produces movement, movement vibration, and vibration sound'. As we will see in Chapter 1, the 'protoplasmic whole' offers Dorothy Boillotat repose, while in Chapter 3 'the Palaeozoic ooze' serves Henry Miller in a story about visual art.⁴⁷ One of the most striking examples of a primordial creaturely gesture comes from one of *transition*'s visual works: the British Surrealist Grace Pailthorpe's ink sketch *Ancestors II, 1935* (Figure I.2). Composed using the psychoanalyst-artist's method of 'graphic automatism', *Ancestors II* is an attempt to portray what Michael Remy describes as the 'authors of those enigmas we cannot solve because they are part of, and they inspire, our own interior transformations'. The image is full of the orifices and protuberances of psychoanalytic visual iconography, but with a distinctly animal emphasis.⁴⁸ The shapes suggest mouths, noses, internal organs – even canines and apes. But the longer one looks, the more emerges. Fossils, shells, fins, anemones and sand dunes offset the sketch's more 'red-blooded' visual clues. As Wendy Williams and Linda Wheeler put it, describing the critical field of animal studies, there is an 'animal part' here that demands attention.⁴⁹ Jungian mythic structures of the psyche, semi-primitivist art discourse and the detectable sounds of science all emerge as productive lines of enquiry. As Jolas himself wrote after temporarily suspending the magazine in 1930, *transition* sought 'a sense of the fabulous in terms of the Twentieth Century'.⁵⁰ This 'fabulous', I suggest, is distinctly animal.

Figure I.2 Grace Pailthorpe, *Ancestors II*, 1935, ink. Printed in *transition*, 26, 1937

Studies of literary modernism and the animal are therefore a vital framework. One of the earliest and most important studies in this field is Margot Norris's groundbreaking *Beasts of the Modern Imagination* (1985). Norris offers an intellectual history of what she terms 'the biocentric tradition', from Darwin to Nietzsche, Kafka, Ernst and Lawrence. Broadly opposed to anthropocentrism – the measure of humanity in all things – Norris's artists shared a post-Darwinian articulation of 'disanthropic and misanthropic' non-human expression, specifically in the 'self-reflexive animal metaphor'. Inheriting the revolutionary perception of form in nature from Darwin, they were united in an anti-idealist, anti-metaphysical vision of the world. With an inbuilt hostility towards mimesis itself, she argues, the biocentric tradition was all but over after the 1930s, with the advent of the Second World War. Norris reads the history of the Third Reich, with its appropriations of both Darwin and Nietzsche, as a falsification of biocentric thought, which was itself an 'affirmation of the animal', forever open to its own reanthropomorphisation, to its own destruction via the cultish notions of 'physical prowess, racial destiny, and genetic constitution'. Prior to this extinguished biocentrism, artists such as Ernst worked with creaturely figurations as 'biological possibility' and 'biocentric performance'. Following the beasts in her canon of modernism leads Norris to a confrontation with her own 'utter naïveté about the vexed and oxymoronic nature' of the term 'animal imagery'. I share this problematic. The animals in *transition* are totemic, serviceable: freighted symbols rather than textually fortified agents. It is true that some artists' animals reveal an anti-anthropocentric sensibility, but to suggest that this is characteristic of the magazine would be a misleading reduction. Instead, I follow Norris's lead when she posits that 'the biocentric vision speaks with no strictly homogenous voice, and everyone will hear a different call in the wild cry of the beasts of the modern imagination'.[51]

A subsequent definition of biocentrism by Oliver A. I. Botar offers a helpful extension of Norris's work, and gets us closer to the experimental art and writing in *transition* that the present study takes up. Botar highlights a late nineteenth- and early twentieth-century biocentrism that was rooted in a neo-romantic tradition reactive to the materialism and 'excessive' positivism of contemporary science. As an 'open intersection of discourses', biologistic cultural expressions drew from the *Lebensphilosophie* (life philosophy) most forcibly present in the work of Nietzsche, Georg Simmel and others: a heterogenous body of thought that was preoccupied with teleological concepts of growth force or holism, and that in biology included the resurgence of Jean-Baptiste Lamarck's belief in inherited evolutionary characteristics and linear, progressive species development. Botar helpfully breaks down this philosophical and biological paradigm shift into a typology of organicism, moving on to the extremely influential work of Ludwig Klages, who sought – although he was anti-Semitic – to debunk the ennobling notion of *Geist* that directly fed into the biologism of 'blood and soil' in Nazi ideology. Like Norris, Botar is at pains to point out the intellectual malleability of biocentrism as a concept that fuelled political anarchism and socialism on the left just as much as cultural nihilism on the right. The lasting feature of this disparate tradition lies in the anti-anthropocentric *Weltanschauung* (world view) that is present to a degree across the diversity of its adherents.[52]

I am also indebted to the wider field of animal studies – driven by pioneering scholarship from Steve Baker, Cary Wolfe, Jacques Derrida, Giorgio Agamben, Gilles Deleuze, Félix Guattari, Steve Connor, Matthew Calarco and others – which crosses disciplines in its quest to interrogate speciesism, the ethics of the other, agency, subjectivity and consciousness across the abyssal human–animal border, in order to critique human sovereignty.[53] Critics have largely focused on animals that are subjected to our systematic cruelty: the beasts enslaved in intensive farming, used in experiments or barbarically tortured and killed in abattoirs. Philip Armstrong and Carrie Rohman have joined the conversation with explorations of modernist literature in terms of 'structures of feeling' at odds with Western, post-Enlightenment rationalism that explore the radical alterity of the animal and the twentieth-century 'eruption of linguistic convention', tracing, as Rohman puts it, a 'reckoning with the animal'.[54] Informed by these theoretical approaches, I wish to extend Tim Armstrong's insight – that animals vanish from modern life with the rise of the metropolis, and that modernism offers a mournful reflection on that loss – and focus on the anthropomorphic, non-mammalian weave of much of the writing under investigation.[55] Texts that project human meaning onto the animal are still forms of animal writing. The tradition of the fable, which folds the animal kingdom into a typology of human error, pride and folly, is still capable of profoundly anti-humanist insight, as Gregor Samsa in Kafka's story – a powerful meditation on modern sickness and compassion fatigue – so amply demonstrates.

Primordial Modernism

This book focuses on just four primordial creatures, following the metaphors through *transition*'s four most significant contexts: the amoeba and the influence of Surrealism; the fish and Joyce's ichthyological, evolutionary play; the lizard and *transition*'s proximity to a questionable, regressive side of modernism in the work of Gottfried Benn; and the bird and the essential romanticism of Jolas's editorial and poetic vision at the heart of the magazine. *Transition* did more than any other magazine of the interwar period to introduce French Surrealism, its immediate artistic neighbour, to an American audience. There was so much Surrealism in *transition*, in fact, that it became known erroneously in the press as the *American Surrealist Review*, much to Jolas's chagrin. By 1933 Jolas publicly disavowed the movement, stating that 'the impulse of the revolution of the word owes its genesis to such precursors as Arthur Rimbaud, James Joyce, the Futurists, the early Zürich Dadaists, certain experiments of Gertrude Stein's, and Léon-Paul Fargue. It owes nothing to Surrealism'.[56] Yet in 'Literature and the new man', an editorial published just a few years earlier, Jolas had defined his project as a response to Surrealism. Here he 'differs' from the Surrealists' 'definition of reality' but concedes that 'they were the only ones to recognise the importance of the explorations into the subconscious world'. Echoing the 'Proclamation', which was itself partially derived from André Breton's 1924 treatise 'Introduction au discours sur le peu de réalité', Jolas's logic is therefore fairly fluid, in need of explication via his artists and writers.[57]

Exhibiting an organic holism that David Bennett has analysed as central to the magazine's Jungian orientation, Jolas writes that the 'creator' or poet 'find[s] the bridge between the primal and the objective worlds' and 'consciously fuse[s] his discoveries into an organic whole'.[58] This is a vital component, and it finds form across the journal through one animal metaphor in particular: the amoeba. The protozoic single-celled organism can be found across modern art, but in this case it helps us understand *transition*'s character. Metaphors and images of these blob-like and earliest life forms come up through Surrealism as figures for abstraction itself. In *transition* they also bring up questions of the nationalist aspects of anglophone responses to the French movement, which in turn take us to contemporary accusations that the magazine was stale or out of date. In July 1936, for instance, looking back over *transition*'s development, Edward Alden Jewell defined its activities as 'a sort of eager hashing and re-vamping of the avant-garde mumbo-jumbo sovereign in elite circles ten or fifteen years back'.[59] In the face of such a charge, I will begin at the end of *transition*'s life, with its relationship to a modernism ossified in the Museum of Modern Art in New York. This was a moment in *transition*'s history that included a good deal of such 'hashing and re-vamping' but also had an uncharted aliveness – an element of what I tentatively call an 'amoebic mode', or animalised abstraction.

Turning towards contemporary biologism and a further question of the signifying animal, Chapter 2 considers *transition*'s most famous serialisation: Joyce's 'Work in progress'. The journal was known informally as *la maison du Joyce*, with almost every issue containing a new instalment alongside glossaries, essays and homages to this extraordinary text.[60] Here I address the 'Shem the Penman' episode, published in October 1927. Joyce's 'apology and his boast', 'Shem' offers a self-reflexive figure of the artist.[61] He is also a fish, and a stinking one. How does the fish help us understand Joyce's satirical and expressly biological usage of received ideas about degeneracy, specifically in relation to the writing process? Evolutionary biology during the years when Joyce was drafting and publishing 'Shem' was fraught with contradictions and obsolescent theories, and, as I will argue, it seems clear that Joyce worked insightfully with source texts. By comparing artefacts from the period to the metaphorical weave of Shem's fishiness (in mind, body and linguistic excess), we might usefully posit that this fishiness is a primordial animal gesture that allows Joyce to write in defiance of social Darwinist appropriations of evolutionary theory.[62] This was certainly known at the time. Writing in *Forum and Century* in 1939 about the newly published *Finnegans Wake*, Mary Colum suggested that the book would be read by 'people interested in [. . .] the racial mind and the racial experience'.[63] The fish, I contend, opens up such a reading.

'Lizard', the third chapter in this book, confronts a more explicit form of racism during the early 1930s: the nascent eugenics in the critical writings of the Expressionist poet Gottfried Benn. Barely considered in anglophone modernist studies, Benn's place in *transition* is difficult to overstate. In his inclusion in the journal, we see how Jolas was enraptured by Benn's formulations of 'primal vision' or 'primal unity'. A variant of the organic whole, this was expressed through a series of texts that conceptualised vision in terms of a reptilian organ of the brain: the pineal eye. Organising my analysis under the sign of the signifying reptile, therefore, I consider Benn's writing both in and beyond the magazine. How was he promoted? What was the logical conclusion of his proto-fascist polemics? What do we do with the fact that a cohort of English-speaking poets and writers were enamoured of Benn's quasi-scientific style? Alongside a consideration of the multitude of signifying reptiles found across the magazine, in this chapter the pineal eye emerges as a primordial theme. As twenty-first-century readers, we are witnessing the deeply alarming rise of populist alt-right movements in both Europe and America, and as such it is especially pressing to attend to the attractiveness of writers such as Benn, Bernard Faÿ, Pierre Drieu La Rochelle and Georges Pelorson, all of whom were published in *transition* and went on to collaborate to varying degrees with the Nazis.[64]

Despite (and sometimes because of) its publication of such illustrious or notorious authors as Joyce and Benn, *transition* was not always well received. Many who read the journal decried what one critic called 'that irritating hodge-podge of genius and nonsense'.[65] This was due partly to Joyce's impenetrability and partly to the prevalence of Surrealism, but mainly to Jolas himself. As we will see, his sustained, transcendent notion of the 'vertical' in poetry sometimes grated on critics' nerves: the soaring heights of aesthetic experience seemed out of kilter with the times, yet they formed the wellspring from which the magazine drew. As Kramer and Rumold observe, Jolas's enduring optimism in attempting to 'unite the extraordinarily diverse representatives of the avant-garde in a Revolution of the Word' was a 'response to the conflicts and chaos of the interwar era'.[66] This legacy was not fully appreciated at the time, however. Charges of pretentiousness were rife, both during and after *transition*'s lifetime. Igor Stravinsky relished such supercilious comments, recounting, for instance, an incident in his memoir. 'I remember [Aldous Huxley] leafing through a copy of *transition*,' he writes, 'reading a poem in it, looking again at the title of the magazine, reflecting for a moment, then saying, "backwards it spells NO IT ISN(T) ART".'[67] Such quips were sufficiently widespread for Jolas to embrace them: he frequently printed bad press as mock endorsements for future issues. The *transition* circle met with praise, too. Reviewing Jolas and Sage's 1929 edition of *Transition Stories*, an unsigned reviewer at *The Dial* referred to 'our esteemed contemporary *transition*' and its important echo of 'the very shouts and cries and steam-whistles and radio-ed advertisements of the time'.[68]

The journal's reception is thus closely related to its fourth and final primordial creature, which in this study is also the odd one out: the bird. Where the other animals in the texts under discussion belong to the primordial 'soup', emerge from the Mesozoic era or possess a chthonic 'third eye', the birds in this chapter are decisively 'higher' than the evolutionarily 'low', and are indicative of what Jolas calls 'the distant horizons of my aerial imagination'.[69] They are implicated in his selection, translation and arrangement of texts, sometimes at the cost of the subtlety of the original poem. They are present in Jolas's focus on vertical poetics, which increased as the journal went on. They are fundamentally romantic symbols of flight – the 'Icarian principle' on which Jolas based his career.[70] Jolas's birds, as this chapter suggests, help us understand how he produced what the poet Barbara Guest describes as 'by far the most provocative international magazine [of] the era', as well as constituting his constant faith in the Revolution of the Word – a faith that has, until recently, led to his being all but erased from studies of modernist culture as too out of keeping with other artists and writers during those crisis years.[71] Yet despite the apparent naivety of his romantic leanings, Jolas was more than aware of the precarity of cultural life after the onset of the Second World War, and the end of *transition*'s run. 'Everything I believed in for Europe has crumbled overnight', he wrote to Sweeney in July 1940. 'But I have to go on.'[72] In those turbulent interwar years, long after *transition*'s editor dreamed of scorpions and ashes, his artists and authors produced what I call a primordial modernism, a contradiction in terms that befits the magazine. We must begin by accommodating the schismatic nature of *transition*, which is most usefully framed by Mansanti as a 'schizophrenic discourse'.[73] As metaphors for schismatic consciousness and ambivalent national identities, and as revealing instances of transatlantic cultural exchange, *transition*'s animal metaphors are as far from the human as one can imagine. They are of the ocean, the river, the arid land, the nest. They buzz, or swarm or ooze, or fly from a prehistoric past, even as they come to signify experiments in artistic futurity.

Notes

1. Jolas, 'Dementia praecox', unpublished MS, 1917–18. Box 17, Folder 319, Maria and Eugene Jolas Papers, Beinecke Rare Books and Manuscripts Library, Yale University. For a finding aid, see Young, 'Guide to the Eugene and Maria Jolas Papers'. Subsequent references to this archive will be indicated by the Box and Folder numbers followed by an indication of the collection as the Jolas Papers. Jolas later published an entire edition of his poetry, edited by Oscar Williams and Gene Derwood, in *Rhythmus* in 1924. See also his *Secession in Astropolis* (1929), *Mots-déluge* (1933), *I Have Seen Monsters and Angels* (1938) and *Wanderpoem* (1946).
2. 'Although I was a dissident Catholic, I was nevertheless *still* a Catholic,' Jolas explains, testifying to a faith 'to which I have adhered – with rebellious interruptions – throughout my life'. Jolas, *Man from Babel*, 4, 155.
3. Jolas arranged for astrological consultations and the production of his star chart on at least two separate occasions: there are two distinct charts, one in French and the other in German, dated 1939 and 1946 respectively. Box 26, Folder 484, Jolas Papers.
4. Jolas, *Man from Babel*, 36.
5. Pound, 'Dr Williams' position', 395; Eliot, 'Periodicals: English'; Stein, *Autobiography*; Bracques et al., *Testimony*. For a contemporary account of the falling out between Stein and *transition*, see Vulliet, 'Americans'.
6. Jolas et al., 'Proclamation'.
7. For a more detailed overview of Jolas's contact with Solveen's circle, see Mansanti, 'Between modernisms', 730–2. See also Jolas, *Man from Babel*, xvii–xviii; Arp et al., 'Poetry is vertical', 148.
8. For an inestimably useful reading aid, see Silet, *transition*.

9. See Jolas's 'New vocabulary', 'Inquiry about the malady of language' (1935) and 'Malady of language' (1935).
10. Jolas, *Man from Babel*, 276. Jolas is quoting his 'Paris diary' fragments regarding his refusal to incorporate the mechanistic (or technological) into his vision of language as a modern 'mythos'. See ibid. 35; Box 13, Folder 255, Jolas Papers.
11. See the Modernist Journals Project at http://modjourn.org/ (last accessed 18 June 2018), the Blue Mountain Project at http://bluemountain.princeton.edu (last accessed 18 June 2018) and Monoskop at https://monoskop.org (last accessed 18 June 2018).
12. For a path-breaking study, see Hoffman et al., *Little Magazine*. For foundational studies in the field, see Rainey, *Institutions of Modernism*; Morrisson, *Public Face*; Churchill and McKible, *Little Magazines*; Katz, *American Modernism's*; Ardis and Collier (eds), *Transatlantic Print Culture*; Scholes and Wulfman, *Modernism*; White, *Transatlantic Avant-Gardes*; Brooker and Thacker (eds), *Oxford Critical*; Collier, 'What is modern periodical studies?'
13. McMillan, *transition*; Jolas, *Man from Babel*; M. Jolas, *Maria Jolas*. For an example of such a memoir and its portrayal of *transition* via 1920s celebrity culture, see Putnam, *Paris*.
14. Perloff, 'Logocinéma'; Rabaté, 'Joyce and Jolas'; North, *Camera Works*; Monk, *Writing*.
15. Kiefer and Rumold (eds), *Eugene Jolas*; Mansanti, *La revue transition*; Mansanti, 'Between modernisms', 736.
16. Cole, 'What is the avant-garde?'; Parks, 'Kind of higher'; Taylor-Batty, *Multilingualism*; Wilson, *Modernism and Magic*; Kelbert, 'Eugene Jolas'; Hatch, 'Eclectic/subversive period'; Grass, 'Democratic languages'.
17. Rumold, *Archaeologies*, 120, 123, 125–6; Miller, *Late Modernism*; Goldman, *Modernism*, 27.
18. Williams, letter to James Laughlin, 23 January 1938, in Witemeyer (ed.), *William Carlos Williams*, p. 26.
19. Kindley, 'Ismism', 33.
20. Finney, 'Eugene Jolas', 49–52.
21. Rahv, 'Literary class war', 8; Gold, '3 Schools'.
22. Mansanti, 'Between modernisms', 736.
23. The *transition* Kafka translations were the first available in English, appearing over a decade before the Edwin and Willa Muir translations that were to popularise the author in the United States in the late 1940s. Kafka, 'Metamorphosis', trans. Jolas (1936, 1937, 1938), originally published as *Die Verwandlung* (1917). Masson, 'Combat de poissons', 'Le coquillage', 'Le piège', 'Animal pris'.
24. For a close reading of *transition*'s many spider metaphors and their links to Nietzsche's philosophy of language, see Setz, 'Nietzsche's spider'.
25. *Transition*'s reincarnation after 1948 under the editorship of Georges Duthuit and others is beyond the scope of the present study. It was a primarily French journal of philosophy and criticism, with regular contributions from Jean-Paul Sartre, Jean Wahl and others.
26. Schwitters, 'priimiitittiii'.
27. Éluard, 'In company', 113. Originally published in Éluard, *Les dessous*.

28. Space does not permit me to discuss the broader history of insects and the avant-garde. The popular entomologist Jean Fabre (1823–1915) was a significant influence on such artists and thinkers as Luis Buñuel, André Masson and Roger Caillois, and Breton's circle was fascinated by the femme fatale nature of the praying mantis. See Caillois, *Edge of Surrealism*; Cheung, 'Mask, mimicry, metamorphosis'; Begin, 'Entomology'; Golston, 'Petalbent devils'.
29. Einstein, 'Bebuquin', 298–9, 301, originally published as *Bebuquin oder Dilettanten*.
30. Jung, *Psychological types*, para. 758.
31. Einstein, 'Bebuquin', 299.
32. Jolas, *Mots-déluge*. For a review of this work, see Soupault, 'Mots-déluge'. See also Jolas, *Words from the Deluge*, with illustrations by Yves Tanguy.
33. Einstein, 'Bebuquin', 301.
34. Jung, 'Instinct'. See also Noll, *Jung Cult*, 40–1.
35. Jung, 'Psychology and literature'.
36. Jung, 'Psychology and poetry', 36–7.
37. Rumold, *Archaeologies*, 120.
38. Griffin, *Modernism and Fascism*, 105.
39. Smith, *Theories of Nationalism*.
40. Hayes, *Historical Evolution*; Kohn, *Idea of Nationalism*.
41. Griffin, *Modernism and Fascism*, 107, 123–4.
42. Shils, 'Primordial, personal, sacred'. See also Özkirimli, *Theories of Nationalism*, p. 49, p. 72.
43. See Silet, *transition*, 53, 56, 100–1. Rumold, *Archaeologies*, 122.
44. Richards, 'At other times', 65, 67, 74–5, 77.
45. Mansanti, 'Between modernisms', 736.
46. Oparin, *Origin of Life*; Haldane, 'Origins of life'. For a useful overview of the concept, see Fry, 'Origins of research' and *Emergence of Life*.
47. Recht, 'Fire fanfare', 150; Huebner, 'The road', 112; Rao in Benn et al., 'Inquiry', 160–5; Boillotat, 'Sensing', 11–12; Miller, 'Cosmological eye', 327.
48. Remy quoted in Robertson, *Surrealism in Britain*, 49. Pailthorpe's contribution to British Surrealism and her role as a trained psychoanalyst have been significantly overlooked. For two introductory texts, see Milner, 'Eeriest couple' and Pailthorpe and Mednikoff, *Sluice Gates*.
49. Williams and Wheeler, 'Editorial'.
50. Jolas, '*transition*: an epilogue', 187.
51. Norris, *Beasts*, 2, 1, 23, 17, 43, 224, 25.
52. Botar, 'Defining biocentrism', 15–16, 24, 26, 29, 30, 31.
53. Baker, *Postmodern Animal*; Derrida, 'Animal that therefore' and 'Say the animal responded?'; Agamben, *The Open*; Deleuze and Guattari, *Thousand Plateaus*; Connor, 'Thinking perhaps begins'; Calarco, *Zoographies*.
54. P. Armstrong, *What Animals Mean*, 4; Rohman, *Stalking the Subject*, 27–8.
55. T. Armstrong, *Modernism*, 149–52.
56. See Jolas, 'What is the revolution', 125. On the question of the journal's misrecognition and the author's personal engagement with the movement, see Jolas, 'Surrealism', 29.

57. Jolas, 'Literature', 14. *La révolution Surréaliste*, which ran to twelve issues between December 1924 and December 1929, is a clear intertext here. Breton, 'Introduction au discours'. Jolas doubtless read this in its original prior to his interview with Breton (a rare coup for an English-speaking publication) for his regular column in the *Chicago Tribune*. See Jolas, 'Rambles' (1925). See also Breton, 'Introduction to the discourse'. The 'Proclamation' features the same quotation from Rimbaud's 'hallucination' of the Word as is found in Breton's writing and manifestos, as well as the explicitly Surrealist notion of a 'metamorphosis' of reality.
58. Jolas, 'Literature', 14. Bennett, 'Periodical fragments', 485.
59. Jewell, 'Whichness'.
60. The phrase is accredited to Marcel Brion. See McMillan, *transition*, 179.
61. Tindall, *Reader's Guide*, 137.
62. Space does not permit me to focus on the influence of Henri Bergson's mystical biology or the history of early twentieth-century vitalist philosophy in connection with Joyce or modernist literature more broadly, although it is a well-established field. See Burwick and Douglass (eds), *Crisis in Modernism*; Antliff, *Inventing Bergson*.
63. Colum, 'Life and literature', 158.
64. Bernard Faÿ was a historian and later Vichy collaborator who believed in a worldwide Jewish conspiracy. He was likely published in *transition* via Elliot Paul, *transition*'s co-editor during its first year. Both Paul and Faÿ were friends with Gertrude Stein. See Faÿ, 'Travel and flight'; Faÿ's contribution to Jolas et al., 'Inquiry among European', 260–1; and Faÿ, 'Essay on poetry', 241–7, in which he describes poetry as so many flies about a dung heap. Rochelle, another French fascist, appears during 1927, seven years prior to his conversion to Hitlerism. For his appearances, see Rochelle, 'Young European', and two commentaries: Paul, 'New nihilism', and Sage, 'Young European'. Georges Pelorson was a Vichy collaborator and appears on numerous occasions in *transition*. For bibliographical details, see Silet, *transition*, 124–5.
65. Georges Currie reviewing *transition* in the *Brooklyn Eagle*. Quoted in *transition*, 18 (February 1929), 290.
66. 'Note on the text' in Jolas, *Man from Babel*, xxxix.
67. Stravinsky and Craft, *Dialogues*, 42.
68. Anonymous, 'Briefer mention', reviewing Jolas and Sage (eds), *Transition Stories*.
69. Jolas, *Man from Babel*, 17.
70. Jolas, 'Atlantica poem', unpublished typescript, n. d, c. 1938. Box 12, Folder 241, Jolas Papers.
71. Guest, *Herself Defined*, 165.
72. Jolas, letter to James Johnson Sweeney, 14 July 1940. Box 59, Folder 1390, Jolas Papers.
73. Mansanti, 'Between modernisms', 724–5.

I

AMOEBA: FIGURES OF ABSTRACTION, SURREALIST INFLUENCE AND THE REVOLUTION OF THE WORD

> My fingers trace behind the moving word.
> The words are there, white;
> Or is the shroud white?
> Or can I see the words eating themselves
> Into the darkness?
>
> Evan Shipman, 'Premonition', 1928

Early in 1935, *transition* moved to New York. After years of production in Paris and The Hague, Eugene Jolas transferred operations to offices on West 42nd Street. Just ten blocks north, over on West 53rd Street, the Museum of Modern Art (MoMA, then still a five-storey town house leased from John D. Rockefeller) was getting ready to open its exhibition 'Cubism and Abstract Art'. The retrospective was held on 2 March–19 April 1936, not long before Jolas moved back to Paris in the autumn to set about editing the tenth-anniversary, final issue of *transition*, which was released in spring 1938. As part of the MoMA exhibition, the museum's director, Alfred H. Barr Jr, composed a large flowchart showing all the branches of modern art movements from the 1890s onwards. A mass of black and red arrows and networked 'isms', this image was used on the exhibition catalogue cover, press release and poster. It hangs in the museum to this day (Figure 1.1). The 'diachronic chart of tributary movements' moved down a vertical axis of years, ending with 1935. This gave the impression of two parallel forces emerging into the 'present' of Barr's scheme, two 'great rivers' derived

PRIMORDIAL MODERNISM

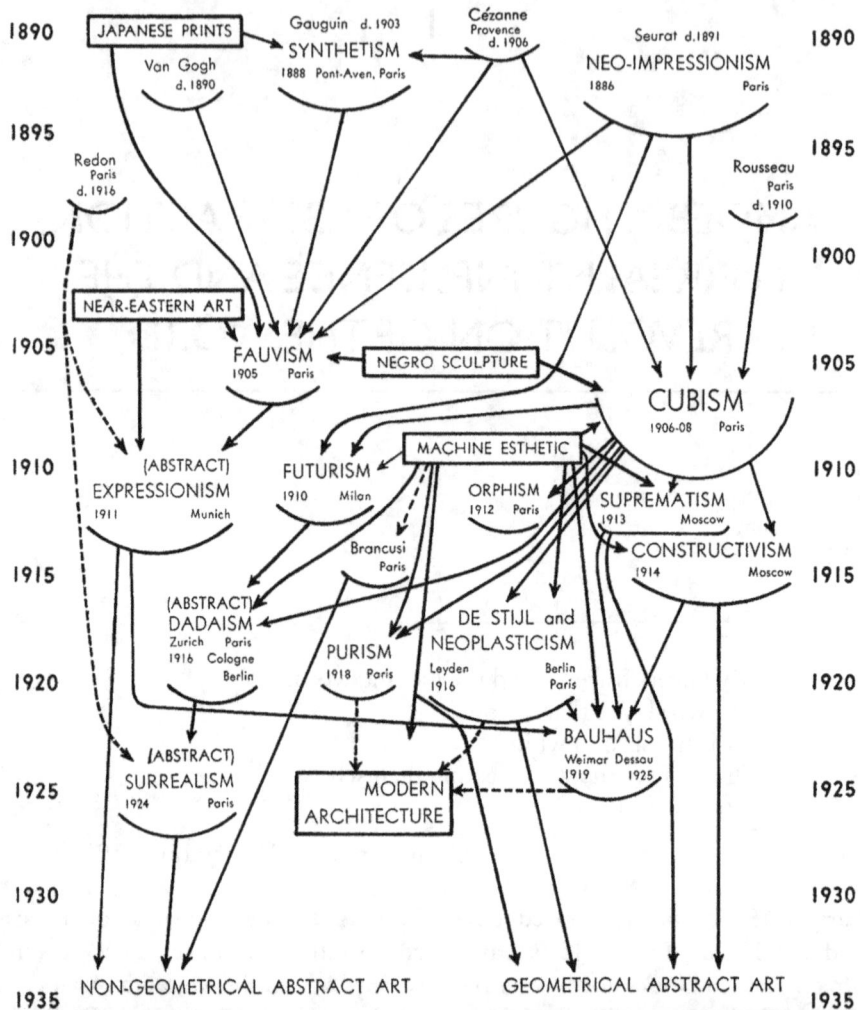

Figure 1.1 MoMA exhibition catalogue cover. Alfred Hamilton Barr Jr, *Cubism and Abstract Art*, 1936. Digital image © Museum of Modern Art/Scala Florence, 2014

from Impressionism.[1] Barr thus promoted a dialectical tendency between two overarching types of abstraction. One he named 'geometrical abstract art', as found in the work of Piet Mondrian or the Russian Constructivists Antoine

Pevsner and Naum Gabo, presented as an offshoot of Cubism. The other he named 'non-geometrical abstract art', with a lineage that stretched from Paul Gauguin to Henri Matisse, and from Fauvism to Expressionism, Dada and Surrealism, as seen in the work of Jean Miró, Hans Arp, André Masson and others.[2] The chart stands today as one of the most notorious critical tools in the history of American modernism: a document of formalist, elitist, androcentric canon formation, which produced a bleached concept of abstraction that many art historians would critique for years to come.[3] But there is something in this historic moment that relates to Jolas's magazine. In the catalogue text accompanying the image, Barr reaches for an animal metaphor. 'The shape of the square', writes the director as he contemplates canvases by Kazimir Malevich and Wassily Kandinsky, 'confronts the silhouette of the amoeba.'[4] The amoeba – the protozoic, single-celled organism at the very origin of life on earth – offers Barr a shorthand, a symbolic category for what he calls 'biomorphic abstraction'. Barr was likely thinking of a 1934 Kandinsky gouache entitled *Composition*, the most contemporary work shown in the exhibition (reproduced in *transition*), and *Striped*, also from 1934, a monochrome plane of black and white vertical bars framing a foreground of multicoloured biomorphic shapes.[5]

It would be easy to dismiss Barr's amoeba as a mere quip, a blob of organic matter that served merely to augment his narrative. But this ignores a crucial context. In Barr's curatorial mind, the amoeba appears as a handy opposition to the aesthetic grids of compositional form – a principle, or optic, for modern organic art. This is hardly new: consider Goethe's fascination with botanical processes, certain literary tendencies to revert to nature, or indeed any holistic vision of fertility throughout art history. But unlike such earlier modes of thought, Barr's schema pitted the organic against the prismatic forms of Cubism which, as Glen Macleod has argued, had been inspiring literary works such as Gertrude Stein's *Three Lives* (1909) for over twenty years.[6] Scholars have examined 'gridded' elements in both the visual arts and literary articulations of modernity ever since (especially) Dirk Van Hulle's work on the formal opposition between organic and geometric poetics.[7] When one considers the chart's 'non-geometric' half, Barr's formalism is especially apparent. The confluence of arrows from Odilon Redon, Abstract Expressionism, Constantin Brâncuşi and Surrealism converges around the date of André Breton's 'First manifesto of Surrealism' (1924), then leaps directly to the present. Although the same is true of the geometrical lineage, the accompanying text's glossing of the non-geometric contemporary mode as 'biomorphic abstraction' applies the term loosely and without due citation. Barr's lack of awareness of the historical context out of which his own formalism has appeared thus relies on the looseness of the 'amoeba' itself as a distinguishing feature.[8]

Modernism's eventual arrival in MoMA came about with the aid of at least a decade of what Dickran Tashjian calls 'cultural brokerage': the translation and showcasing of European works of literature and art for primarily American readers.[9] Yet despite Tashjian's pioneering work, there remains a paucity of critical analysis of Surrealism's early influence in America, due largely to the assumption that it started in 1940 with Breton's move to New York. But as William Hogan put it, writing in 1938, '*transition* supported Surrealism a decade before *Harper's Bazaar* had even heard of it'.[10] Samuel Putnam too, writing six years earlier, also identified this significance. Responding to a literary fracas in which the *Secession* editors sought to make claims as to 'WHO BROUGHT DADA TO AMERICA' (seemingly oblivious of Marcel Duchamp, Arthur Cravan, Francis Picabia, Man Ray and others), Putnam dismissed the whole 'imbroglio' as a misapprehension:

> The answer is, NO ONE BROUGHT DADA TO AMERICA! No one, certainly, before Eugene Jolas, although Margaret Anderson may have made something of an attempt. And what Jolas and the old *transition* brought was not Dada but a version of *Surrealism*.[11]

A critical focus on this cultural brokerage – which was the very business of the modernist magazine – is now essential. Recent developments in periodical studies have opened up the field, as Susan Rosenbaum's and others' work makes clear, by exploring how journals offered exciting paper art galleries.[12] Between 1927 and 1938, *transition* brought Surrealism to America more strongly than any other magazine. As Tyrus Miller has written of the readers and writers of the time, 'if one wanted to familiarise oneself with Surrealism and its fellow travellers, *transition* was not a bad place to start'.[13] In this case, we can narrow the focus to the primordial animal par excellence. Barr's use of the amoeba as a figure for abstraction has a history not just in the visual arts but in *transition*'s literary texts, and it leads us to a broader consideration of the nature of the magazine's encounter with the Surrealist movement.

There is evidence to suggest that *transition* was a major influence on Barr. One of the few magazine office documents to have survived the Second World War is a subscription list from around 1936 that bears Barr's name. (Other listed subscribers include Georges and Sylvia Bataille, Sylvia Beach, Samuel Beckett, Constantin Brâncuși, Albert Camus, Aimé Césaire, Harry and Caresse Crosby, Alberto Giacometti, Jacques Lacan, Valery Larbaud, Michel Leiris, André Malraux, André and Rose Masson, Maurice Merleau-Ponty, Adrienne Monnier, Pierre Reverdy, Jean-Paul Sartre, *Vogue* fashion editor Lucien Vogel, Jean Wahl and Richard Wright.)[14] A professional affiliation between *transition* and MoMA also developed via James Johnson Sweeney, whom Barr appointed as a curator in 1935.[15] Sweeney was co-editing *transition* from New York prior to Jolas's relocation from Paris, and was simultaneously compiling the catalogue for MoMA's 'African Negro Art' exhibition (18 March–19 May 1935).[16] Barr was certainly exposed to *transition*: as well as being a one-time contributor, reporting on Soviet art in 1927, he also regarded Joyce as one of his 'pet modernists', as Alice Goldfarb Marquis points out.[17] One wonders whether the Surrealist material published in *transition* after April 1927 appeared in Barr's art history classes at Wellesley, which he designed to explore the 'modernist interpretations of art'. He encouraged his students to read as many new art and literary journals as possible, especially those featuring European avant-gardist material.[18] Easily acquired in New York through the Gotham Book Mart, *transition* was among the most prominent of such titles. It is possible that Barr's pedagogical use of *transition* in his classes might even have affected sales. As Frances Steloff wrote to Jolas in 1939, the number of copies sold went up considerably during this period.[19] Although missing from both Marquis's book and Sybil Kantor's illuminating work on the MoMA director, it seems likely that the Jolases' magazine played a significant role in Barr's intellectual approach.

The history of the life sciences is another context for Barr's figuring of abstraction through an amoebic silhouette. Especially after the First World War, when thousands of returning soldiers were tested for amoebic dysentery, the nature of this single-celled protozoon was part of the public imagination.[20] Barr perhaps also knew that Kandinsky's Parisian works of the mid-1930s bore the direct influence not only of Paul Klee's, Joan Miró's and others' biomorphic forms, but also of developments in microbiology and its illustrations of single-celled organic life, insect and fish embryos, nematodes, placental structures, sea polyps and other oceanic creatures.[21] Tim Armstrong has discussed creative responses to interwar developments in the life sciences among British poets and authors who were in touch with the forefront of biology via British scientists such as J. B. S. Haldane, Joseph Needham and H. S. Jennings. Armstrong suggests that there is a visible 'biological style' in interwar writing, born from a mixture of Henri Bergson, other vitalist influences, and creative engagements with developments in medicine, biology and sexological discourses.[22] This relates to the biological conception of the self promoted by Surrealists themselves. On 11 June–4 July 1936, less than two months after the MoMA show ended, a major Surrealist exhibition took place at the New Burlington Gallery in London. Reporting on the event in September, the *International Surrealist Bulletin* included a lecture by Hugh Sykes Davies entitled 'Biology and Surrealism', which outlined recent psychoanalytical ideas about repression via endocrinological features of physical (and thus not solely psychical) structures.[23] The cultural climate in which Barr's amoeba appeared, therefore, suggests that his opposition between biomorphism and geometrical art reflected more than the cultural imperialism it has come to represent.

Barr's ahistorical approach to abstract art did not escape contemporary criticism. In 1937, Meyer Schapiro highlighted a glaring absence in Barr's analysis: the social, political and historical realities of the culture from which art was produced. Schapiro interpreted Barr's 'biomorphic abstraction' as a form of artistic atrophy, 'a violent or nervous calligraphy' expressed in 'amoeboid forms, a soft, low-grade matter pulsing in an empty space'. For Schapiro, this creative vacuity culminated in a Surrealist pessimism of 'bones, grotesque beings, abandoned buildings and catastrophic earth formations'.[24] Between Barr and Schapiro, then, amoebic shapes were cast in two different ways. Barr's embodied a valiant 'organicism' in art that confronted a mechanical vision of modernity. Schapiro's, conversely, encapsulated a reactionary moment when the revolutionary spirit of Surrealism was exhausted. Taken together, these two ideas of abstraction – as a site of both the Surrealist movement's vitality and its decline – help us approach the literary texts discussed below. As Charles Bernstein writes of abstraction, 'it's as much the ambidextrous and amphibious as the ambivalent'. But when one turns to literary texts, abstraction can also be a 'self-reflection of the semiotic process of representation', an imaginative space where a creature as basic as an amoeba might enable the writer to articulate the limitations of representational language.[25]

To explore the nature of such texts, I turn first to the amoeba's scientific conceptual history as a useful contextual background. I will then outline *transition*'s various 'amoebic silhouettes', which were primarily emergent from francophone Surrealist texts and visual works. I argue for a loosely defined amoebic mode here: a creative impulse towards abstraction in a literal, almost biological manner. This approach reveals certain American contributors as engaging with Surrealism, often through the same amoebic mode. Finally, I consider the ways in which the amoeba, as a loosely defined reading tool, can illuminate American Surrealism, and with it *transition*'s legacy in modernist culture.

Amoebas and the Word

Amoebas have been a categorical challenge to biologists ever since their discovery by August Johann Rösel von Roselhof in 1755, and they have served in scientific history as an exemplar rather than a type.[26] They are the building blocks of life, studied for their instructive value, as almost every living organism can trace its basic features back to the amoeba's organic processes. In 1878, the biologist Joseph Leidy extolled this 'wonderful creature', one of 'the lowliest of the lowest class of animals, a mere speck of the thinnest jelly endowed with the usual attributes of all living things'.[27] Leidy and other late nineteenth-century biologists were drawn to the cell's behaviour, but agreement over nomenclature remained elusive. Attempts to clarify the confusion of amoebas reached an apex in 1926, when Asa A. Schaeffer described thirty-nine new species and created eleven new genera, sparking classificatory debates that continue to this day.[28]

Amoebas currently occupy the taxonomic group protists, or as the biologist Chris Reid puts it, 'everything we don't really understand'.[29] They have frequently moved around divisions among the animal, vegetable and fungal groupings of life. As eukaryotic microorganisms, amoebas constitute a unicellular, mobile, fluid-dwelling and living material of the (now outdated) class of protozoa, meaning 'first life'. Their amorphous shapes feature pseudopodia, temporary limb-like projections that allow movement. En masse, and on land, they also form slime moulds, a sporulating spread of various fungus-like substances. Named Proteus after the Greek god of the sea, amoebas appeared in Carolus Linnaeus's 1758 *Systema Naturae* as *Volvox chaos*, then as *Chaos proteus* in 1767. The 'amoeba' was eventually named as such in the 1830s; the most visible species, *Amoeba proteus* (Figure 1.2), was named in the late 1870s. Disputes around the naming of 'giant amoeba' species such as *Chaos carolinense* persisted into the late 1930s.[30]

While a select group of microbiologists argued over the nomenclature for this miniscule creature, Eugene Jolas, Maria Jolas and Elliot Paul were preparing to publish a circle of writers and artists engaged with aesthetic – but equally exemplary – amoebas. In a text entitled 'Balls, or simple error' that was designed to send up avant-garde abstraction in film and literature, Whit Burnett, the future founder and editor of *Story* magazine, employs an amoeba metaphor. In the midst of a raucous scene of cabaret dancers, 'flapper slayers' and jazz, the text suddenly switches register to a wry, encyclopaedic voice. 'When more closely seen on a telescope from a precarious position on a slack wire', the text declares, 'it will be readily observed that amoebae, in times of stress, conjugate rather than divide.' The prose then falls back into a play on music and movement:

> Mr Oliver Wedgewood Homes [. . .] put down the telescope, or rather, we see him pick up the wriggly rubber trombone. Wriggly rubber notes

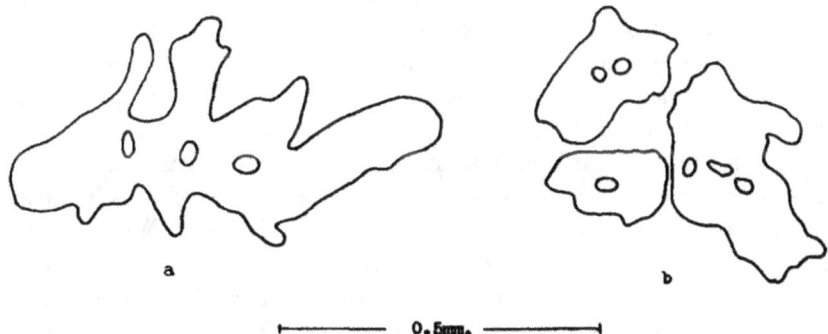

Camera lucida sketches of the division of a trinucleate Amoeba into three progeny, containing respectively 1, 2 and 3 nuclei. a, parent 3 days before division; b, progeny about an hour after division.

Figure 1.2 *Amoeba proteus*. Illustration of organism before and after reproduction by binary fission, 1924. From Joseph Levy, 'Studies on Reproduction in *Amoeba Proteus*' (1924), 147. © Genetics Society of America

fill the wriggly rubber room, and the wriggly rubber bars writhe in wriggly rubber tunes [. . .]. Note follows note, [. . .] and the room is all black rubber bouncingballs and gently dancing snakes.[31]

Burnett's 'conjugation' of cells is a passing reference, a scene in which a Surrealist telescope turns up living things, then plays on the repetition of 'wriggly rubber' as an aural commingling or 'conjugation' of a different order. The text keys into both a microscopic and an aural plasticity of form and movement.

Shipman's 'Premonition', quoted at the head of this chapter, is another example. Dedicated to André Masson, it portrays the American poet beholding the biomorphic forms of the Surrealist artist's work. Words form a living substance, as if at the bottom of the sea, surfacing and propelling the vision. 'Can I see the words eating themselves', the speaker asks, 'into the darkness?' The rest of the poem evokes a 'cloth' as an image of the space on which words stitch, but where they also grow: a space of living language, cast as an 'icy vigilance' where the great death of silence looms large.[32] Some of Jolas's more abstruse poetry was also regarded in what we might call an amoebic metaphorical manner. 'This is indeed the abysmal slime of language', wrote a journalist in 1932, 'from which nevertheless may be dredged up strange and wonderful things.'[33]

Amoebic Silhouettes

A little over two weeks after *Cubism and Abstract Art* closed in New York, on 5 May 1936 the artist and frequent co-editor at the *Nouvelle revue française* André Lhote delivered a lecture on 'L'inconscient dans l'art' at the Institut Métaphysique in Paris. The talk was printed in the *Gazette des Beaux-Arts* for its summer issue, then translated by Jolas for *transition*'s penultimate issue the following year.[34] Lhote took a strikingly similar approach to Barr's with regard to questions of abstraction. Incorporating the Surrealist practice of automatic writing into a more multimedia discussion, Lhote reflected upon on his own version of the 'non-geometrical' organic principle, an idea that had apparently emerged at the same time on both sides of the Atlantic. This 'vital and profound urge', he wrote, lies in the curve: the curve upon the canvas but also by the hand, another visual idea of an internal or ineffable force. Where Barr saw amoeboid shapes, Lhote invoked the sweep of modern art's curves as resembling 'the marvellous twisting of a plant drunken with liberty and pleasure'. Extending the organic, living vegetable image, his text compares non-geometric abstraction to 'the tendrils of creepers that unroll like the interiors of sea-shells' and that 'never stop tracing their dizzying flourishes'. Lhote then described automatic 'graphism' as a 'verbo-visual automatism' before linking Surrealism to a genealogy of art through the 'tangles of algae', 'long-haired inter-twinings' and 'vegetable, human, rocky or cloudy arabesques' of Matthias Grünewald, Hieronymus Bosch and El Greco. Like Barr before him, Lhote sought defining principles, and he turned to the same categorical space, that of the amoeba: the protoplasmic substance of the most basic forms of life.

Lhote's essay was a belated version of the cultural anthropology that had so fascinated modernist authors earlier in the century via influential works such as James Frazer's *The Golden Bough* (1890) and Freud's *Totem and Taboo* (1913). The text belongs to that earlier discursive history, as the artist-critic mentions the 'dreaming and patient savage' as a quality in art that might respond to the corruption of modernity. But he goes further. In Lhote's discussion, art goes beyond the human – beyond even the animalised human of the 'primitive' – in search of 'primordial rhythms'.[35] His essay is neither strictly primitivist nor even anti-humanist. It is abstractionist, in a way that is representative of the literary abstraction the reader can find across *transition*. If we put aside the taxonomical intimations of both Barr's and Lhote's arguments, each critic thinks with the amoebic shapes of animal-vegetable, metamorphotic, primordial life.

Transition's most obvious amoebic image had appeared almost a decade earlier. Yves Tanguy, who went on to illustrate the cover of Jolas's 1941 poetry collection *Words from the Deluge*, often painted what Roger Caillois described in 1975 as 'giant amoebas'.[36] Such forms are visible in the untitled painting that Jolas reproduced in *transition*'s February 1928 issue (Figure 1.3).[37] Tanguy's seabed scenes are dominated by amorphous cellular life forms, which Caillois goes to some lengths to describe:

> Pouches quivering from a common frost despite their watertight membranes; wheezy ganglions, suckers and feelers, all crawling, exploring, and sucking; a tentative growth of mushrooms and elastic, tenacious warts that are unbalanced and bloated, the crust of a planet disinfected by its acid colours. [. . .] It is merely disorienting. It functions by threatening us with distant biologies that are irremediably foreign, sealed off, lazy, and corrosive.[38]

Like Schapiro, Caillois also sees Tanguy's amoebas as indicative of a 'vacant metaphor' in many artworks of the period. They are part of the Surrealist movement's 'evocative sorcery predicated on the use of the image', he argues, an element in which the 'stubborn indulgence of personal simulacra' privileges the sign to the point of meaninglessness. A member of Bataille's *Documents* circle, Caillois contributed to a wider critique of Bretonian Surrealism, and in that respect he is not directly relevant to *transition*, but the terms of his rejection are useful nonetheless. He objects to the application of an easy biologism in the visual realm, which he sees as a scientised version of the exotic. In what follows I will consider the extent to which the amoeboid metaphorical impulse appears in *transition*'s literary texts.

Figure 1.3 Yves Tanguy, *Painting* (1928). Reproduced in *transition*, 11, February 1928. © ARS, NY and DACS, London 2018

Two foundational figures who inspired the Surrealist movement and appeared in *transition* were Arthur Rimbaud and the pseudonymous Comte de Lautréamont (Isidore Lucien Ducasse). Both authors articulated abstracted ideas about the 'primal matter' of language, and both offer early examples of what we can broadly term an amoebic mode of writing. In November 1929, Stuart Gilbert translated an essay by the young Roger Vailland that had previously been published in the latter's short-lived journal *Le grand jeu*. In 'Arthur Rimbaud, or war on Man!' Vailland discusses Rimbaud's *Une saison en enfer* in terms of the poet's urge to obliterate his sense of selfhood: to fall, 'and in falling dwindl[e] to formlessness, gripped by the panic of infantile dreams when, transformed into a pin', the poet must 'choose a path immune from the trajectory of suffocating pillows'. Implicitly suspicious of Freudian dream analysis – the pillow that suffocates – Vailland quotes Rimbaud's line (which was also a source for the 'Revolution of the Word' manifesto) that 'the old poetic lumber used to figure largely in my alchemy of the word. Now I accustomed myself to pure hallucination.' Just as Lhote visualises 'graphism' in the plastic arts, Vailland reformulates the psychoanalytic concept of automatic writing. The imagined primal matter of language allows Vailland to read Rimbaud as a poet who embraces the abandonment of the idea of 'self' in favour of pure 'matter'.[39] This anticipates Lhote's more art-historical theorisation of the quest for primordial rhythms in modern art. In both, one finds a 'language of absolutes', to cite Schapiro's questioning of Barr – albeit in a pessimistic tone.[40]

This principle also propelled another anglophone version of Surrealism in *transition*. In 1938 Herbert Read wrote of the 'metamorphosis of language' as closely aligned to the practice of automatic writing. Almost exactly the same idea emerges: a reflection on Surrealist poetics, combined with a suspicion of psychoanalytic understandings of narrative and followed by a call to return to the word, the matter of poetry. Read echoes the original formulations of automatic writing by Breton and others, taking it to mean 'a state of mind in which expression is immediate and instinctive – where there is no time-gap between the image and its verbal equivalent'.[41] A leading member of the Surrealist circle in London, Read was likely aware of Vailland's take on the 'suffocating pillow'.[42] Both critics were invested in an approach to Surrealist poetics that was distinct from a Jungian or Freudian context and aimed at the bulkier category of abstraction: a space apart from representational language, but seen in non-spiritual, non-metaphysical terms.

It is in this context that we might approach the most formative Surrealist (or rather, reclaimed Surrealist) author. Lautréamont was a largely unknown figure whose *Les chants de Maldoror* (1868–9) gained a cult status among the Parisian circle. The discovery by Soupault and Breton of the last known copy of Lautréamont's *Poésies* (1870) in the Bibliothèque Nationale was, as Hal Foster puts it, 'one of the foundational legends of Surrealism'. *Transition* played a part in this rehabilitation. In October 1927, Jolas republished a portion of John Rodker's *Maldoror* translation, and the chosen passage draws on a similar idea to that found in Vailland's Rimbaud. Both signal an abstract characterisation of 'the Word', here in an image of animalised, enlarged perception. This is a quality one finds throughout *Maldoror*, from an archangel crab scuttling on the rocks, to the unnerving plumed birds with which the unholy Maldoror communes on a gleeful descent into evil. However one sees Lautréamont – whether as a nineteenth-century diabolist or, as Wyndham Lewis declared in his attack on the *transition* circle, as no more than an 'inverted moralist' – this animalised focus on perception offers a connective line to other texts.[43]

The selected Lautréamont passage is a longing paean to the tumultuous sea, with a repeated refrain: 'I salute you, ancient ocean!' Maldoror's narrative voice rejects the vanity of a humankind that forever believes in its own beauty. The narrative whorls through the primeval water, with frequent references to animals, smallness and fragmented scenes of modernity:

> Ancient ocean, whose waves are crystal, you resemble somewhat those azure marks to be seen on the bruised backs of cabin boys; you are an enormous bruise upon the earth's body; I like that analogy. So at first sight of you, a prolonged sigh of sadness passes, which might be imagined as the murmur of the suave breeze, leaving ineradicable traces upon the deeply moved spirit, and the crude origins of man, when he became acquainted with abiding sorrow. I salute you ancient ocean.[44]

Maldoror returns to the ancient aquatic mass as a symbol for the origins of humanity (and its 'tiny eyes'), contrasted with the 'octopus with a silken stare'.[45] This juxtaposition reaches to the enormity of nature, with its prehuman time and scale. It also draws attention to its own constructedness, as Maldoror congratulates himself on his own linguistic skill ('I like that analogy'). Like Vailland's Rimbaud, the text is concerned with a non-human yet living signifying space where a poetic conception may emerge. Lautréamont's *Maldoror* is a constant acknowledgement of humanity's imprisonment within consciousness, yet it refuses any description of an edifying spirit or soul. Like Lhote, Vailland and Read, therefore, it offers a figure for abstraction.

Scholars have explored this quality. Taking stock of Lautréamont's significance during the period, Anna Balakian frames the author's volatility as a response to the impact of Darwinism, expressed with recalcitrant sentimentality or extreme romanticism. Lautréamont 'cannot quench his passion for the infinite', she writes. 'If it is true that he shares the destiny of the animal, then his own unanswered but unabated longing for the infinite must exist in the lowliest creatures.' This longing – part of his rejection of human hypocrisy – is located in a primordial sea.[46] Jolas was attuned to this quality. In October 1927, he hailed Lautréamont as a saviour of the American literary scene, positing the author as a beacon, an illuminating presence he saw as missing on the other side of the Atlantic. 'The American poet needs the immense impulsions of a Lautréamont', he declared, who has 'liberated the imagination and dispelled our fear to enter into darkness. [...] He lets us see into the occult beyond, where new and demonic visions people our solitude.'[47] This 'darkness' gestures towards both a subconscious and a non-human realm.

The sign of the ancient ocean is also at the forefront of Tristan Tzara's poem 'L'homme approximatif', which Jolas translated and printed in the June 1930 issue, prior to Tzara's publication of the work in a single-authored volume.[48] 'The approximate man' echoes not only Lautréamont's predilection for the lowliest creatures, but also Vailland's scepticism regarding the 'pillow' of dream symbolism, despite Breton's clear influence.[49] 'The approximate man' moves through a primordial landscape, as if it had been composed in front of an Yves Tanguy canvas:

> I inhabit the music in the stove where shadows bake
> a tear – cold trace of a lizard – is enough – dazzling negligence
> to put out in each lamp the silence that buries us in pillows of dawn

The poetic voice employs a clash of ephemeral realms – music and the lizard's footsteps – as a gesture towards a similarly anguished idea of an infinite space:

> from the extreme points of luminous longitudes
> from the lofty gaze of the fatigue of snows
> imperfect returns of long magic meditations
> to the seasons here below
> soaked in those algae swarming with transparencies
> of the mantling of heteroclite eternities dragged in the mud down here
> eye always new to the return of things[50]

Tzara's landscape develops through the poem with a gathering sense of war. Images of battle and the silent fields where soldiers have died are met with broadly amoebic metaphors, in a deliberate invocation of the constructedness of the abstract figure. The 'soft fields of edelweiss where legions of honor grow wild', for instance, are cloaked in the warped symbolism of 'let the anemone face lick the steep moon stain'. This technique carries through the poem: the voice moves from modern industrial scenes to the amoebic symbol of eternity, captured as an imperfect return. 'Hangars of the years of slag' and 'asphalt brains' portray the early twentieth century, an image soon swamped in the abject ancient ocean. The salt of the sea comes to signify a zeitgeist – 'the salt of your age rises to the surface of the water' – but it does so as a naturalist principle that in no way reduces to organic holism the confusion and fear of modern consciousness.[51] Tzara's imagery has a direct antecedent in his earlier Dadaist texts, where the microbiological figures as an emblem for the movement. In his 1918 'Dada manifesto', for instance, Tzara invokes bacteria as an image for Dada's non-utilitarian uselessness, its resistance to all meaning, and he writes that 'the first thought that comes to these minds is of a bacteriological order'. Tzara also talked in 1922 of the movement as 'a virgin microbe that insinuates itself with the insistence of air into all the spaces that reason hasn't been able to fill with words or conventions'.[52]

In light of these instances, we might say that the amoebic principle does more than simply reproduce the logical category of the absolute. It calls upon clashing images of urban asphalt scenery, a salty living sea, and the inescapable play of language. This is evident in the following two moments in Tzara's text, which are indicative of the technique in the poem as a whole:

> the pores of the earth open with those of the skin
> and the stretched out hands the still soft shell wounds
> [. . .]
> and by following the coasts and the landslides of metaphors
> the eyes of the numbers are filled with the time struck in the game of
> the arts[53]

Tzara alludes to Lautréamont's outrage and horror at humanity's hypocrisy, now in a post-war world. If we compare the two, we might claim that the amoebic mode is a very literalised, cooler version of the fiery metaphysics experienced several generations before, employing the lowliest vector of animality as part of a meditation on the limits of the power of the Word. Or, as Tzara puts it:

> where languages make their dregs foam down to the last swallow
> and all the final disappointements [sic] and their fire ducts
> which seal the pagan repast to the silences of the rock[54]

This 'foam[ing] down' of language to its animal base is found in further works by European writers, and Jolas, as editor and translator, had a unique influence. Describing what he called the disintegration of the Word in the organic sense of decomposition, Jolas championed the work of another major figure: Léon-Paul Fargue.[55] Impressed by Fargue's neologisms, his 'slashe[d] syllables' and ability to 'buil[d] new words from root vocables and introduc[e] [. . .] an element entirely unknown before', Jolas describes an amoebic current at work in the francophone materials displayed in his journal, whether officially Surrealist or outside the movement.[56] In 1949 Jolas crystallised this editorial drive, reflecting on the fact that *transition* was the first to translate Fargue. 'In looking back', he wrote, 'it is probably no exaggeration to say that a new literary style resulted from this heightened esthetic awareness, a style that broke with the imagist-objectivist tradition in order to seek a symbolic form.'[57] This form was metaphorical and thematic. It gravitated towards the idea of an ancient aquatic mass, and towards the lowliest animals as a metaphorical terminus: an articulation of the proximity of chaos and the Word. Fargue's *transition* texts frequently allude to Lautréamont, most notably 'Tumult', translated by Maria Jolas and published in February 1928:

> this need to escape from the center of gravity in your human thought, this desire to go out with the eye of a fly, this rage about the accounts of the earth, do you hope to establish its net price, that is very hard; your questions solved, everything is worse than before; you always forget the principal thing, you have not seen anything in the way of waste, your seams rip first one place then another! your fastest trains go forward like a child's drawing, the smoke badly made; the constructions of your finest brains roll under the table, Descartes' crystals badly distributed, underfed molecular decreasing[58]

Fargue's prose moves in a similar stream to Tzara's verse. The 'underfed molecular decreasing' offers a metaphoric juxtaposition of ancient and modern scenes, as the reader is invited to imagine a microscopic image as well as one of malnourishment. This extract is likely to have been of special interest to Jolas because it expresses his own sentiments so closely. In a December 1927 editorial entitled 'On the quest', Jolas too described this 'need to escape from the center of gravity in [. . .] human thought': 'the hunger for evasion, which is the symbol of our generation, can find expression in certain definite ways'.[59] This bears a resemblance to Fargue's invocation of the forgotten 'principal thing' – 'a certain definite' expression akin to Tzara's 'foaming down' of language.[60]

American Animalcules

The Surrealist influence on American texts is especially visible during *transition*'s early years, from its beginnings as a monthly publication to the issue containing the Revolution of the Word 'Proclamation' (issues 1–16/17, April 1927–June 1929), prior to what Hugh Ford has called *transition*'s more 'hermetic' phase.[61] During the years 1927–9, *transition* was one of the only vehicles for American-European literary culture. The *Little Review* had published Surrealist content during its 1914–29 run, and there were other publishing ventures that focused on Franco-American avant-garde literary work and became better known for cultivating what Vassiliki Kolocotroni calls the '*surrealisand* American intelligentsia', but these publications would not build momentum for several years.[62] William

Carlos Williams's revived *Contact: An American Quarterly Review* appeared in 1932, offering a contemporary vector for Surrealist material. Albert Skira's *Minotaure* appeared in 1933; William Phillips, Philip Rahv and Sender Garlin founded the *Partisan Review* in 1934; Charles Henri Ford and Parker Tyler's *View*, the most substantial periodical to print such material, began in 1940. As Tashjian has shown, it was *transition* that most inspired Ford during these earlier years.[63] This period also marks a second phase in Surrealism itself. When it started in 1924, the movement centred on Breton's essentially expressive poetics, which drew from such elements as the automatic text, ideas of the unconscious, dream symbolism, the marvellous, convulsive beauty and objective chance. But by the latter part of the decade it was Pierre Reverdy's notion of the 'Surrealist image' that drove developments. Surrealism proliferated across different art forms, from photography to activism and aesthetic theory as well as verse, prose and the visual arts, and it did not always adhere to Breton's official edicts.[64]

Breton cites Reverdy in the 'First Surrealist manifesto' as having originally defined the Surrealist image. Defined as two or more divergent realities operating in the mind at once to produce a poetic effect, it was a 'pure creation of the mind', in Reverdy's words – a jarring, schismatic image, predicated on the divergence of forms involved in the metaphorical impulse.[65] In terms of the Surrealist influence on American poetry, Rosenbaum regards the Surrealist image as the movement's most 'enduring legacy', evident in 'an understanding of the poem as enacting and inviting a dialectical action of mind, a new way of knowing'.[66] *Transition* certainly bears this out. A good example appears in October 1927 with a poem by Reverdy himself. 'Inn' speaks of the beloved as akin to a shadow. This shadow is first presented as a traditional crepuscular light, but it is also framed as vice and futility where 'ideas die', and the elusive object of the lover is itself like a draining, fading light:

> It is fading and we have seen nothing
> Of all that passed we have retained nothing
> So many words that rise
> Stories one has never read
>   Nothing
> The days swarming at the exit
> The cavalcade has vanished at last
> Down there between the card-players' tables.[67]

The poem begins in a romantic and pastoral mode, but soon turns to an alienated scene of lost glory in a metropolitan recess – a space of gambling, of words seeping out to nothing. If the Surrealist image hinges anywhere in this example, it is on the word 'swarming', with all its infinitesimal animal potential. The 'swarming' of days amid 'so many words' conflates diverging units of time and language, much as the abstracted image of the ancient ocean – the amoebic space – in the preceding examples offers an organic material that simultaneously promises and refuses meaning. When we turn to *transition*'s American texts, this idea is useful primarily as a point of difference: in this body of responsive American writing, the Surrealist image often surfaces with levity.

Archibald MacLeish is a prime example of a jocular take on the Surrealist image. Although a relatively minor poet, MacLeish published a series of five poems in September 1927.[68] All of these works pose questions about modern artistic production and meaning, with the majority of the cycle written in comedic verse that gestures towards Surrealist ideas. Of the five – which appear towards the back of the issue, after an extract from Robert Desnos's novel *La liberté ou l'amour!* and various reproductions of Surrealist artworks – 'Birth of eventually Venus' is especially suggestive.[69] Like Reverdy's 'swarming' days, the poem centres on miniscule, aquatic, pre-human life. Here is the poem in its entirety:

> Cast up by the sea
> By the seventh wave
> Beyond the sea reach
> In the rubble of weed and
> Wet twig
> The not yet amphibious
> Animalcula
> Gasps and wiggles on the beach
> Gathering her long gold hair about her
> And gazing with pure eyes
> Upon the unknown world.[70]

At first glance, the poem is a straightforward retelling of the myth of Aphrodite's birth. Cronos, the first and youngest of the Titans, overthrows his father Uranus, god of the sky, castrating him and hurling his genitals into the sea. The froth of the waves caused by this act then spurs Aphrodite, or Venus, to appear from the water on a scallop shell. In the last lines the poem recalls her divine beauty as portrayed in famous paintings of the goddess by Sandro Botticelli (c. 1486), Alexandre Cabanel (1863) and William-Adolphe Bouguereau (1879). Or rather it would do so, were it not for the power of the central lines. Again:

> The not yet amphibious
> Animalcula
> Gasps and wiggles on the beach

The poetic voice stages the 'birth' as an amoebic event, caught between gods and beasts. The anthropomorphism is anchored in that knowing use of the word *animalcula*. Etymologically, the word stems from the post-classical Latin *animalculum* meaning 'small or low animal', deriving from the form *animal* plus '-cule', or '-cle', a suffix denoting a lesser element or entity as in 'particle', 'article' or 'vesicle'. But the word has several meanings. 'Animalcule' could mean a low or miniscule creature. It could also refer to minute aquatic life, such as protozoans and other motile single-celled organisms: this use of the word stretches from the seventeenth to the twenty-first centuries, and constitutes a more technical, microbiological usage.

MacLeish is also aware of the word's third, rarer meaning: spermatozoa. In this largely obsolete sense, 'animalcule' can mean either a single spermatozoon or the imagined embryo inside the spermatozoon, according to the eighteenth-century paradigm of preformation. With three related meanings, the poem deploys a powerful ambiguity in this parodic origin myth. Instead of being delivered upon a scallop shell, Aphrodite could be in the company of single-celled oceanic organisms – or sperm. 'Not yet amphibious' serves to strengthen the biological register, and 'gasp[ing] and wiggl[ing]' suggests sexual reproduction. The poet asks the reader to suspend the divine image in favour of the primordial animal, underlined with the humorous aspect that Aphrodite came from a severed penis frothing up from the sea.

This comedic quality is also present in William Carlos Williams's *transition* contributions, which are responsive to Surrealism in a similar manner to MacLeish's texts.[71] 'Theessentialroar', published in January 1928, apes the form of an automatic text, with constant non sequiturs, one running sentence, and no punctuation aside from occasional capitalised emphases.[72] Williams plants his narrative voice in the midst of New York City's 'roar', its noise and clatter of conversation, traffic and fragments of cultural life: 'a very nice lady smiles like the translation of a norse saga [*sic*] that the sea has left when the plug slips through the pipe, the toss and danger of the cold sea is dead in English'.[73] Williams's prose bears a resemblance to that of Benjamin Péret, another founding member of Breton's movement, who co-edited *La révolution Surréaliste* and is translated in *transition*. 'In a clinch', which appeared in the following issue, is a translation of part of Péret's then unpublished novel *Death to the Pigs*, written in 1922. Featuring a talking clay pipe, it envisions America as a sea of pigs, with the red, white and blue of capitalist greed woven into the supposedly automatic text. Like Reverdy's 'swarming' and MacLeish's 'animalcula', Péret's central conceit is a speaker likened to a fly trapped in a wine carafe, with a host of animals greeting him on a journey. He beholds a hybrid 'sardine-butterfly' who joins him, offering comfort before transforming into a signpost and smashing the glass; this is followed by an encounter with a talking 'small white mole with dragon-fly wings', a singing pig, porcupines, 'frightened birds' and 'enormous rats which jostled and crushed one another', all of which leads the speaker to conclude: 'and since that day I have wandered over the world'.[74] Where Williams's narrative voice is caught in 'theessentialroar' of urban noise,

Péret's articulates a Parisian metropolitan scene through the miniscule (and drunken) insect. In both, all is open to ridicule – even Surrealist abstraction itself. Although not strictly amoebic, Péret's prose is bolstered by animalcules.

Transition contains a possible source for this comedic mode. A significant number of American contributors to the magazine had an ambivalent if not openly dismissive attitude towards Surrealism. For some, such ambivalence is a front, a defensive mask concealing lines of influence. This is especially apparent when Jolas publishes responses to a questionnaire entitled 'Why do Americans live in Europe?' The responses are made in grand terms such as the 'spiritual failure of America' or the respondents' 'vision' of themselves 'in relation to twentieth century reality'. One of the items on the questionnaire asks about the nature of the 'revolutionary spirit of the age'. This is expressed, Jolas explains, in such movements as communism, anarchism – and Surrealism. Robert McAlmon is characteristically high-minded: 'Surrealism may be like Dada; nothing.' Emily Holmes Coleman is sceptical, declaring herself 'an incurable romantic' before dismissing out of hand any politically engaged connection between art and revolution – expressing a surprisingly conservative belief in aesthetic autonomy. Lansing Warren, a reporter for the *New York Times* and staff member on the European edition of the *Chicago Tribune*, is similarly dismissive, but lighthearted. He avoids Surrealism, he writes, because 'one gets in trouble with the twentieth century. The only way one can live with it peaceably is to find a nice quiet minority and crawl into it and lie low'. Surrealism, anarchism and communism 'are all too vigorous for me': 'what I am looking for is some ism that's more latent, more unobtrusive'.[75]

The questionnaire's more hostile responses are equally instructive. Contributors who state their unwillingness to countenance the importance of the Surrealist movement are often the very writers most marked by its influence. The journalist, writer and translator Pierre Loving, for example, regards Surrealism as no more characteristic of the twentieth century than the 'bousingots', the 'noisemakers' of countercultural resistance that were characteristic of 1830s France. Citing Petrus Borel as a truly revolutionary figure from the 'hell-raising fringe of the Romantic movement', Loving regards Surrealism as a 'new species' of bousingots, 'far inferior in passion and force'.[76] His statement is misleading, however. A regular journalist for such titles as *The Nation* and the *New York Herald*, and author of *The Gardener of Evil*, a 1931 novelised portrait of Baudelaire, Loving contributed creative work to *transition* that was clearly written directly under the movement's influence.[77]

Two further examples illustrate this early American response to Surrealism, again from contributors with journalistic and editorial backgrounds. The poet and publisher Walter Lowenfels flatly rejects the terms of the questionnaire, stating that Surrealism is not revolutionary but 'reactionary'.[78] Written before Lowenfels co-founded the Carrefour Press in 1930 with Michael Fraenkel, and before he became editor at the Pennsylvania edition of the *Daily Worker* in the late 1930s, this statement masks an artistic (if not political) engagement that is evidenced in his creative contributions to the magazine. 'Solstice', for instance, published in the summer 1928 number, is a poem directly engaged with Reverdy's 'Surrealist image'. Footfalls are not soft but 'surgical' slices in this poem; snow is not virgin, but 'being born'.[79] Lowenfels may reject Surrealism on political grounds, but he works with, rather than against, the poetics of the movement.

Jolas's fellow *Chicago Tribune* journalist and writer Leigh Hoffman was similarly influenced by Breton's circle. Hoffman is the most dismissive of the questionnaire's respondents. 'The little group of surrealists – fighting, groping, experimenting – are expressing the chaos of their age, which is a difficult and wholly transitory task', he writes, concluding that 'their works are as temporal as the passing seasons'.[80] If one turns to his creative contributions to *transition*, however, one finds the strong intertextual presence of the 'black Pope' himself – Breton.[81] Hoffman produced two short prose works: 'Anamnesis' in the February 1928 issue, and 'Catastrophe', published in the summer of that year.[82] Although bearing the stamp of solid, journalistic, realist prose, both texts offer mischievous takes on aspects of translations of works by Breton published in *transition*. 'Catastrophe' is a short and whimsical prose piece in which the narrator chases his own head around the city, and it features frequent and disorienting encounters with women. 'I could see my head about a hundred yards in advance waiting for me to catch up', the narrative voice recounts, through 'crowded thoroughfares and down deserted, narrow byways' of a bustling city scene.[83] The text echoes the opening chapter of Breton's *Nadja* (1928), which had been translated in the previous issue.[84] More pointedly, Hoffman writes with an awareness of a lesser known 1927 text by Breton, 'Introduction to the discourse on the dearth of reality'. This was originally published in winter 1924, just a few months after the release of the 'First Surrealist manifesto', in Princess Marguerite Caetani di Bassiano's international review *Commerce* (1924–32), a major source for *transition*'s European content.[85]

A 'neglected but fundamental' document of the movement, 'Discourse' frames a series of attacks on narrowly defined conceptions of reality in relation to literary form.[86] Breton writes of the regard for mountains and seas as an imprisoning 'classic mind', leading to an attack on what he regards as the enslavement of language. 'Language can and should be torn from this servitude'; 'no more description from nature, no more sociological studies [...] Silence! After you, my beautiful language!' The suspension of disbelief, a prerequisite for realist narrative, is a mere fetish, he goes on, 'which needs must try on the white helmet, or caress the fur bonnet', and the fantasies of idle creation are but 'absurd automatons, perfected to the last degree'.[87] Breton moves from this sense of bankrupted classicism to free the power of language from reason, utilitarianism and verisimilitude. This culminates in an image of the biblical creation story as akin to an artist's blank canvas:

> Must poetic creations assume that tangible character of extending, strangely, the limits of so-called reality? May the hallucinatory power of certain images and the true gift of evocation which certain men possess, independently of the faculty of memory, no longer be misunderstood. The God within us does not, indeed, rest on the seventh day. We still have the first pages of Genesis to read [. . .] We know by certain signs that the great illumination follows its course.[88]

Hoffman's 'Anamnesis' is a direct response. The word 'anamnesis' has several meanings: the recollection of an entire history via one consciousness, an invocation of a previous life, or the part of the Christian Eucharist which recalls the passion, resurrection and ascension of Christ. Hoffman's omniscient narrator is also an omnipotent god. The text's central consciousness stands at the dawn of time on a silent, Precambrian earth, before any living thing. He then articulates his own creation of humans, before jumping to a modern bourgeois life of womanising and drinking. The narrator acquires an automaton of a woman 'to comply with my every whim', a 'perfect and admirable dummy' that evokes Breton's image of realism as so many 'absurd automatons, perfected to the last degree'. With a nod to Breton's scepticism towards sublime visions of nature, Hoffman's narrator also sculpts a mountain so that he might show a nameless woman the scene, order her to write down his words, and then destroy the entire landscape in a wrathful godlike fashion.[89] Where MacLeish's Surrealist image hinged upon the transformative 'animalcula', here the reader sees a fascination with Breton's call for Genesis – for an artistic freedom to create and recreate origin myths, unrestrained by the 'absurd automatons' of reason.

To return to the scene of MoMA's formalist abstraction, then, it seems clear that *transition* was one of Barr's literary antecedents, and it engaged in the biomorphic abstraction that would turn up in the mid-1930s as the 'amoebic silhouette'. Especially in its early years, the magazine provided a conduit for such Surrealist concepts and poetics as dream analysis, the automatic text and the Surrealist image, with a thematic link concerning this miniscule, pre-human, aquatic, abyssal creaturely poetic. In designating these qualities an 'amoebic mode', I have invoked a necessarily malleable approach encompassing protozoa, animalcules, the ancient ocean and microbiology. After all, Barr's pronouncement for the visual arts, although questionable, articulates the structure of a metaphor.

An 'inevitable coition with abstraction'

If the first category of Surrealist influence and the amoebic mode rests with comedy, the second rests with a combination of marked locales and depictions of ancient time. Where the examples above reveal authors seeking to reconfigure the origin myths of language and religion, others look to the prehistoric past. Poets and authors explore disjunctive clashes of ancient and modern time and space, using geological imagery, with recurrent poetic reflections on the 'protoplasmic' or organic origins of life. Although Alexander Oparin's concept of the 'primordial soup' at the dawn of life would not reach a wide English-speaking audience until 1938, the reader can detect an early fascination with the most biologically distant, most ancient living world. This second category of amoebic abstraction in *transition* is also more distinct from (although still influenced by) the Surrealist texts that were often printed alongside it. It is indicative of a younger generation of American writing nurtured in the magazine, and it forms the final part of this discussion.[90]

An early example comes from Bryher. In 'Different focus', part of a series of poems printed in *transition*'s third issue, the poetic voice shifts from the modern realm of the city to the primordial realm of the Jurassic era. The reader hears of an insurmountable gap between the speaker and the lost object of her love. As in MacLeish's poem, there seems to be a direct allusion to the Surrealist emphasis on unusual configurations of objects, here transposed to a clash between space and time. With its staccato rhythm and continuous image form, I quote the poem in full:

> It's not you,
> it's everything you were,
> lights reflected from a skyscraper,
> lights from revolving disks,
> words so of this day,
> un-old, untold.
>
> Sounds of your voice,
> your brain,
> your asthenic modern head,
> ears,
> picking up the wireless of the world,
> transmitting it again.
>
> Shells inland
> on the bed of a long forgotten dried up sea,
> so old that they are young,
> prehistoric things,
> pterodactyl wings,
> stride of dinosaurs in sand;
> if you are brittle and dry
> and needing

> something I cannot even understand,
> to be carried by the wind
> from the sea,
> detached and unrelated,
> it is for you to decide this,
> not me.[91]

Bryher clashes against a naturalist mode with the dissonance of a dinosaur print beneath a skyscraper. The image is a trace, a series of recordings, from city lights to transmitters to the acoustics of a shell, a fossil or a footprint. The voice searches for polarities and confronts the dry origins of the ocean: a space we might usefully call amoebic, or a stand-in notion for origins, reached with a call to the oldest animals ('so old that they are young'). It is the formlessness of abstraction, but in a particularly metropolitan, American setting. The large industrial city is plunged to the seabed, and all for the lover's ultimate resignation – the end of intimacy.

This juxtaposition of the ancient and modern reappears in a poem by Blanche Matthias, published two issues after Bryher's appearance. Matthias was a regular art critic for the *Chicago Tribune*, and had likely encountered Jolas in Paris the mid-1920s or earlier. She also worked for the *Chicago Herald*, the *Examiner* and the *Chicago Evening Post*, as well as contributing creative works to *All's Well*, *The Forum*, *Pagany*, *Prairie*, *Poetry*, *This Quarter* and *transition*. Although discussion of her life is limited to a few footnotes in studies of Chicago's modernist art scene or of her artist friends (who included Georgia O'Keeffe and Margery Latimer), Matthias is an important voice in this case.[92] Like Bryher's verse, Matthias's poem 'The formless ones at Carmel Point' also conveys some primordial qualities of nature. Rather than in the city, this poem evokes a scene on the Californian Big Sur shoreline, Matthias's 1920s home. Again, I quote in full:

> Figures of shadow
>   ooze from the rocks
> And are sucked back
>   into the rocks.
> Humans in terror moved by the space left empty
> Huddle together, and build cities.
> They cannot escape;
> They cannot get free;
> Enchainment is compelled by mist and fog
> By clouds, and the steadiness of wind
>   uninterrupted by the going of the false dawn
>   or by the impenetrable freshness
>   of that which links all nights to all dawns;
> Or the oozing and sucking of rocks.[93]

Those opening and closing lines, with the 'oozing and sucking' of the rocks bookending the poem, set up an ecological vision in which urbanisation is a dismal crust upon the landscape. The poem bears a strong resemblance to Robinson Jeffers's later 'Carmel Point'. Another of Matthias's contributions in this cycle is dedicated to the 'poet in Tor House', the residence Robinson and Una Jeffers built in the early 1900s.[94] Jeffers's poem, written in 1938 and published in his 1954 collection *Hungerfield*, could almost be a copy of Matthias's. Its scene of encroaching humanity also centres on the 'pristine beauty' of Carmel Point's 'outcrop rock-heads' before 'the spoiler' of housing development. Jeffers's well-known ethos of 'inhumanism' is clearly stated in the closing lines of his poem. If it is a copy of Matthias's text, it is a more plaintive cry:

> We must uncenter our minds from ourselves;
> We must unhumanise our views a little, and become confident
> As the rock and ocean that we were made from.[95]

Whether or not Jeffers is borrowing from his friend's 1927 verse, a point of difference between the two situates Matthias's *transition* context. It is there in that repeated verb 'ooze'. The evolutionary connotations of this word are unmistakable: the reader might envision the tidal pull of the ocean, but also, again, the 'primordial ooze'. There is a living, breathing presence in this otherwise lifeless landscape, and a deliberately abstract design. 'Figures of shadow / ooze from the rocks' is an amoebic metaphor that strains towards a time beyond humanity. This was perhaps the quality in Matthias's poetry that came to Jolas's mind when, after reading a selection she had sent to him in 1940, he wrote in a letter that her work 'get[s] near the kernel of things, an inward thinking, a musing in images'.[96] Certainly, in his June 1929 editorial 'Logos', Jolas attributed the same quality to Bryher's and Matthias's poems:

> The sharpness and power of the metaphorical vision gives [the poet] a superiority in understanding and the primordial creation of life. [. . .] This should be made through a technique of the word that is parallel with the incentive guiding the evolution of the images in his mind, because we are beginning to realise that, by putting words together in identical and repetitive relationship, we arrive ultimately at creative abortions, and are not faithful to ourselves.[97]

Jolas was evidently responding to what was arguably *transition*'s most influential Surrealist work in this transatlantic context, which had been translated by Maria Jolas in the previous issue: Robert Desnos's essay 'The work of Man Ray'. A mere three pages long, Desnos's essay frames abstraction as focused on perception and animation. He begins with a description of the 'most primitive' animal life, coupled with a belief that he has alighted upon an imagined untapped world of perception:

> Our only exploration of the Universe has been with the aid of senses corrupted by prejudice. Our vision of the world when reduced to its minimum is the same as that of the most primitive missing link: doubtless the blind fish in the depths of the ocean constructs his mythology among the aromatic sea-weed in spite of the entire collection of gods which man strives to force from matter. With the awakening of our senses, we decreed that chaos had been dispersed. But there are other forms of chaos surrounding us and we have no way of dividing these into water, air, earth, or fire. There is an infinity of senses which we lack. The conquest of just one of them would revolutionise the world more than the invention of a religion or the sudden arrival of a new geological era.[98]

Anticipating Lhote's art-historical piece quoted above, this extraordinary introduction to Ray focuses on the curvature of the artist's work as an important feature, much like the primordial, 'sinusoidal' curves of verbo-visual graphism in Lhote's essay.[99] But Desnos takes the principle further than Lhote. 'The spirals twine in and out like supple brains', he writes, attributing to the curvature of Ray's pictures a strangely lifeless quality, albeit 'with nothing dead about them'. By moving between images of abstraction as both alive and somehow 'fugitive', like the moment between facial expressions, Desnos creates an influential and arguably amoebic principle of abstraction. It is a figure one is both drawn to and wary of, like a precipice above a ravine. 'But we dare not lose ourselves bag and baggage herein', he writes, 'despite the reiterated balls of our likeness in the depths of the water.'[100] It is through this image of abstraction – alluring, amoebic, abyssal and on the brink of chaos – that we might best consider *transition*'s amoebic mode. More than simply an anticipation of Barr's formalism, these are metaphors of the most primitive missing link. This is not to say that such writing reflects a dearth of critical, political or artistic engagement with the world from which it was produced. On the contrary: just as the ambivalent and comedic responses to Surrealism outlined above reveal a subtle, careful attention to the movement on the part of its so-called sceptics, so these final examples reveal a comparable complexity, marked by a more geological vision and returning repeatedly to primordial scenes of life. Like Desnos's warning that 'we must not lose ourselves', *transition*'s authors often express that same pull towards abstraction, but they do so guardedly, unwillingly, aware of its vagaries.

By the end of *transition*'s eleven years, this ambivalence found form in the works of another overlooked *transition* author, Dorothy Boillotat (later Dorothy

Donnelly), which offer a final example of the amoebic mode. Boillotat was an award-winning poet who later wrote *The Golden Well*, a structuralist 'anatomy' of symbols, myths and fables.[101] In a 1931 letter to the poet, Jolas wrote as if to a protégée: 'you are the only one in America whose writing seems to me to be going in the right direction'.[102] Of all the authors drawn to *transition*'s particular literary culture of abstraction, Boillotat was certainly among the most engaged readers of the magazine, as her titles alone indicate. 'Escapes', 'Decaying', 'Heritage', 'Sensing', and 'Dream of the end of time' all appeared in the latter half of *transition*'s run, from issues 18 (November 1929) to 27 (April–May 1938). All reveal a close and careful engagement with Surrealism. 'Escapes', first, shows the clear influence of Marcel Noll's early contributions, which had been translated by Eugene Jolas, Elliot Paul and Maria Jolas and published between April 1927 and March 1928.[103] 'Decaying', like Jolas's 'Logos', is suggestive of a direct response to Desnos, Bryher and Matthias, and indeed to a 1928 contribution from Paul Bowles entitled 'Entity', in which the primitive figure of the spiral recurs as a mystical presence.[104] In Boillotat's text, the speaker considers various manifestations of organic permanence, but these are countered with images of transience and fragility. Several recurring figures of abstraction dominate: spirals, the sea and a 'katabolic' worm – a creature that is connected to a downward spiral of fragmentation and disintegration and yet is foundational, at the origins and also the undoings of life. A worm, one might add, is like an amoeba: 'in the heart of the world, feeding and crawling, ceaselessly crawling and feeding'.[105]

Between these poles of description, Boillotat considers the 'sameness of things': 'the sameness of things is too strong with the immobile strength of still, deep water'. By counterpoising the tension between the permanence and impermanence of life, Boillotat is able to create a passage of creaturely imagery that stands in for a reflection on language. 'There is only a vast katabolism', her speaker reflects, 'and building is to be broken.'[106] This writerly pull towards an abstraction that moves through particular animal metaphors is a characteristic feature of Boillotat's work. In 'Sensing', the speaker refers again and again to the curvatures of nature. These are not strong, absolute or fixed, but are like tissues of gossamer, liable to break:

> Whorls of conversation spin finer and finer amid amber tea until I know and fear the inevitable coition with abstraction. A diaphanous rope confusing as ether fumes strangles me and I am tangled in its multitudinous coil. I cannot breathe unless I break the fragile spirals and crumple the crystal webs and shatter with a bass discordance the too perfect shells woven, ring on ring, of conscious rhythms into faultless curves. Is there a door and can I flee from this mothwing world with its excessive refinement of skeletons of the spirit?[107]

The speaker continues this theme: she attempts to 'hold a word', but cannot. She is overwhelmed by the 'inevitable coition to abstraction'. 'Is there a door?' she asks. 'Is there a door and can I flee?' Boillotat's voice confronts the oncoming abstraction of experience in an ambivalent manner, much like Desnos. Her text both moves towards and pulls back from this impulse: a 'pagan joy' desired and distrusted, something against which she must become 'an embryo in the womb of life and sense all with the aboriginal shock of firstness'. In the end, this ambivalence around abstraction – that 'inevitable coition' – reveals the idea of total perceptive immersion in the world, and of a Revolution of the Word in which language could enact such change as a fantasy, perhaps even a foolhardy one. In that 'firstness', moreover, might the reader hear the non-human? Boillotat's narrator talks of a 'knot of wood' as akin to solidity, structure – as that 'which could be broken but not dissolved by thought into abstraction'.[108] The grandeur of such a fantasy is knowingly embedded in its articulation, finally, as the speaker can only ever imagine such a desire, rather than live it.

The 'inevitable coition with abstraction' is, in the end, an ultimate source of fear and ambivalence in Boillotat's texts, suggesting a shift in the magazine away from an earlier moment in Surrealist poetics, towards a more responsive body of work that often rests its reflections on the primordial animal. A 1929 prose work from H. Christopher Holme entitled 'Art and revolution', for example, brings the markedly American accoutrements of modernity into play before invoking a more European current of abstraction. 'And all the time machines clocked tumultuously', the narrative voice says, 'tapemachines, refrigerators, printing-machines, powerplants. A face loomed in his mind, abstracted from the conversation, large, ugly, monstrous.'[109] The text concludes with a verse segment entitled 'Abstract!', with an imperative exclamation mark bringing a shade of parody to the fore, and the not-quite-human homunculus invoking an earlier stage of evolution:

> Light-spattered homunculi
>   fumble aspiring upwards.
> The airy wastes of liberty
>   allure but cannot hold
>   Matter with immaterial chains.
> The momentary, red sun wanes
>   into oblivion, reaching
> lost tentacles of tired illumination
>   into the putrid genesis
>   of half-reality[110]

With these 'lost tentacles of tired illumination', Holme is characteristic of a community of American writers working in the milieu of Surrealist abstraction, whether comedically like MacLeish, or more sensitively like Boillotat. 'I would revert to the amoeba', Boillotat writes in 1935, 'and know all through the primal sense. I would fold upon and envelop completely the thing, not touch it merely with the tips of pseudopodia, which, sensitive, are presently my fingers. I would know it with the protoplasmic whole.'[111] It is fitting that the final issue of *transition* reproduces a canvas by Wassily Kandinsky entitled *Composition, 1937*: this is Barr's formulation writ large, so many amoebic silhouettes encased within the grid of the square (Figure 1.4). To turn finally to the literary equivalent, Boillotat's is not a holistic vision of nature, but an encroaching one, 'corrosive and lazy', as in Caillois's sense of Tanguy's amoeboid shapes. Boillotat's amoeba marks an awareness of this corrosion, this vortex of abstraction, in spite of – and perhaps because of – over a decade of the journal in which it was formed. The protozoic signifying space – what I have tentatively called an amoebic mode – enables a reading of this literary-historical junction, which is especially evident across *transition*'s pages.

Figure 1.4 Wassily Kandinsky, *Composition, 1937*. Reproduced in *transition*, 27, April–May 1938

Notes

1. Foster, 'At MoMA', 14.
2. Barr, *Cubism*. Although MoMA ran its companion show 'Fantastic Art, Dada, Surrealism' later the same year (7 December 1936–17 January 1937), Barr never compiled a chart for those movements. Macleod, 'Visual arts', 195.
3. For a critical overview of Barr's formalism, see Kantor, *Alfred H. Barr*, 314–53. For a gendered critique, see Pollock, 'Moments'.
4. Barr, *Cubism*, 19.
5. I am grateful to Bernard Vere for pointing this out. Kandinsky, 'Composition, 1937'.
6. Macleod's examples of Cubist influence on modernist literature are Stein's *Three Lives* (1909), Eliot's *The Waste Land* (1922) and Stevens's *The Man with the Blue Guitar* (1937). Macleod, 'Visual arts', 200–2.
7. See especially Kraus, *Originality*, 9–22; Mitchell, '*Ut pictura theoria*', 351; Mitchell, *Picture Theory*, 213–40; Hulle, 'Growth'.
8. As Jennifer Mundy points out, Barr uses the terms 'biomorph' and 'biomorphic abstraction' without explanation, even though Geoffrey Grigson originated them a year before. Grigson, 'Comment on England' quoted in Mundy, 'Naming of biomorphism', 63.
9. Tashjian, *Boatload of Madmen*.
10. Hogan, '*transition*'s tenth anniversary', preserved in Box 60, Folder 1400, Maria and Eugene Jolas Papers, Beinecke Rare Book and Manuscript Library, Yale University. Subsequent references to this archive will be indicated by the Box and Folder numbers followed by an indication of the collection as the Jolas Papers.
11. Putnam, 'If Dada comes', original emphasis. For an early theorisation of American surrealism, see Hays, 'Surrealist influence'. Hays argues for Charles Henri Ford's and other poets' interpretations of the Surrealist movement in terms of what he calls 'poetic fundamentals' (ibid. 202).
12. Rosenbaum, 'Exquisite corpse'. See also Pawlitt, 'Surrealism'.
13. Miller, 'Poetic contagion', 19.
14. Subscribers list, c. 1936. Box 60, Folder 1402, Jolas Papers.
15. Sorenson, 'James Johnson Sweeney'. See also Brennan, 'Multiple masculinities'.
16. Sweeney, *African Negro Art*.
17. Barr, 'The LEF'; Marquis, *Alfred H. Barr Jr*, 40.
18. Marquis, *Alfred H. Barr Jr*, 43. Marquis credits the quotation to an unsigned article in the *Boston Evening Transcript*, 27 April 1927.
19. Steloff, Gotham Book Mart, letter to Jolas, 26 May 1939. Box 59, Folder 1385, Jolas Papers. Further correspondence between Jolas and Faber, the magazine's British distributor, suggests UK sales were up in 1938 too: the journal generated a slim profit during the magazine's final year. Faber Press invoice issued to Jolas, 17 August 1938. Box 59, Folder 1384, Jolas Papers.
20. Lankester, 'Parasitic amœbæ'.
21. Vivian Endicott Barnett has shown direct parallels between Kandinsky's Paris period and his well-thumbed encyclopaedia dating from the mid-1910s. He reveals suggestive images under the volume's 'Zoology' and other entries as major sources for Kandinsky's work. See Barnett, 'Kandinsky and science'.

22. Armstrong, 'Biological tropes', 103. See also Price, 'Finite but unbounded'.
23. Davies, 'Biology and Surrealism'.
24. Schapiro, 'The nature', 142.
25. Bernstein, 'Disfiguring abstraction', 490.
26. Reynolds, 'Amoebae'.
27. Leidy, 'Amoeba proteus', 235.
28. Schaeffer, 'Taxonomy'.
29. Quoted in Jabre, 'How brainless', para. 1.
30. Kudo, '*Pelomyxa*', 480. See also Mendelsohn, 'Lives'.
31. Burnett, 'Balls', 124.
32. Shipman, 'Premonition', 135.
33. 'Gessler', 'Slants', *Honolulu Star-Bulletin*, 17 September 1932, n.p., preserved in a scrapbook in Box 13, Folder 259, Jolas Papers.
34. Lhote, 'L'inconscient'. I quote from Lhote, 'Unconscious in art'.
35. Lhote, 'Unconscious in art', 86, 90.
36. Tanguy (cover), in Jolas, *Words from the Deluge*; Caillois, 'Surrealism as a world of signs' in *Edge of Surrealism*, 329, originally published as 'Le Surréalisme comme univers de signes' in *Obliques* (1975).
37. Tanguy, 'Painting'.
38. Caillois, *Edge of Surrealism*, 330.
39. Vailland, 'Arthur Rimbaud or war', 66–7, 69, 70. Originally published as Vailland, 'Arthur Rimbaud ou guerre'.
40. Schapiro, 'The nature', 124.
41. Read, 'Myth', 184.
42. See Read's edited collection *Surrealism* and his article 'Beyond realism'. I am grateful to Charlie Dawkins for bringing the latter to my attention.
43. Foster, *Compulsive Beauty*, 42; Lautréamont, 'From the lay', 109–10; Lewis, 'Diabolical principle', 69.
44. Lautréamont, 'From the lay', 109–10.
45. Ibid. 109.
46. Balakian, *Surrealism*, 58.
47. Jolas, 'Enter the imagination', 160.
48. Tzara, 'Approximate man'. Jolas likely worked from Kra's 1929 volume: Tzara et al., *De nos oiseaux*. Tzara published the work as a stand-alone piece in 1931 as *L'homme approximatif*.
49. Cardinal, 'Tzara, Tristan'.
50. Tzara, 'Approximate man', 325.
51. Ibid. 325–6.
52. Tzara, 'Dada manifesto 1918', and 'Lecture on Dada' (1922) in *Seven Dada Manifestos*, 4, 112. Quoted in Miller, 'Poetic contagion', 21.
53. Tzara, 'Approximate man', 327, 329.
54. Ibid. 328.
55. Léon-Paul Fargue was not a Surrealist: he was part of the French Symbolist poetry circle associated with *Le Mercure de France*. That Jolas misrecognised his author's allegiances is secondary to the qualities in the work he wished to call upon for a new generation of American writers.

56. Jolas, 'Revolution of language', 110–11.
57. Jolas, *Transition Workshop*, 15.
58. Fargue, 'Tumult', 59–60. Other Fargue texts in the magazine include 'Aeternae memorie patris', 'The drug', 'Plus je vais', 'Exile', 'The alchemist'.
59. Jolas, 'On the quest', 194.
60. Translations of Fargue and others by the Jolases had a direct influence on subsequent anthologies. Whilst putting together a volume of French poetry translated by anglophone poets, the novelist Paul Auster wrote to Maria Jolas requesting permission for this text, along with a series of other Surrealist offerings in *transition*. Auster, letter to M. Jolas, 4 April 1981. Box 28, Folder 525, Jolas Papers. Auster (ed.), *Random House Book*.
61. Ford, 'Foreword', ix.
62. Koloctroni, 'Minotaur in Manhattan', 87.
63. Tashjian, *Boatload of Madmen*, 158–9.
64. Miller, 'Poetic contagion', 19.
65. Breton, *Manifestoes of Surrealism*, 26.
66. Rosenbaum, 'Exquisite corpse', 270–1.
67. Reverdy, 'Inn'.
68. MacLeish, 'Vernissage', 'Birth', 'Poem', 'Project' and 'Poem dedicated'. The cycle was not incorporated into MacLeish's collected poems for another fifty-five years: see MacLeish, *Collected Poems*, 502–5. *Poetry* published these works in 1980 in the same order as they had appeared *transition*, under the title 'Five lost poems'.
69. Desnos, *La liberté*. This was debuted in *transition* as 'Liberty or love'. The Surrealist artworks in question are Tanguy, 'Landscape', Miró, 'Drawing', Arp, 'Arping' and M. Ray, 'Section of film', which all appear between pages 113 and 114.
70. MacLeish, 'Birth'.
71. Williams published a mix of poetry, fiction, editorial content, articles and reviews in *transition*: Williams, 'Dead baby' (1927), 'Voyage to Pagany' (1927), 'A note', (1927), 'Winter', 'Theessentialroar', 'Letter', 'Improvisations', 'George Antheil', 'A point', 'The somnambulists', and 'Simplicity of disorder'.
72. Scholars have explored Williams's engagements with Dada and Surrealist aesthetics, both before and after this period. See Schmidt, *William Carlos Williams*; Tashjian, *Skyscraper Primitives*; Macleod (ed.), *Williams and Surrealism*.
73. Williams, 'Theessentialroar', 50.
74. Péret, 'In a clinch', 55–6, 59–61. See also Péret, *Death*.
75. Stein et al., 'Why do Americans', 99, 110–11, 113.
76. Ibid. 109–10.
77. Schwartzburg et al., 'Pierre Loving'. See especially Loving, 'Praying insects'.
78. Stein et al., 'Why do Americans', 107.
79. Benefiel and Wheeler, *Guide*, 5; Lowenfels, 'Solstice'.
80. Stein et al., 'Why do Americans', 101.
81. This was Breton's moniker in New York circles by around 1940. Kolocotroni, 'Minotaur in Manhattan', 88.
82. Hoffman, 'Anamnesis', 'Catastrophe'.
83. Hoffman, 'Catastrophe', 77.

84. Breton, 'Nadja (opening chapter)'. It is worth noting that this extract appeared at the same time as the French edition of the novel. It is possible that Breton authorised the translation for promotional purposes. See Breton, Nadja.
85. Breton, 'Introduction', originally published as 'Introduction au discours'. See also Breton, Introduction au discours. For further discussion, see Chenieux-Gendron, 'Poetics of bricolage'. Commerce operated under the directorship of Valery Larbaud, Léon-Paul Fargue and Paul Valéry. Early issues of transition bore the same font and layout, were of the same size, and included many translations of works which had originally appeared in the French journal. See Levie, Commerce.
86. Lomas, 'André Breton's "Subject"', 5.
87. Breton, 'Introduction to the discourse', 130, 141–2.
88. Ibid. 142.
89. Hoffman, 'Anamnesis', 67–9.
90. Oparin, Origin of Life.
91. Bryher, 'Different focus'.
92. For a brief biographical overview, see Stark, Guide, 4. See also Matthias, Wish to Sing.
93. Matthias, 'Formless ones'.
94. Matthias, 'Altar stone'.
95. Jeffers, 'Carmel Point' in Hungerfield, 97. For a discussion of Jeffers's 'inhumanism' and the context of ecocriticism, see Keller, 'Green reading', 605–6.
96. Jolas, letter to Blanche Matthias, 13 February 1940. Box 3, Folder 54, Jolas Papers.
97. Jolas, 'Logos', 28.
98. Desnos, 'Work of Man Ray', 264.
99. Lhote, 'Unconscious in art', 96.
100. Desnos, 'Work of Man Ray', 265–6.
101. Donnelly, Golden Well.
102. 'Administrative/biographical history: The Walter and Dorothy Donnelly family papers, 1887–1976', University of Central Florida Special Collections, at http://ucfarchon.fcla.edu/index.php?p=collections/controlcard&id=20# (last accessed 25 June 2018).
103. Boillotat, 'Escapes', 'Decaying', 'Heritage', 'Sensing' and 'Dream'. Noll, 'Two poems', 'From a notebook' and 'From a note book'.
104. Bowles, 'Entity'.
105. Boillotat, 'Decaying', 50.
106. Ibid. 48.
107. Boillotat, 'Sensing', 11.
108. Ibid. 11–12.
109. Holme, 'Art and revolution', 163.
110. Ibid. 165.
111. Boillotat, 'Sensing', 15, 11–12.

2

FISH: EVOLVING THE ARTWORK IN JAMES JOYCE'S 'SHEM THE PENMAN' (1927)

Yet may we not see still the brontoichthyan form aslumbered.
James Joyce, *Finnegans Wake*, 1939

Science is not a heartless pursuit of objective information. It is a creative human activity, its geniuses acting more as artists than as information processors.
Stephen Jay Gould, *Ever Since Darwin*, 1977

In October 1927, *transition* published its seventh issue. As with previous numbers, its centrepiece – in some ways its *raison d'être* – was the seventh instalment of Joyce's 'Continuation of a work in progress', the ongoing serialised project that in 1939 became *Finnegans Wake*.[1] The instalment is known as the 'Shem the Penman' episode, and much has been written on the subject of the eponymous artist, a semi-autobiographical figure. 'Shem' is one of the more accessible entry points to the 'Work in progress', and it has been read predominantly through the figures of the artist and the artwork. Such readings reveal Joyce to be highly responsive to his critics. He is the 'penman' of loving pastiches of *transition*, and of less than loving ripostes to Wyndham Lewis's polemics.[2] What remains less commented on, however, is a distinctly non-human, primordial metaphor in the text: Joyce writes Shem as a fish. Whether in words pertaining to types of fish, fishy parts, fishy food, fishy bile, fishy ink or the single declaration 'Fish!'[3] Joyce enacts a connection between the animal and the artist through the context of the life sciences. Specifically, he does this through repeated allusions to contemporary evolutionary theory. The narrator Shaun asks 'the first riddle of the universe: when is a man not a man?'[4] From this early intertextual reference to the German embryologist Ernst Haeckel to the closing, cleansing arrival of the river-mother Anna Livia Plurabelle, the reader is in a discursively biological realm, and the fish is never far off.[5]

The fish can be any sea-dwelling, gill-bearing vertebrate without limbs or digits. It is the backboned creature furthest from humans. We think of fish as unfeeling, unthinking fodder, swirling the ocean in shoals. They appear throughout myth, art, literature and folklore as symbols of plenty, fertility, knowledge, even immortality. During the late 1920s and early 1930s in particular, morphologists, palaeontologists and many other scientists were frequently engaged in studies of living and prehistoric species of fish, which formed part of the texture of debates around the nature of adaptation.[6] The 1920s also saw the term 'land invasion' enter popular consciousness, as scientists questioned the point at which the earliest fish began to evolve limbs.

Despite the wealth of knowledge the fish has given to biological study, it is defined by what it lacks. The fish lacks the appendages or digits that become claws or feathers or fingers. It lacks anything that points towards sentient subjectivity. A paradox lies between this bodily lack and the sheer fecundity of the fish in its art-historical legacy. As symbol or specimen, the fish can help us think about the spaces between what is known or written and what is unknown or erased. For although the fish is a marker of lack (of fingers that might write, for instance), there is a strong association between this animal and writing. The early Christian symbol for Christ, the ichthus, is the result of an acrostic. The word 'ichthus' (in Hellenistic Greek ἰχθύς, 'fish') is formed from the first letters of the Greek words for 'Jesus Christ, son of God, saviour' (ησοῦς Χριστός, Θεοῦ Υἱός, Σωτήρ, *Iesous Christos Theou Uios Soter*). Yet biologically, as the great evolutionary 'root' of vertebrate life, the fish is a creature of primordial origins, of the prehistory or absence of a Logos.

This strong association between fish, creation and the Word is pertinent to my reading of Joyce's primordial modernism. In the beginning was the Word and the Word was God, we hear in the Christian Gospel of John (1: 1–5); specifically, the Word was flesh, and that flesh was Christ (John 1: 14–15), the ichthus of Jesus Christ, son, and saviour. Parallel to this theological line of association lies a diversity of symbolic fish with which 'Shem' is directly engaged, where we find fish linked to creation and the Word. Evolution, degeneration, extinction and generation also move through the text. Informed by scholarship from Len Platt, Scarlett Baron and Paul Bowers that has addressed Joyce and biology, I posit a reading that moves from these Christian fish into more secular territory. For the evolutionary fish is the fish at the 'bottom' or beginning of the tree of life, and this is highly suggestive for my deliberately partial approach to *Finnegans Wake*. Joyce's fish are also highly racialised: the colder, harsher Shaun in the text expresses contempt for his brother Shem by using a eugenicist's voice. Joyce does something, I suggest, with Shem's 'lowness', his fishiness. Rather than simply representing either bodily lack or the traditional symbol of plenty, Joyce's fish in the Shem episode become a primordial expression of modernist writing.

This chapter is formed of four parts. The first addresses the symbolic legacy and tradition of fish and inscription as an art-historical texture present in 'Shem the Penman'. The second contextualises Joyce's episode via the historical connections between fish and contemporary evolutionary theory. The third part considers how Joyce moves from evolutionary fish as a site of degeneracy and lack into a modulated linguistic space where Shem's excremental self-production returns to a fish of plenty or knowledge, precisely through its filthy, 'low' inscription. This prompts questions, discussed in the final part, as to how we might theorise Joyce's fish as a primordial modernist articulation that is at home in *transition* and is part of the magazine's wider project. In the epic world of *Finnegans Wake*, a novel 'about everything', lies a creative project intimately connected to Jolas's vision for his magazine.[7] When we take this small part of the 'Work in progress' and read it as it appeared, valid points of connection emerge. Samuel Beckett wrote about the 'Work in progress' in an essay originally published in *transition*, and his words are apt here: it is '*not about* something; *it is that something itself*'.[8]

God, Fish, Word

The symbolic fish is pervasive. As well as being the ichthus, in Hellenic mythology the fish symbolises the divine source of life; sacred fish indicate a hope for immortality, which is in turn a variation of the Egyptian Oxyrhynchus fish that devoured the phallus of Osiris.[9] In Hebrew mythology, Leviathan is the hostile sea monster, whale of chaos, that is slain by Yahweh and killed at the end of all time (Isaiah 27: 1). Leviathan transmutes in later rabbinical tradition to become the great fish, the food of the faithful at the coming messianic banquet.[10] In chthonic terms, Mesopotamian fish symbols denote life itself, as well as the idea of rebirth.[11] Various fish symbols appear as rhomb or lozenge shapes, signifying the female vulva and accentuating the ubiquitous image of fertility, as in the Masonic iconography of the Venn diagram-shaped *vesica piscis*. In art, after a significant absence of fish from eighteenth- and nineteenth-century painting, the twentieth century saw renewed attention being given to this animal, particularly by Paul Klee. As the catalogue of the 1953 London gallery exhibition 'The Fish in Twentieth Century Art' puts it, it has a close association with the psyche:

> Before [Klee], [the] fish had a carnal attraction; it appeared as a victim caught by the fisherman [. . .] But Klee's fish could not fulfil any material function; a mysterious creature, in complete harmony with its surroundings, its form is compact [. . .] [It] seems, more than the mammal, more than the bird, to be part of the element in which it lives. No wonder that the fish became the favourite in a period which found new revelations in the region of subconsciousness and of inorganic matter; which became attracted by any exoticism and by any force that could not be grasped by the intellect.[12]

Twentieth-century writing is no exception in this 'region of subconsciousness'. One thinks of Santiago's words in Ernest Hemingway's *The Old Man and the Sea* (1952): '"Fish", he [says] softly, aloud, "I'll stay with you until I am dead."'[13] The play of symbols in such an example is about encircling forms of God-man and fish.[14] Virginia Woolf's *Between the Acts* (1941) creates a psychical symbol in the fish pond, again joining the fish to depths, water and the mind.[15] In these examples, the fish is a symbol for a cluster of associations between identity and individual consciousness. Hemingway's grand imagery may be very different from Woolf's synaptic pool, but in each there exists a legacy of the connection between the fish emblem and religious modes of inscription.

Joyce writes from within this tradition in a number of ways, as well as away from it. As Ingeborg Landuyt points out, even before one turns to the text in detail, there is a deliberately biblical tenor around the number seven and its place in both *transition* and the final *Wake* text as Book One Chapter Seven. The seven days of creation, seven years of plenty and famine in Egypt, seven petitions of the Lord's Prayer, seven words on the cross and seven sacraments – the Bible is full of significant septuplets.[16] Prior to its 1925 publication in *This Quarter*, Joyce worked on the passage under the informal title 'Shem – Ham – Cain – Esau', a clear allusion to the marked brother cast out of paradise who committed seven crimes and would be punished sevenfold.[17] The importance of the Shem chapter's engagement with Genesis should not be underestimated, although in this case the focus on the connection between fish and creation will allow a more delimited discussion.

Structural as well as genetic aspects are also significant here. As Roland McHugh observes, 'Shem' is part of a process whereby 'consciousness strives with passionate intensity for unattainable ideals until in I.7 it attains madness'.[18] In Joyce's sign system, the siglum for Shem is ⊂; Shaun is ∧; the ultimate male protagonist, HCE or Humphrey Chimpden Earwicker, is ⊓; the ultimate female protagonist is △, ALP or the alma mater, the river – the delta. Shem and Shaun as a duality are ⋏. Shem is a principle of life, Shaun death. Shem offers up a symbol of the elm tree, Shaun a stone. If we take the dualism to its crudest level, ⊏ is the artist, ⋏ the scientist.[19] Book I in its entirety is a presentation of ⊏ by ⋏. ⊏'s words are made in the text to introduce a 'notion of time',[20] as ⊏ is an association with time, with the elm's growth, and with the river of time, the △.[21] In Shem lies a principle of life, a growth force, which cannot settle straightforwardly as a simple allusion to Cain.

Regarding the fish in the passage, critics have pursued diverse lines of enquiry. Numerous scholars, including Harry Levin, William York Tindall, Patricia Morley and others, have underlined a deep connection between HCE and the Irish mythological identification of Finn MacCool with the Salmon of Wisdom and Solomon-Salmon.[22] Such critical approaches revel in Joyce's extension of Christian and pagan totemic fish in proliferating mythological allusions. The symbolic fish legacy may be inverted, played with, and readable through the text, but such allusiveness is not all. Shem is the sham artist, and beyond Shaun's slander, he is a keeper of ideas of creation. Writing in the voice of the brother's distaste, Joyce articulates such ideas of creation via particularly contemporary evolutionary principles. Although the reader is forced into Shaun's eugenicist mindset, the fish is nonetheless, for Joyce, a highly charged site of artistic production.

We first encounter, in 'Shem's bodily getup', a series of deformities and asymmetrical failings, as the narrator attempts to encompass what 'this hybrid actually' looks like. Describing first his head, the list includes 'a trio of barbels from his megageg chin'. The barbel, a European freshwater fish of the carp tribe (*Barbus vulgaris*), has fleshy filaments which hang from its mouth, here corrupted on Shem's fish-like whiskered face.[23] Over the page a disjunction emerges among wet, dry, warm and cold. We learn that, with 'eelsblood in his cold toes', Shem also possesses a 'salmonkelt's thinskin', with that 'kelt' indicating a spent fish, the male after spawning. The highlighting of the fishy thin skin might lead the reader to immediately imagine the opposite, in the sense of a person having a thick skin – or rather, of Shem as categorically not having one, and thus as oversensitive or neurotic in Shaun's terms. There is a more pertinent insult here too: Shaun's barb points to a particularly male and bodily sense of sterility.[24]

This continues with the most melodic refrain in the text: 'Shem was a sham and a low sham and his lowness creeped out first via foodstuffs.'[25] Shaun's pointed mockery extends to his brother's diet, including how he 'preferred Gibsen's teatime salmon tinned, as inexpensive as pleasing, to the plumpest roeheavy lax or the friskiest parr or smolt troutlet that ever was gaffed between Leixlip and Island Bridge'.[26] As types of salmon, the lax and parr are distinct from the kelt, denoting a rich fertility. This is underlined by the geographical placing: Island Bridge is the point where the Liffey becomes tidal. As McHugh notes, Leixlip too means 'salmon leap'.[27] In effect, Shem is a sham not only for being like the spent and saggy salmon, corrupted in body, but also for eating questionable tinned fish instead of the fruits of the river. This opposition recurs in the modulated play on fish and meat in a grotesque (though juicy) sense of edible meat which is beyond Shem:

> None of your inchthick blueblooded Balaclava fried-at-beliefstakes or juicejelly legs of the Grex's molten mutton or greasilygristly grunters' goupons or slice upon slab of luscious goosebosom with lump after load of plumpudding stuffing all aswim in a swamp of bogoakgravy for that yude![28]

Along with the racial othering in this line at the word 'yude', a derivative of 'Jew', the slur aligns fleshly fecundity with meat, a consumable carcass which Shem, the 'piscivore', cannot manage. In the 1939 edition, Joyce adds the words 'somatophage merman' to the passage, further emphasising a disparity between 'good' and 'bad' kinds of carnivores.[29] 'Somatophage', meaning body eater, is an internally proliferating term, as Joyce inflects the later text with the obscure compound 'somatopsychic', in its dual sense (according to the *Oxford English Dictionary*) of both 'of or pertaining to awareness of one's own body' and 'arising from or pertaining to the effects of bodily illness on the mind'. The term produces an image of the hybridised fish-man as an eater of bodies: not in the carnivorous, red-blooded sense, but as a piscivore, an eater of fish bodies, and hence of his own body – a self-consumption linked to illness. The text thus bears a striking resemblance to a 1920 sketch by Paul Klee entitled *Mann Fisch Mann Esser*, published in *transition* in November 1929 (see Figure 2.1). In this image, an open-mouthed humanoid torso appears as a cross-section diagram, with arrows pointing into the mouth and a similarly poised fish inside the stomach. The diagrammatic form creates almost a flow chart, indicating circular processes of consumption within the androgynous subject. The figure has a strong jaw, serrated teeth and haphazard dugs. The stomached fish, and the further stomached humanoid figure inside the fish, creates a sense of infinite regress. Both the eyes and the teeth are ichthyological. The very face is fishy, like Shem's 'getup'. Joyce may have seen the image elsewhere, or discussed it with Jolas. Jolas is likely to have been struck by the pineal, even vaginal 'eye' upon the head – a vestigial, primordial organ discussed in the next chapter.

Whether or not Joyce saw Klee's sketch in or after 1920, Shaun's description of the 'somatophage piscivore merman' works its way through the magazine. The text's wordplay instates a similar series of imagined organic borders – between clean and dirty, fertile and barren. 'Foodstuffs' signify Shem's place

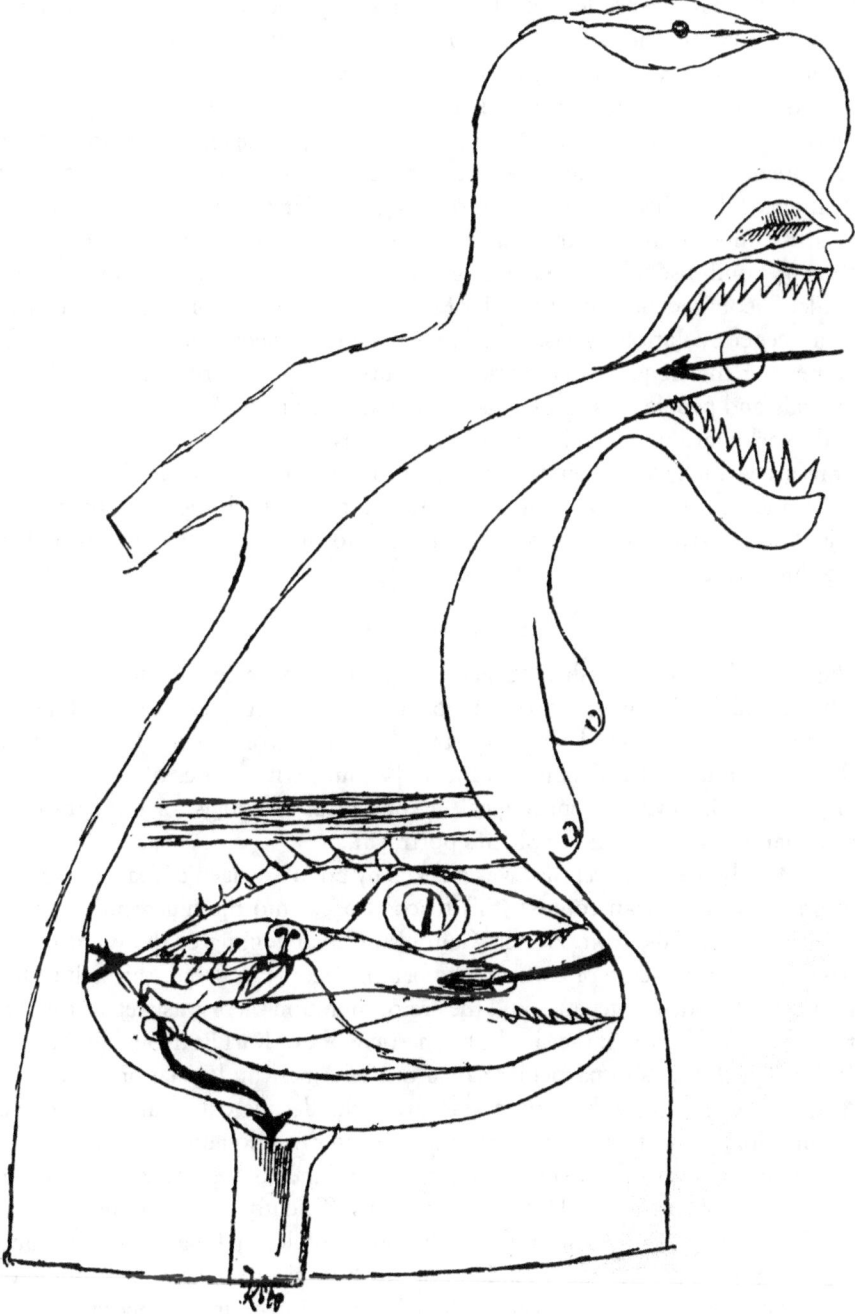

Figure 2.1 Paul Klee, *Fish-Man; Man-Eater* (1920). Reproduced in *transition*, 18, November 1929

beneath the assumed order. Like the Klee drawing, such borders and order figuratively 'point' to the fish as a symbolic pivot between the polarities of filth and fecundity. As an early movement of the episode, this fish-of-borders or fish-not-flesh is central to Shaun's sustained mockery of Shem. As well as theological and mythological allusions, therefore, the episode brings a linguistic play around the corporeal, 'low' type. Shaun looks down upon Shem as a 'canaille', a type of delinquent described by the Italian sociologist Cesare Lombroso as a criminal, swarthy, inborn, asymmetrical and racially other degenerate; as Landuyt has shown, Lombroso was a source from which Joyce took copious notes.[30] The reader encounters not only the fish of plenty and its inversion, but also the fish of a deeper evolutionary vision. After all, Shaun speaks in a eugenicist voice, expressing the frequent assumption of a taxonomically ordered hierarchy of animals and people. Shaun racialises Shem at every turn. Words such as 'coon' and 'blackguard' are coupled to Semitic threads in the text, and Yiddish inflections are virtually spat from the younger brother's mouth. We see Shaun simply enjoy meting out his abuse. Although the text casts such logic as absurd, we might press harder on the historical context informed by eugenic discourse during this period.

Strabismal Stemmings

Shem's portrayal uses fish language that necessitates attention to contemporary eugenicist discourses. From the outset, Shem is of 'aboriginally' dubious 'stemming'.[31] We hear of Shem as 'strabismal',[32] a word that splices together the clearly audible 'strabismus' (a form of squint) with echoes of 'stratify' and 'abysmal'. This evokes genealogical, taxonomical orderings, or cartographies of racial 'lines', as central to Shem's portrayal.

The early twentieth century was marked by popular eugenic ideas. Especially in an Anglo-American context, this reached back into the nineteenth century and into the 1930s, from Francis Galton's original coining of the word in the so-called positive sense of encouraging healthy people to breed, through to the impact of Mendelian genetics and the era of mutation theory, as well as the statistical quantification of race in the biometric work of Karl Pearson and W. F. R. Weldon. The 1920s in particular saw a raft of American legislation instituting 'negative' eugenics, with many cases during the decade culminating in forced sterilisation. Almost every biologist interested in evolution and working during this period was to some extent a eugenicist, so inherent was racism within the life sciences of the time.[33] This would not be sufficiently critiqued until around 1935, with the publication by the evolutionary biologist Julian S. Huxley and the anthropologist Alfred C. Haddon of *We Europeans*, a deep questioning of the hitherto blanket assumption of white, Nordic, European or otherwise Aryan racial superiority.[34]

Len Platt has offered a pioneering study of scientific racism in relation to *Finnegans Wake*. Reading the history of Aryanism through the text, he sees an enormous cultural convergence in the nineteenth century between the deployment of 'highly romantic historiographies' and progressive narratives of development:

> Just as they wreck ideas of racial and linguistic purity, the larger design and aesthetic principles of the *Wake* are also fundamentally incapable of subscribing to notions of biological linearity and progress historiography. The *Wake* makes an assault on race from different perspectives, where scientific racism and its attendant discourses appear not so much as a species of knowledge in its own right, but as a perspective, or series of perspectives, that had a major impact right across the academy and, through that, into the mainstream of Western culture generally.[35]

Focusing on Victorian economics and the ideologies underpinning social Darwinism, Platt writes:

> By the end of the century the science of race had become hugely reinforced and greatly sophisticated. Now liberals, progressives and conservatives alike were subject to what were perceived to be the hard facts and inexorable logic of Lamarckian and Darwinian biological science.[36]

Platt's work is an invaluable point of departure, especially when we look more closely at the specificity of that 'inexorable logic'. As Peter J. Bowler points out, by the end of the century many were proclaiming nothing less than the end of Darwinism, specifically around the validity of natural selection theory. Although evolutionism in its profoundest Darwinian sense – the existence of a mechanism driving adaptation – remained unquestioned, neo-Lamarckian ideas, especially in American palaeontology, gave rise to a wealth of alternative theories, propelled largely by an explosion of fossil discoveries throughout the decade. Jean-Baptiste Lamarck had famously committed the heresy (as it came to be perceived) of believing that a parent animal might pass on acquired characteristics as part of the adaptive process, generation by generation. The notorious example he gave was the giraffe, which, stretching up for foliage time and again, elongates its neck enough to lead to longer-necked offspring, by tiny increments. Heretical as this became, in the 1920s biologists were prepared to reopen the question of acquired characteristics and the adaptive process, during an era of fraught debate among biologists as to how creatures evolve.[37]

Joyce was thus writing during a time of profound change in the life sciences. Darwin published *On the Origin of Species* in 1859, and within a decade almost all scientists had accepted evolution as a fact, as Stephen Jay Gould has shown; however, 'the debate about causes and mechanisms was not resolved (in Darwin's favour) until the 1940s'.[38] In 1942 Julian Huxley named this period the 'modern synthesis': a coming together of previously disparate biological discourses and new methodologies in genetics, when almost all of the organicist theories of inner growth forces were swept away as obsolete.[39] But between 1875 and 1925, during Joyce's lifetime, biology underwent what historians have called the 'eclipse' of Darwinism. This era is often overlooked, even by historians of evolution, since many of its theories were cul-de-sacs or blind alleys, holding onto teleological logics in the face of natural selection's apparent raw materialism. Even Mendelian genetics, a primarily neo-Darwinian school of thought regarding random genetic mutation, was strongly influenced by the anti-Darwinian theory of evolution by sudden saltation.[40] Building on Platt's work, therefore, we might look at ostensibly 'pure' science, rather than sociopolitical ideology, and consider significant information pertinent to Joyce's text.

Although various short-lived theories were on the wane in semi-popular arenas such as natural history journals, public-facing science writing, museum displays and encyclopaedias, one concept in particular persisted, and it resonates in 'Shem': the concept of orthogenesis, or evolution by straight lines. Orthogenetic theory underpinned many assumptions in eugenic discourse. Literally meaning 'straight creation', orthogenesis was a reactionary movement in the various disciplines practising this type of work, from palaeontology to comparative anatomy and morphology.[41] Many scientists were interested in resuscitating orthogenesis, because it offered a non-Darwinian model for development: it was the antithesis of the random and haphazard machinations of chance inherent in natural selection. As Gould points out, orthogenetic theory 'became a touchstone for anti-Darwinian palaeontologists, for it claimed that evolution proceeded in straight lines that natural selection could not regulate'. Certain trends, once started, could not be stopped, even if they led to extinction. The Irish elk's horns and the sabre-toothed tiger's fangs were the most popular 'cases' of orthogenesis put forward during the 1920s: such adaptations were thought to develop their own momentum and ultimately lead to extinction. The theory did not face any counter-attacks until the following decade.[42] The scientists behind orthogenesis, a group Michael Ruse has called the 'palaeontological pack', comprised several generations of biologists who enjoyed swashbuckling, competitive geological finds and adventurous voyages. The group was headed by Edward Drinker Cope.[43] Cope, followed by his student Henry Fairfield Osborn, came up with a series of related theories, often in papers written in impassioned, unscientific prose. Concepts as wonderfully named as bathmism (from the Greek βαθμός, meaning 'step' or 'beginning'), aristogenesis, autogenesis, entelechy, nomogenesis, ortho-selection, rectigradation, archaesthetism, kinetogenesis, katagenesis and microzymism were thinly veiled attempts to impose a teleological order upon evolution – by any name other than God's.[44] Yet they were also dedicated scientific attempts to explain and order species' non-adaptive characteristics, the features of the organism that are either overdeveloped or not useful to survival. As Bowler writes, 'the willingness to admit an important role for non-adaptive trends thus allowed a shift of emphasis away from habit and behaviour towards purely biological mechanisms of directing variation that were beyond the organism's voluntary control'. The hypothesis of regular development, as promulgated by Cope, Osborn and others in the early twentieth century, was thus 'a vestigial influence of nineteenth-century idealism upon twentieth-century biology'. But a deeper current exerted a simultaneous influence, too. The opportunity for anti-Darwinian conceptions was apposite, especially for palaeontologists and other biologists who were working with the fossil record and determined to discover this imagined natural law.[45]

One of the most influential areas where orthogenesis drove contemporary thought was in the museum display, and elaborate representations of the tree of life were founded on its logic. One such picture comes from a powerhouse of 1920s palaeontology: the American Museum of Natural History (see Figure 2.2). One biologist in particular figures prominently in this context, specifically for his contemporary work on fish. William K. Gregory, Osborn's student, went on

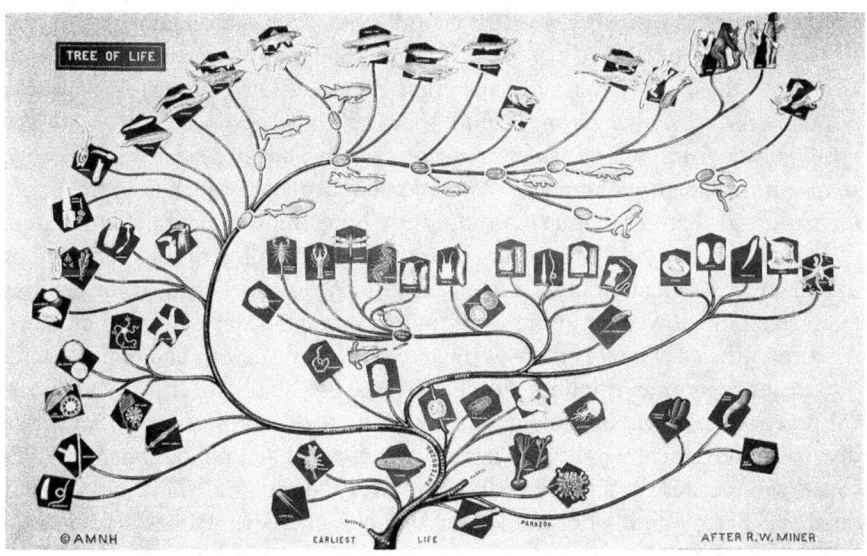

Figure 2.2 R.W. Miner, 'The tree of life'. Diagram hanging in the Darwin Hall of the American Museum of Natural History, August 1927. Photograph by H. S. Rice and Irving Dutcher. © Image No. 312029, American Museum of Natural History Library

to curate the Hall of Fishes and become the first editor of *Natural History*. His ichthyology offered a challenge to prevailing concepts of the time.

Figure 2.2 shows the American Museum of Natural History's public display of the tree of life as it appeared in the Darwin Hall in August 1927. Given the persistence of recapitulation theory and the idealism of orthogenesis, one can look upon the stemming points – what Georges Cuvier named *embranchements* – as indications of the points at which life moved from sea to land, with the fish as the driving force through all the higher developments.[46] Gregory directly influenced the understanding of these stemming points, as biologists began to question the evolution of fish fins into tetrapod limbs. The early twentieth century saw palaeontological work excited by the theory that the first amphibians evolved from crossopterygians, primitive fish from the early Devonian period, about 416 million years ago. In 1915, Gregory spotted two instances where scientists working independently had each advanced the theory that this group of fish possessed fins that could be used as a structural model for the origin of the earliest amphibian limb.[47] Following this discovery, the geologist Joseph Barrell published a paper suggesting that climatic stress was the causal factor behind the 'land invasion', that is, that the first air-breathing fish were responding to drought. Methodologically, Gregory's work at the museum, and much of this period of ichthyology, was functional, morphology-driven palaeontology.[48] But as Ronald Rainger's history of the American Museum of Natural History shows, Gregory's subsequent work on the evolution of fish was instrumental in his growing scepticism towards orthogenesis.[49] In 1927, the year Joyce's 'Shem' appeared in *transition*, Gregory published a scientific paper that eventually became the basis of his popular study *Our Face from Fish to Man* (1929).[50]

Our Face from Fish to Man is a curious book. The lay reader is given some snapshots of Gregory's and others' functional morphology, including the transformation of the non-mammalian inner ear bone into the mammalian system of inner ear bones, and the evolution of the jaw, with illustrations throughout like the one shown in Figure 2.3 from *Scientific Monthly*. The diagram gestures from fish to the lower vertebrates, through to mammals, primates and humans. As before, the *embranchements* of the tree of life are smooth and continuous.

Gregory's work exemplifies a time when the essentially descriptive teleological practice and logic of biology gave way to more empirical work: an active discursive movement was at play in both professional and public spheres during Joyce's composition and publication of the 'Work in progress'. This shift necessitated a less ideologically driven mode of thought, and Gregory was instrumental in the major reformations underway in the discipline, which was slowly uncoupling itself from eugenics. However, the shift was far from clear-cut. On the one hand, Gregory's work at the museum on fish evolution led him into the fields of myology and osteology, addressing the evolution of musculature and bone. This

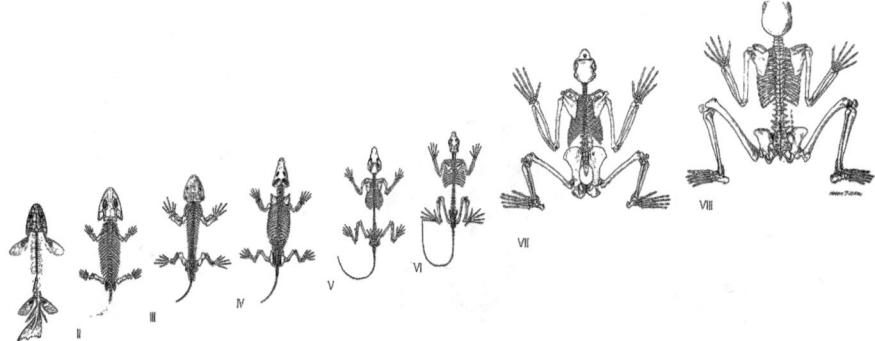

FIG. 1. MAN'S DEBT TO THE LOWER VERTEBRATES
SPECIMENS POSED IN PRIMITIVE TETRAPOD POSITION IN ORDER TO SHOW MAN'S INHERITANCE FROM THE LOWER VERTEBRATES OF EVERY BONE IN THE SKELETON.

I. DEVONIAN LOBE-FIN (*Eusthenopteron*).
II. CARBONIFEROUS AMPHIBIAN (*Microbrachium*).
III. PRIMITIVE PERMO-CARBONIFEROUS REPTILE (*Seymouria*).
IV. PROGRESSIVE TRIASSIC PRO-MAMMAL (*Cynognathus*).
V. PRIMITIVE MAMMAL (*Opossum*).
VI. PRIMITIVE LEMUROID EOCENE PRIMATE (*Notharctus*).
VII. TYPICAL ANTHROPOID (*Chimpanzee*).
VIII. MAN.

Figure 2.3 Helen Ziska, 'Man's debt to the lower vertebrates'. From William K. Gregory, 'The origin, rise, and decline of *Homo sapiens*', *Scientific Monthly* (1934), 482. © American Association for the Advancement of Science

became an influential discipline for Gregory's students.[51] As early as the mid-1910s, with his advancement of the fin-to-limb evolution hypothesis, Gregory was sceptical about orthogenesis.[52] His ichthyological work in the following years moved towards parallel questions of human evolution, in sharp contradistinction to the views of his mentor, Osborn. In 1927 Gregory published a paper entitled 'Two views on the origin of Man', in which he repudiated Osborn's belief in orthogenesis outright: 'I must attack his whole argument, in so far as it is based upon his studies of mammals other than primates, as a series of analogies, unsupported by direct evidence and outweighed by many definite facts of record.'[53] Gregory's functional morphology raised productive questions about evolutionary transitions from the earliest fish to humanity. Contra Osborn, then, Gregory insisted on a more empiricist method in evolution theory, thereby enacting a major development in the field, away from its progressivist rhetoric.

On the other hand, while such developments were occurring within the discipline, the popular side of this science remained fundamentally marked by racial schemas. The frontispiece to *Our Face from Fish to Man* (Figure 2.4) uses the standard model of the day for museum displays. The artist incorporates an S-shaped curve to denote the branch of the tree of life from fish to human, working steadily up towards the whiter-than-white 'European' at the top. The diagram directly informs the displays which Gregory oversaw in his curatorial role at the American Museum of Natural History, which were a regular feature of the Biology Hall until at least 1949 (Figures 2.5 and 2.6).[54]

Figure 2.4 Helen Ziska, 'Our face from fish to Man'. Frontispiece to William K. Gregory, *Our Face from Fish to Man*, 1929. © Image No. LS262–16, American Museum of Natural History Library

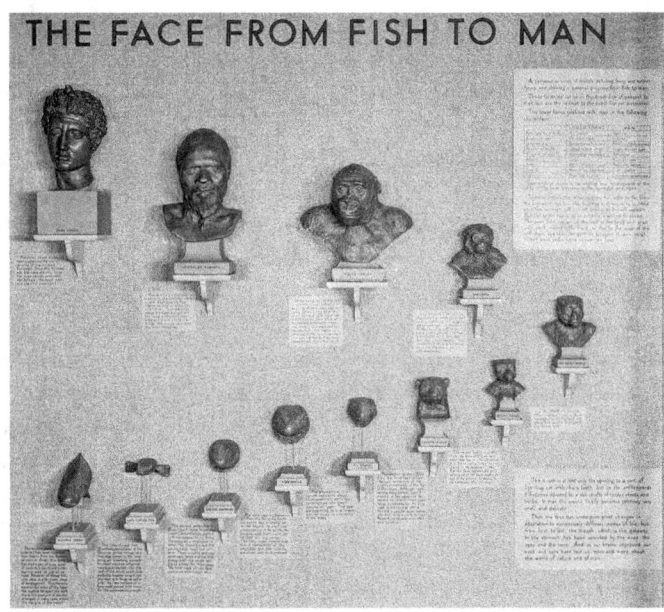

Figure 2.5 'Our face from fish to Man'. Installation in the Biology Hall of the American Museum of Natural History, c. 1932. © Image No. 314251, American Museum of Natural History Library

Figure 2.6 'The face from fish to Man'. Installation in the Biology Hall of the American Museum of Natural History, 1949. Photograph by Thane L. Bierwert, August 1949. © Image No. 320564, American Museum of Natural History Library

As much as Gregory questioned Osborn, his work was still part of an inherently racialised paradigm: the statue of David, so often utilised in these models, bears an air of Aryan superiority over the dark-skinned subject labelled Aboriginal or 'mongrel', which is positioned between the Neanderthal and the post-Enlightenment (white) man. By the mid-1920s, Osborn, now the director of the American Museum of Natural History, was writing patently racist accounts of human development. As Ruse points out, he saw the racial mixing born of modernity as degeneration, denial of divine order and anarchy.[55] Nevertheless, Gregory's dissent counteracted this current and represents a much broader period of reform within the discipline. Perceiving the Galton Society (which was essentially an organ for the International Congress of Eugenics, over which Osborn presided in 1921, and at which he gave an address in 1932) as elevating a political and social agenda above scientific discussion, in 1930 Gregory resigned as secretary for the organisation, and in 1935 he left the Society completely because of its overtly racist ideology.[56] During this period orthogenesis went from being widely accepted to all but disproven. Such was the climate of ideas during Joyce's production of the 'Work in progress'.

The year 1927 in particular is important. In that year the Supreme Court upheld Virginia's eugenic sterilisation statute by enforcing it on Carrie Buck, an eighteen-year-old deemed to have a mental age of nine. The *Buck* v. *Bell* case is significant not only for its temporal coincidence with Joyce's text, but also because of its historical place in a much broader history of eugenics which demands separate discussion. The case fuelled a resurgence of similar lawmaking that led to the enactment of new statutes in sixteen states during the late 1920s and early 1930s. However, although the landmark case of *Buck* v. *Bell* marked the institution of forced sterilisation in the United States, Edward Larson points out that it was in fact a historical apex of eugenics policy and practice. In America, the number of sterilisation rulings dropped steadily after 1927. Such eugenic policies and practices had often been propelled by orthogenetic theory, which was soon in decline in scientific discourse. Nevertheless, in terms of the international context, American eugenics led the way for related legislation throughout Europe, a movement that only changed direction when faced with its own logical conclusion in Nazi Germany. 'In some ways', Larson writes,

> American eugenics became a model for other countries. [. . .] Beginning with the passage of Germany's Law for the Prevention of Genetically Diseased Progeny in 1933, modelled in part on California's compulsory sterilisation law, every Nordic nation in Europe adopted stern eugenics legislation.[57]

Morphology itself was also in decline during the mid-1920s, and as the most pedagogical wing of the discipline (exemplified by Gregory and the American

Museum of Natural History) it was soon perceived as a descriptive practice positioned somewhere between science and art. According to the palaeontologist Alfred Romer:

> [Gregory was] essentially an artist by disposition [. . .] and this gave him an invaluable feeling for form, for morphology. Now that I look back on it, he was in my youth the only man in North America who had a knowledge of the basic structure of the skull in lower vertebrates.[58]

As a turning point in popular evolutionary discourse, then, 1927 marks the moment when the morphological mode of pattern-seeking science experienced its own historical need to move beyond idealist (and racist) logic.

Joyce may not have read Gregory's publications in *Nature*, or visited the Darwin Hall, but, as various scholars have shown, he was directly engaged in the historical moment in evolutionary biology. Baron has explored links between *Ulysses* and late Victorian Darwinian science, for instance, and Bowers has investigated the significant overlaps between Darwin's *The Descent of Man* and Chapter I.6 of the *Wake* in particular.[59] A line in the 'Proteus' episode of *Ulysses* stands out in this regard, indicative of the author parodying the kind of mid-1920s natural science exemplified by Gregory, in which the face of a fish metamorphoses into that of a human. Looking out at the river and seeing the rotting carcass of a dog, Stephen ponders the order of the universe: 'God becomes man becomes fish becomes barnacle goose becomes featherbed mountain.'[60] With this jocularity but keen awareness in mind, I wish to extend the focus of Baron's, Bowers's and Platt's work by considering the more specific scientific moment outlined above, during which Joyce composed the 'Work in progress' and published it in *transition*. I refer to two vital texts: his notebooks, and the 1910–11 *Encyclopaedia Britannica*.

If we turn to the *Finnegans Wake* notebooks composed between 1926 and 1927, reproduced with scholarly apparatus by Brepols Press, a hitherto unidentified source stands out. Scans VI. B. 172 and 173, as the editors' transliteration shows, include geological and glacial periods, eoliths (flint tools from the Stone Age), and several names for various ape-like hominid 'discoveries' of the time, including Java Man from 1891 and Piltdown Man from 1912 – the latter ostensibly a 'missing link' that was revealed to be a hoax some years after Joyce's death. Joyce also lists Cro-Magnon humans, the quality of the jaw of the Heidelberg Man and the 'Grimaldi Negro', as it was then called.[61]

The editors do not name a source here, but Joyce's list of subjects bears a strong resemblance to Osborn's hugely popular *Men of the Old Stone Age*, which was first published in 1915 with further editions running into the mid-1930s.[62] As we have seen, Osborn was a strong proponent of orthogenetic theory, as evinced in the book's preface, where he writes of 'the theory for which I believe very strong grounds may be adduced, that all these races represent stages of advancing and progressive development'.[63] This logic is present throughout the study, which shows frequent graphs and illustrations of intermediary prehistoric humans, couched in progressivist rhetoric. The table of contents includes the same topics as those listed by Joyce, in the same order: geological time periods, glacial periods, eoliths, a section on the Heidelberg Man, then sections on all the so-called races of humans that we can see in Joyce's notebook. In his final sections Osborn includes some eye-wateringly eugenic speculation about Cro-Magnon skulls being of modern European 'type', and Cro-Magnon language as somehow present in modern-day Basque Country dialect.[64] This similarity strongly suggests that Joyce read Osborn's book, which was advertised by Scribner's in a September 1918 issue of *The Dial* – an issue that carried an article by Scofield Thayer on Joyce's early work – as 'the first full and authoritative presentation of what has actually been discovered up to the present time in human prehistory'.[65]

If it is true that Joyce read Osborn, he did so parodically, lightly – arguably aware of the museum director's fallible logic. Joyce must have loved the word 'Cainozoic', which is prevalent in Osborn's text: his artist figure Shem is in part modelled on Cain, and that suffix '-zoic' marks the taxonomic group 'zoa' and the first geological traces of life. Most telling among the various examples indicated in the notebook is a line that appears early on in the *Wake*. The word 'Neanderthal' turns up as 'what a meanderthalltale to unfurl and with what an end in view of squatter and anntisquattor and postproneauntisquattor!'[66] From 'Neanderthal' to 'me-and-a-tall-tale-to-unfurl' with 'an end in view' is a relation analogous to a vision of evolution that is very much of its time, and a vision of narrative – of storytelling – that is very much Joyce's own.

If we pursue this analogous relationship further, a second line of enquiry emerges from what Platt has shown to be one of Joyce's most famous source texts: the eleventh edition of the *Encyclopaedia Britannica* (1910–11).[67] It is probable that Joyce read pertinent information in the encyclopaedia regarding contemporary evolutionism: the layout of the text is itself suggestive. The entry for 'Evolution' is a long piece of text in columns. Towards the end of the entry there are several indented words in bold type, likely to catch the eye in an otherwise densely packed page of text. These are: ontogeny, phylogeny, comparative anatomy, bionomics, biometrics, segregation and bathmism.[68] A casual reader could thus flip through these pages, and his or her eye would be drawn to a full gamut of contemporary thought and methods that would be proven years later to be wrong or bad science. In the penultimate section of the encyclopaedia's 'Variation and selection' essay, for instance, one can find a section devoted specifically to orthogenesis.[69]

The author of these entries, Peter Chalmers Mitchell, touches on the neo-Lamarckian school of evolution, which he describes as 'particularly active in America'. With the light touch characteristic of encyclopaedic writing, he offers a reflective overview. He considers that in spite of being let down by its interpretation of heredity, neo-Lamarckian theory is nonetheless robust in its 'zealous study of the living world and the detection therein of proximate empirical laws'. In the entry for 'Variation', Mitchell devotes more than ten column inches to orthogenesis as a means to further assess the rift between Darwinian and Lamarckian versions of selection theory. Surprisingly, he concludes by fully supporting orthogenesis:

> The past history of the organic world displays many successful series and these, as they have survived, must inevitably display orthogenesis to some extent; but it also shows many failures which indeed may be regarded as showing that the limitation of variation has been such that the organisms have lost the possibility of successful response to a new environment.[70]

That the *Encyclopaedia Britannica* presents such openness to orthogenesis in 1910 demonstrates the currency of the concept, at least in the popular channels of dissemination most likely to reach Joyce. By the time Joyce drafted 'Shem', however, the notion of an inherently ordering force driving evolution was under significant strain in professional circles, as Gregory's work hints. In a 1902 speech to the Linnaean Society in London, William Diller Matthew denied the importance of orthogenesis, considering it 'utterly impossible' that a species could 'continue specializing in some particular direction beyond the point where specialization is of use'. Matthew's scathing attack on Osborn goes so far as to figure the fossil hunter as himself a sabre-toothed tiger, a snooty, anthropomorphised animal-cum-palaeontologist who thinks of himself as 'a really high class animal':

> It all belonged to him ... to him and his race. Individually or jointly none of the inhabitants of the plain dare dispute his sovereignty; bloody and merciless tyrants though they were, none could successfully resist them. Well might he stand, fearless and majestic, viewing the scattered, timid groups of great pachyderms from which he intended to select his next victim.[71]

Furthermore, in 1911 Edward Hayes compared the development of biology as a science proper with that of sociology, emphasising that the doctrine of forces undermined empirical writing and yet was pervasive across divergent fields as part of the 'outgrown' school of vitalism: 'only a remnant of reactionaries', he writes, 'continue to make use of the concept of "vital force"'.[72] Yet despite such controversy, the residue of vitalism persisted into the 1930s in the work of Osborn, Cope, and even Gregory.

Joyce was evidently invested in contemporary biology. While arranging publication of a bespoke edition drawn from the 'Work in progress' in 1929 – a series of stories released by Harry and Caresse Crosby's Black Sun Press – Harry Crosby suggested that Joyce might choose someone to preface the work. Although neither were available and the job went to C. K. Ogden, Joyce put forward the names of two prominent biologists, both of whom were highly involved in the latest debates between supporters of neo-Lamarckian and neo-Darwinian theories: Julian Huxley and J. W. N. Sullivan.[73] Further evidence lies in the text, which is suggestive of Joyce's parodic engagement with these palaeontological, neo-Lamarckian tendencies towards orthogenetic 'strabismal' 'stemmings'. Earlier in the book we read of a 'turk', 'all over which fossil footprints, bootmarks, fingersigns, elbowdints, breechbowls, a. s. o. were all successively traced of a most evolving description'.[74] In 'Shem' there are similar hints to the reader that Joyce is aware of the 'vestigial' quality of this thinking, and thus of its creative potential. At one point, for instance, Shem is in a compromised position when he 'got the charm of his optical life when he found himself at pointblank range blinking down the barrel of an irregular revolver of the bulldog with a *purpose pattern*, handled by an unknown quarreller'.[75] Alongside the more obvious political implication here in terms of the extinction of the Irish at the hands of the 'Irregulars' (with the 'quarrellers' also 'guerrillas'), the reader might hear an implicit sense of orthogenetic conceptions of evolution – effectively a stamping of some kind of 'purpose pattern'. The reader might also hear the randomness of natural selection. Baron reveals how Joyce writes passages of *Ulysses*'s 'Oxen of the Sun' episode in the style of Thomas Huxley, 'Darwin's bulldog'. Here Joyce uses the word 'bulldog' but hands the biologist a gun and a 'purpose pattern' – a teleological concept. The purpose pattern suggests the purposefulness implied in the more popular understanding of Darwin's theory as 'the survival of the fittest', a phrase in fact coined by Herbert Spencer. Baron goes on to show how Joyce replicates Darwin's oscillation in *Origin* between referring to 'Nature' and to 'the Creator' when Leopold Bloom hears medical students coldly discussing 'the survival of the fittest'.[76]

Shem's prostrate position beneath a gun, and possibly beneath life itself, in that 'irregular revolver' places him at the mercy of all the permutations of this image and its evolutionary possibilities. That 'unknown quarreller' 'hand[ling]' matters is not necessarily God but a debate concerning the remnants of teleological thought, a semi-metaphysical persistence of biological determinism. It is this 'purpose pattern' too which threatens to obliterate Shem, who is a non-adaptive degenerate just as much as he is an over-adapted, navel-gazing artist – effete, yet a producer of filth. Whoever the 'unknown quarreller' that possesses the 'purpose pattern' might be, Shem stares down the barrel of his own extinction.

Whatever the extent of Joyce's awareness of the neo-Lamarckian 'moment' in which he lived, whether he is sending up the Shaun-like Henry Fairfield

Osborn or parodying outdated vitalism, it seems fair to suggest that Joyce instates a significant connection between the fish, evolution and the word. 'Young Master Shemmy' is 'at the very dawn of prehistory'[77] (in *Finnegans Wake* this is 'young Master Shemmy on his very first debouch at the very dawn of protohistory'[78]), 'seeing himself such and such'. The Greek root word in the 1939 edition is *prôtohistoria*, meaning first knowledge, or history of the earliest times. In the 1927 version of the episode, this is printed as 'prehistory' – the pre-human, prehistoric planes of time that Shem's lowness signals. Coupled to this geological origin point, the 'dawn of prehistory' is related to Joyce's sense of the writing process itself. In an October 1923 letter to his patron Harriet Weaver, Joyce invokes an embryological definition of writing:

> The construction is quite different from *Ulysses* where at least the ports of call were known beforehand. [. . .] I work as much as I can because these are not fragments but active elements and when they are more and a little older they will begin to fuse themselves.[79]

As well as being indicative of alchemical properties, elements that grow and fuse could be read as embryological or cellular – as evolutionary. The latter three implications come together, both in the language and play of the prose, and in relation to the contemporary imagination.

'Bedood and bedang and bedung'

If the fish as an evolutionary degenerate allows the reader to engage with the messiness of biological discourse during the time of the text's production, it is another form of mess to which I now turn. For, as it progresses, 'Shem the Penman' changes gears. Shem moves from being the abominably low to being the abominable producer of filth. However, Joyce connects the fish-artist and his product to a sense of something that counters his younger brother's castigations: he enacts a defence. There is a resistant kind of textual fishiness that returns the reader to the nexus of inscription and creation with which this chapter began.

Towards the end of the episode, Shaun begins to hint at how Shem 'winged away on a wildgoup's chase across the kathartic ocean and made synthetic ink and sensitive paper for his own end out of his wit's waste'.[80] Is Shem now a flying creature, enacting – as Robert Boyle puts it – an Aristotelian type of cleansing, emptying motion? Is the artist (with a degree of puerile wordplay) now the 'katharsis-purgative' operator? How does the fish enter in? The accompanying sounds of 'art', 'Arctic' and 'arse' (as source, sea or extremity) are part of what Boyle deems to be Joyce's 'bitter scatological pun' over the subsequent page of text. But it is precisely this conflation that gives rise to an excremental aesthetic which spills over the strictures of Shaun's invocation of the fish as degeneracy and lack.[81] There are three key elements to this aesthetic: the introduction of the 'product', the act of producing it, and the single utterance that comes from Shem himself.

First, the introduction of Shem's act combines biological and episcopal registers. As if making a direct nod to the Lamarckian 'heresy' that acquired characteristics in the organism derive from the environment and nature, the narrator answers a rhetorical question about how Shem produces this self-generative art by declaiming in a 'pulpic' voice.[82] A further clause that delays the revelation of Shem's unspeakable act suggests two conflicting world views jostling for position:

> Let *manner* and *matter* of this for these our sporting times be cloaked up in the language of blushfed porpurates that an Anglican ordinal, not reading his own rude dunsky tunga, may ever behold the brand of scarlet on the brow of her of Babylon and feel not the pink one in his own damned cheek.[83]

Joyce invokes two realms of the organism's existence: manner and matter. One hears the echoes of a seventeenth-century mode, a comedy of manners available to a general opposition between nurture and nature. Given the biological contours of the earlier parts of the episode, however, Joyce's words also point to an evolutionist framework, to the major debates between mechanists and vitalists in the life sciences that reach back to Darwin's era. The organism's 'matter' or chromosomal make-up (for Galton, the organism's germplasm) contains the 'data' from which potential genetic mutation may spring through adaptation. In a late-1920s biological context, the organism's 'manner' – character, parental experience, behaviour and environment – was a fiercely contested entity that, as discussed above, underpinned eugenics. Joyce's use of the phrase alongside 'these our sporting times' is significant: the Anglican's language is that which cloaks or hides the particularities of manner and matter.

The reader can still make out the fish. The 'blushfed porpurates', or purveyors of such language, are fatted – they are entitled to powers of obscuration, with the letter of the law on their side. They appear as cardinals in purple robes, with 'porpoises' smuggled into the line. Shem is described earlier in the chapter as possessing a meticulous ability (before an audience that is uninterested in his 'semantics', allowing 'various subconscious smickers to drivel slowly across their fichers', another pun on fish, features and face[84]) to explain 'the various meanings of all the different foreign parts of speech he misused and cuttlefishing every lie unshrinkable'.[85] Here too is the play on fish (albeit aurally, since cuttlefish are not a fish species) in an image of cultivation, but also of ink. This forms an image opposing the Logos of the Cardinals as that which cloaks the manner and matter of 'our sporting times'. The coupling of the linguistic play, of a human-fish species border with the mess of spilt or waste product ink, foreshadows Shem's act of production. Furthermore, the conjunction between the human-fish and bilious ink is Shem's strongest articulation in the entire episode: the self-production of the excremental artist.

A second aspect of Joyce's aesthetic, then, lies in Shem's unspeakable act, which occurs at this point. Written almost entirely in Latin, the passage speaks to a mythological antecedent. It is worth quoting in full, alongside McHugh's translation:

> *Primum opifex, altus prosator, ad teram viviparam et cunctipotentem sine ullo pudore nec venia, suspecto pluviali atque discinctis perizomatis, natibus nudis uti nati fuissent, sese adpropinquans, flens et gemens in manum suam evacuavit* (highly prosy, crap in his hand, sorry!), *postea, animale nigro exoneratus, classicum pulsans, stercus proprium, quod appellavit deiectiones suas, in vas olim honoabile tristitiae posuit, eodem sub invocatione fratrorum, geminorum Medardi et Godardi laete ac melliflue minxit psalmum qui incipit: Lingua mea calamus scribae velociter scribentis: magna voce cantitans* (did a piss, says he was dejected, asks to be exonerated), *demum ex stercore turpi cum divi Orionis iucunditate mixto, cocto, frigorique exposito, encaustum sibi fecit indelible* (faked O'Ryan's, the indelible ink).
>
> (First the artist, the eminent writer, without any shame or apology, pulled up his raincoat and undid his trousers and then drew himself close to the life-giving and all-powerful earth, with his buttocks bare as they were born. Weeping and groaning he relieved himself into his own hands. Then, unburdened of the black beast, and sounding a trumpet, he put his own dung which he called his 'downcastings' into an urn once used as an honoured mark of mourning. With an invocation to the twin brethren Medard and Godard he then passed water into it happily and mellifluously, while chanting in a loud voice the psalm which begins 'My tongue is the pen of a scribe writing swiftly'. Finally, from the foul dung mixed with the 'sweetness of divine Orion' and baked and then exposed to the cold, he made himself an indelible ink.)[86]

Joyce borrows from the Ovidian myth of the birth of Orion, in which the male gods urinate onto the hide of an ox, bake it in the earth and produce offspring. Joyce therefore invokes a classical narrative in which the production of art is akin to the male seed, the conceptual substance of life and of ideas.[87] The Latin carries a boyish delight in such scatological imagery, and on one level simply inverts the 'clean' idea of inspiration. But instead of the gestation, birthing and cultivation of man's conceptual material as structured into the Ovidian text,

Joyce plays with an added idea. The waste products replace the central seed-like substance with the ever blackening, semi-permanent ink.

Joyce's scatological image of the artist is also available for a moral response. Waste – the urine and faeces of Shem's body, and his scratched-at skin – fertilises the earth. Waste is an essential component of any natural cycle. The waste product that Joyce arrives at as a sense of his own art can be read as the future nutrients of an aesthetic landscape altered by his work. The idea of waste as a fertile source of growth brings us back to the paradox of the fish as both lack and profundity, and can be read as an inversion of the idea of the fish as degeneracy and lowness into a productive, aesthetically valuable entity.

The Latin paragraph also enacts something demonic. The use of the word *nigro*, echoed in the notion of ink that burns or stains, is married to *animale*. '*Animale nigro exoneratus*', we read, or in McHugh's translation, 'unburdened of the black beast'.[88] Boyle reads this as either 'black living thing' or 'black air', and it is the ambiguity he finds 'most puzzling of all'.[89] The reader might connect it to the humour of *Dubliners*, the black mass of *Ulysses*, or, as Boyle ponders, the blackness of the 'nightmare of history' in which all the prose is caught, much as for Stephen Daedalus, famously, 'history [. . .] is a nightmare from which I am trying to awake'.[90] There is a political dimension here too, related to an ordering of the subject whereby the black and the animal are racialised, demonised and lumped together as 'other'. Through *animale*, a word on the edge of 'air' and 'creature' – both that which is black and that of which one is to be unburdened – the timbre of the text is distinctly primordial.

A third element of Joyce's fishy aesthetic follows Shem's defecatory act, in his only independent utterance throughout the whole episode. Shem, a piscivore somatophage merman at the opening of the passage – the self-eating fish-man with a predilection for tinned salmon, self-consuming, self-vanishing, self-cavity-making, with an anti-virile presence – now becomes a productive self. An excremental self-production complements his obscenity, carrying with it elements of the species border. The language constantly yet indirectly emphasises the fisherman's nickname for squid as an 'inkfish'. After his defecation, Shem the inkfish artist is – to use the biological discourse – a non-adaptive, unselected, non-natural creation: a degenerate that writes on his own skin:

> Then, pious Eneas, conformant to the fulminant firman which enjoins on the tremylose terrain that, when the call comes, he shall produce nichthemerically from his unheavenly body a no uncertain quantity of obscene matter not protected by copiright in the United States of Urania, or bedeed and bedood and bedang and bedung to him, with this double dye, gallic acid on iron ore, through the bowels of his misery, flashly, faithly, nastily, appropriately, this esuan Menschavik and the first till last alshemist wrote over every square inch of the only foolscap available,

> his own body, till by its corrosive sublimation one continuous present tense integument slowly unfolded all marryvoising moodmoulded cyclewheeling history (thereby, he said, reflecting from his own individual person life unlivable, transaccidentated through the slow fires of consciousness into a dividual chaos, perilous, potent, common to all flesh, human only, mortal) but with each word that would not pass away the squidself which he had squirtscreened from the crystalline world waned chagreenold and doriangrayer in its dudhud.[91]

Shem's articulation links this aesthetic 'production' to evolutionary discourses that we might read as adjacent to, or partially filtered through, the text. Shem, the 'squidself', is now a fish-like creature with not only limbs and digits to write, but also a voice to speak. We should again limit the point by reasserting Shaun's presence here as the eugenicist voice of power. Shaun's mockery of 'pious Eneas' strengthens the impression that Shem is conforming to the 'fulminant firman', a possible reference to the sun god Helios, or to the suddenly developing, thunderous eruption of the 'firman', an order issued by an Oriental sovereign, as McHugh notes.[92] Shaun's narrative contains the possibility that whatever Shem's 'shammeries' are, whatever his self-inscriptive and grotesque production, it is a necessity of a natural order, much as a medieval carnival offers an outlet but not a true expression of subversion. With the earlier phrase 'purpose pattern', the passage opens up the biological context of contemporary orthogenetic thought. There are echoes of those very concepts, so foundational and yet so short-lived, largely defunct a decade or so later, and here again the reader can consider Shem's production as more than a contained 'outlet' for obscenity.

Here are Shem's own words again: '(thereby, he said, reflecting from his own individual person life unlivable, transaccidentated through the slow fires of consciousness into a dividual chaos, perilous, potent, common to all flesh, human only, mortal)'. In his genetic-exegetical approach to this passage, Finn Fordham compares the manuscript variations across these lines in order to consider how Shem's words might translate into a sense of the world. The word 'transaccidentated' is the first crucial moment. Fordham shows that Joyce's neologism 'stem[s] from the jargonised "transaccidentation", a concept that arose in theological debate in the thirteenth century about transubstantiation after Aquinas's readings of Aristotle' and that continued through to Luther. Unlike the Christian sense of transubstantiation – for instance, of the wafer of the Host into Christ's body – transaccidentation denotes a process whereby 'a thing's accidents are replaced (perhaps only in part) by the accidents of something else'.[93]

Joyce's interest lies primarily in the word's heretical implications. But there are also a few compelling reasons to think through an evolutionary line of analysis. 'Transaccidentation' is a highly satisfying description of Darwinian natural selection: genetic 'accidents' or mutations across generations of organisms that spring up, popping into the processes of hard heredity. By Joyce's lifetime this was understood through the enormous impact of Mendelian mutation theory, a principle in early genetic studies of the randomness of mutation from generation to generation. If one again considers the intellectual climate – both neo-Lamarckian and neo-Darwinian theorisations, and new efforts in experimentation in the life sciences, particularly in North America and Britain – and couples it with the idea that Shaun is aligned with the kind of thinking that supports crudely racialised 'natural' histories, 'transaccidentation' is a beacon word, loaded with evolutionary meaning. In this light, Shem indicates an authorial critique: his alignment is against the ideological currents that were positing so much order (instead of randomness), so much progression (instead of process) and so much politicised wrangling over race (instead of empiricist, rigorous research). As Fordham points out, that which is transaccidentated into chaos is a rare reflection of Shem's 'individual person life': 'the terms here are problematic in a way that may have prompted Joyce to nudge them about in revision. Thus he subsequently conjured up the phrase "varied reflection", but then deleted "varied" and put "progressive"'.[94] One draft sees the words 'varied' and 'progressive' (the latter was cut) being tested out in relation to the 'transaccident[ating]' process and, as Shem articulates his being in relation to the surrounding cosmos, the 'slow fires of consciousness into a dividual chaos'. Variation and heredity were the most critical topics of contemporary debate, and the stakes of each were at issue in both the neo-Lamarckian and neo-Darwinian camps. So too was the ubiquitous problematic of 'progressive' narratives of evolution in the widest sense, as Platt has revealed. Indeed, a 'progressive' vision of adaptation provided the overarching logic behind social Darwinian uses of science for political, racially ordered ends – a creeping populist movement of which modernist authors were highly aware.[95]

Joyce's adjective 'dividual' also implies the processes of division – cutting and splicing – as well as reflecting, fusing and growing. These are the same metafictive entities that describe the artistic process, as the Weaver letter quoted above indicates, with Joyce's nascent fragments growing up and fusing in a fertile reproductive mass.[96] Again the evolutionary framework is present. 'Dividual chaos' is suggestive of the chromosomal minuteness of genetic information as it was understood in the 1920s, prior to the mid-century discovery and subsequent isolation of DNA.[97] The Cuvierian *embranchements* of phylogenetic maps of species evolution, such as those produced by palaeontologists like Osborn and Cope, rely on arbitrarily spliced divisions (or 'strabismal' 'stemmings', to echo the *Wake*) born from the need for taxonomical cartographies. Critically, when we read for the nature of that chaos – as Joyce puts it, the 'chaosmos of Alle'[98] – we miss something of the ambiguity.[99] The 'dividual chaos' is that which processes an already 'accidentated' image of life, itself 'unliveable'. The phrase leads to a separation, a sense that one is earthly and the other human-made, or perhaps the other way around. If the unliveable life is transaccidentated in a natural, possibly Darwinian biological process with its own inbuilt chaos, where does this place the 'dividual'? The 'slow fires of consciousness' in this rich formulation are a threshold through which life passes, carried on all the planes of all animal life, only to return to that grounding clause: 'common to all flesh, human only'. Shem's only direct articulation is tucked into this parenthetical moment, which is in turn a vision of life as 'dividual' across an abstracted border. The 'chaos' could be that which comes from human divisiveness (as in the orthogenetic pedagogy so prevalent during Joyce's lifetime), or it could be an extended figure of the 'transaccidendated' processes inherent to life itself. Shaun gives us Shem's voice and offers a closing 'riddle of the universe' to answer the opening question of 'when is a man not a man?' Shaun's castigations move through all the fishy incarnations of the degenerate excremental artist to this powerful 'dividual' chaos. The reader's single direct experience of Shem is thus a creative, literary take on complex evolutionary terms.[100]

Following this parenthetical 'riddle', Shaun relays his brother's writing scene in a distinctly non-human image: 'with each word that would not pass away the squidself which he had squirtscreened from the crystalline world waned chagreenold and doriangrayer in its dudhud'.[101] Aside from the exuberant Wildean allusion, the greens, greys and inferences of age are linked to the earlier fish metaphors. The reader might imagine an oceanic depth, or the silt of a murky riverbed. Fordham here emphasises the word 'dudhud', the vessel of this greenish pigmentation; and as McHugh points out, the Danish word *dødhud* means 'dead skin', while the Welsh *hud* refers to magic, illusions or charms. But there is a further sense of the fish here. By arranging ichthyological imagery around the non-adaptive life, degeneracy and 'racial senility' that inform Shaun's logic, Joyce articulates surface deadness. This is suggestive in an evolutionary framework that contains a vision of writing as a natural force. Prior to the inscription scene, Shaun asks: 'how many piously forged palimpsests slipped in the first place by this morbid process?'[102] Using the same writerly move employed in the 'salmonkelt's thin skin', Joyce again creates an image of surface deadness that is aligned to Shaun's logic – attributing the obverse, which is aligned to Shem, to writing, and accompanying it with an evolutionary fluidity, a principle of deep life or a core life force. Much as dividual chaos potentially resonates with debates around Darwinian natural selection, in Shaun's parting shot of the 'doriangrayer in his dudhud', the dead 'head' or 'magic' (even though it is the magic of a degenerate, aligned to Wildean decadence or fabled Faustian narcissism) is nonetheless logically reliant on its opposite: a 'living' magic and a vitalist conception of life.[103] Joyce's play of opposites takes both sides of these formulations, exposing them all to ridicule.

A further word requires attention here, since it propels the episode towards a geological scene: 'sedimented'. Linked to the image of deepening, darkening substance (which the squidself Shem squirtscreens himself with, forming a black cloud), Joyce uses the word 'semidemented'. It has an echo of sediment, or of sedimentary processes (in the opening pages, Shem drinks 'sedimental cupslips'[104]), as well as of the fluvial, and even the prehistoric. As Shaun's judgement gathers excessive momentum, he describes Shem's birth and youth in a similar register of elemental, earthly time, where,

> after a divine's prodigence you drew the first watergasp in your life [. . .] but slackly shirking both your bullet and your billet, you beat it backwards like Boulanger from Galway [. . .] the cuthone call over the grey bounding slowrolling amplyheaving metamorphoseous that oozy rocks parapangle their preposters with.[105]

The passage evokes the Precambrian period, the geological era prior to the first fossil remains. The movement of rocks and protozoic sludge invokes a pre-animal, let alone pre-human time. It is also the time of the first fish. That Joyce makes a direct play on the slippage of 'sediment' and 'mental' suggests the possibility of a neurological discourse here, too: 'semi-demented' is of course the obvious pun. But those 'oozy' rocks also figure the Precambrian era that so many palaeontologists of Joyce's generation were thinking through in terms of the explosion of animal life on earth.

Such geological imagery serves to heighten what is perhaps the episode's most overarching conceptual concern: teleology. The British neo-Darwinian biologist J. B. S. Haldane is said to have quipped that teleology, to a biologist, is like a mistress: 'he can't be without her, but he is ashamed to be seen with her in public'. As discussed above, the 'purpose pattern' which Shem encounters (from an enemy or a larger creator, a God maybe, or a Joyce outside this Joyce outside this Joyce) is experienced down the barrel of a gun. For Denis Walsh, the idea of teleological immanence indicates how the goals that explain the parts and activities of a system are the goals pursued by the system itself. There is an inherent unity or interaction of goal-directed form and matter or essence: 'in biology, as in any other natural science, one must know both the form and the matter'.[106] Or, in the case of 'Shem the Penman', the 'manner and matter' of the text.

Joyce takes to evolutionary language not for the purposes of a regimented order or an inversely destabilised teleology, but for that same allegorical image of writing itself. The flow of ink becomes 'squirtscreened' from the so-called degenerate's body. Shaun declares that Sham's 'shemming [. . .] conceal[s] your scatophily by *mating*, like a thoroughpaste prosodite, *masculine monosyllables*'.[107] In Shaun's logic, this 'esuan Menschavik' is the 'Irish emigrant the wrong way out'. One of the numerous conjugations of Irish and Jewish slurs from this Anglican-sided voice appears over the page as he implores the reader to, 'for the laugh of Sheekspair', help him out with his epithet: 'semisemitic serendipitist' – 'Europasianised Afferyank!' The chapter's numerous Yiddish and Semitic words are simple racial slurs; in this schema, Shem is nothing more than a 'blethering ape'.[108] 'The simian has no sentiment secretions but weep cataracts for all me, Pain the Shamman!'[109] For Shaun, Shem is proof positive of the racial hierarchy that would prefer to keep the 'Euro-' portion free of the 'Affer-' or African, much like those snaking branches of the tree of life in the museum with the statue of David at the top. Within this circle of logic, though, lies another vision. Shem's 'mating' of 'monosyllables', or his own production, alights at a place where the brothers' voices mix together. The structuring dualities of Shem–Shaun and Cain–Abel break down.

On the final page of the passage, the HCE paternal voice enters the prose. Shem is now deemed to actually be the 'windblasted tree of the knowledge of beautiful andevil'.[110] The change comes about because of Joyce's allegorical link between the fish-like, pre-human figure and degenerate, anti-evolutionary art. In his 1939 revisions, one hears a stark undercurrent of the political appropriation of social Darwinism. Joyce adds a darkly prescient line immediately after the Semitic 'epithet' quoted above, which heightens the sense that the text is like a radio tuning in and out of cultural noises. In parenthesis, Joyce adds: 'heal helper! One gob, one gap, one gulp and gorger of all!'[111] which, as McHugh observes, sounds very similar to 'Heil Hitler! Ein Volk, ein Reich, ein Führer!'[112] However one reads Shem's act of excremental production, Shem's creative power to make words breed renders him a growth force incarnate. The narrative whirls through, finally, to the maternal river voice: 'our turfbrown mummy is acoming, alpilla, beltilla, ciltilla, deltilla'.[113] Alpha, beta, gamma, delta: the progression of first principles in language's blocks of signification unfolds as in a current. Joyce lets the flow of the river, with its current of silt and rock (and fish), wash away the eugenicist voice of Shaun, the 'squidink', and with it Shem's aesthetic, enveloped in an orthogenetic logic that was all but redundant by the time Joyce drafted the episode, but which was integral to the contra-Darwinian biological sciences of his lifetime. The fish, as a pivotal symbol placed between metaphysical and evolutionary ideas of creation, offers artistic potential.

Tongue of the Dumb

The closing three lines of the passage offer a further way to read the aesthetic implications of Joyce's tropological fish. Anna Livia, the maternal river, is

> rapid-shooting round the bends, by the Tallaght's green hills and the pools of the phooka [. . .], as happy as the day is wet, babbling, bubbling, chattering to herself, deloothering the fields on their elbows leaning with the sloothering slide of her, giddygaddy, grannyma, gossipaceous.[114]

In the words 'pools of the phooka' one hears an echo of the Poulaphuca, a chasm in the Liffey south-west of Dublin: a watery crossroads (with a distant echo too of 'fucker'), like this bookending gesture in the text. Although Joyce cannot have known it, the word 'gossipaceous' echoes a letter from Charles Darwin to his botanist friend Joseph Dalton Hooker in 1849: 'I received your two interesting gossipaceous & geological letters', he writes, alluding to the behaviour of a river on underlying rocks. Joyce likely gleaned the word from contemporary slang lexicons.[115] The linguistic movement of the word 'deloothering' is, as McHugh shows, a combination of the Anglo-Irish words 'deludhering' (deluding) and 'sloothering' (blarney), as well as the tucked-in English meanings of 'deluging' and 'delighting', with a hint of 'herring' in the suffix. In the fluidity of the river – the ultimate female protagonist of the text, and in symbolic terms the home of her fish-like offspring – Shem comes through as a play of deluge, delight, delude and blarney.

But as soon as Joyce evokes this watery and geological image, along comes another riddle. The last line echoes the first (quoted above), where the narrator asks, 'when is a man not a man? [. . .] when he is a [. . .] sham', again leafing Christian scripture into the evolutionary prose: 'he lifts the lifewand and the dumb speak. – Quoiquoiquoiquoiquoiquoiquoiq!'[116] Before we think about that final line, which was added to the 1939 text, it seems significant that Joyce here pairs the 'lifewand' with the 'dumb'. The image of the dumb speaking has a biblical antecedent. One can hear Isaiah 35: 6, which (in the King James Bible) proclaims: 'Then shall the lame [man] leap as an hart, and the tongue of the dumb sing: for in the wilderness shall waters break out, and streams in the desert.' This is suggestive of an oncoming sea change, or a flood of divine presence. Echoes of the New Testament are detectable too, from Luke 11: 14: 'and he was casting out a devil, and it was dumb. And it came to pass, when the devil was gone out, the dumb spake; and the people wondered.' Both moments are cathartic, evocative of the passing of a demon and of darkness. This accords Anna Livia Plurabelle her maternal *deus ex machina* function, but it is Shem, the fish at the heart of the piece, who regains his lost power from the length of the preceding episode.

Two types of fish language are available to the reader, therefore: the degeneration paradigm, which leads to Shem's excremental production, and the 'lifewand'[117] or anterior notion of the deep or core image of life, which underwrites Joyce's prose. Shaun's 'deathbone',[118] an Aboriginal silencing instrument, reinstates a racial dimension: Shaun literally holds the language and logic of the eugenicist, yet Shem's artistic productivity prevails. The juxtaposition of 'lifewand' and 'deathbone' also suggests Joyce's engagement with palaeontological discourse. A wand is that which conjures up a vision or a materialisation, an image of previously silent articulation. It casts a spell. That such a spell is 'life' indicates the possibility, again, that an aspect of the orthogenetic 'moment' is filtering through the text: 'growth force' concepts are teleological mappings of a directed flow of life. If 'Shem' contains such an echo, it appears between the father of evolution without divinity and the wrathful God assuaging a demonic presence.

Scholarship that aims to theorise 'late' literary modernism offers a helpful guiding principle at this juncture. In his 1981 study *Horizons of Assent*, Alan Wilde employs the 'transitionalist' sense of the term 'late modernism' as a broad arc of change in literary techniques and concerns, from high modernism to postmodernism. It is not my objective to gauge all the critical voices that have theorised modernist aesthetics between these 'high' and 'post' axes, although as Michael Whitworth attests, the 'transitionalist' assumption in Wilde's and others' critical mappings, which suggest that the 'post' replaces the 'high', remains open to debate.[119] Reading with an eye to changing attitudes towards characterisation, specifically in Christopher Isherwood's generation, Wilde asserts that by the 1930s there is a 'shift to surface'. Where earlier modernists connected truth to depth, late modernism is marked by a different way of seeing, since there is a 'truth [that] inheres in the visible'.[120] 'Shem' can be read as a formative expression of this 'surface', with a fish emblem that is simultaneously an engagement with the Christian tradition of the ichthus (the fish of plenty), a confrontation with evolutionary discourses of degeneration (the fish of lack) and an idea of the artist that produces 'squirtscreened' work (fishes of ink). Where Wilde reads for irony and truth-value, one might similarly read for what the fish emblem offers the late modernist author in relation to this junction between art and science. Joyce's sense of his work as an evolution in or of literature has an important relationship with this textual, primordial fish.

Tyrus Miller has also theorised the 'transitionary' approach to late modernist aesthetics. In his 1999 study *Late Modernism: Politics, Fiction, and the Arts Between the World Wars*, Miller focuses on types of mimetism and authorial self-reflexivity – structures that incite one to (*pace* Beckett) 'mirthless laughter', grotesque corporeality and – most relevantly to 'Shem' – a presentation of the subject as confronting its own decline. Late modernism is here a presentation of:

> an image of subjectivity 'at play' in the face of its own extinction. It prepares the literary ground for the anthropological 'endgame' Beckett would reveal to the world in the 1950s – the theatricalised gestures of the Western subject, rehearsing its final abdication.[121]

Such 'abdication', such 'extinction' – might this be a way of thinking about the tropological fish in Joyce's text? The difference between Beckett's later writings (and the other canonical postmodernisms with which Miller groups them) and late modernism is that there still remains in late modernism a sense of that which may yet redeem a human subject, the maintenance of 'a tenuous hold in the borderland of "mirthless laughter": a mortifying jolt that may yet work to stiffen and resolve'.[122]

Orthogenetic theory reflected a persistent concern with extinction, with the manner and momentum of the phylogenetic trajectory of the organism's decline. This is evident in the thematic (through Shaun) of degeneracy and lowness, and is comparable to Miller's definition of late modernism as an authorial unmooring from 'determinate social, moral, political, and even narrative location' – a fluidity that 'stands in distinction to more traditional modes of satire' and modulates the earlier high modernist stability of authorship's 'orchestrating role'. 'The late modernist', Miller claims, 'may assume neither a stable ground of values nor any commonality with an audience, nor even a subjective ground of form, beyond an anthropological minimum.'[123] Although the fish initially offers this 'minimum', the text progresses to offer a textual production in the face of its own end product or waste, and as such Shem's 'bedood' and 'bedung' are a particularly ambivalent comedy. Structurally too, with his 'lifewand', the 'tenuous hold' is such that ALP's arrival brings back a vitality: the cathartic purge of the river and its march of nature. Miller's work is helpful because it addresses the clash between an imagined obliteration of the subject, and older, edifying, redemptive tropes in earlier modernist writing. The 'Work in progress' appears between these historically divergent modes of thought: from the vestiges of idealist philosophy in the orthogenetic paradigm, to a new, essentially random conception of life via the latest thinking about variation and selection. Joyce's fish also offers remnants of the fable or what we might call a late modernist totemism: a primordialist mode. As I hope to have shown, Joyce filters the cultural noise of 1923–4, 1927 and indeed 1939 through traces of contra-Darwinian science. His fish is a totem which, in the interwar years, offered its author a form of play before a Western subject teetering on the edge of dissolution.

The episode's closing line extends this idea, finally. The babble that Joyce adds after the 1927 manuscript, the 'quoiquoiquoiquoiquoiquoiquoiq', is not only the stammering, mechanical invocation of 'whatwhatwhatwhatwhatwhatwhat', but also a quacking duck, a 'quackquackquackquackquackquackquack' that ends all talk. It is also the puerility, of course, of 'cacacacacaca' – an excremental slew of words that will reappear in *Waiting for Godot* in Lucky's speech at the end of Act I, where the cacophonous quacking and the faecal pun form a dual Joycean sound: 'a personal God quaquaquaqua with white bears quaquaquaqua outside time without extension who from the heights divine apathia divine athambia divine aphasia'.[124] 'Shem' moves from a fish of the lowest 'stemming' to a fish that produces the waste matter of writing. Between the reification of the subject (via Shaun's orthogenetic voice) and its apprehended dissolution, *transition*'s touchstone author creates his degenerate fish-like artist as 'winged away' across the 'kathartic' ocean. Or perhaps, as Boyle emphasises, on a 'wild-goup's chase'.[125]

NOTES

1. Joyce, 'Work in progress'.
2. For a useful historical background to Lewis's anti-Joyce polemics (in his journal *The Enemy*) as they possibly appear in Joyce's 'Work in progress', see McMillan, *transition*, 179–231.
3. Joyce, 'Work in progress', 41. In the 1939 edition this appears as 'Poisse!' As McHugh notes, this suggests not only the French *poisson* but also *poise* (bad luck) or a version of the verb 'to ponce' (p. 177.12). See McHugh, *Annotations*, 177.
4. Joyce, 'Work in progress', 35; *Finnegans Wake*, 170.4–5.
5. See Haeckel, *Riddle*, originally published as *Die Welträtsel* (1894).
6. For a useful introduction to early enquiries, see Bowler, 'Fins and limbs'.
7. Tindall, *Reader's Guide*, 237.
8. Beckett, 'Dante . . . Bruno', 14, original emphasis. Sylvia Beach's edited collection *Our Exagmination*, in which Beckett's essay was reproduced, gathered together early Joyce criticism that had originally been published in *transition* under Joyce and Beach's direction. Beckett's essay originally appeared in *transition*, 16/17 (1929).
9. Hooke, 'Fish symbolism', 535.
10. Goodenough, *Jewish Symbols*, vi, 14, figures 15, 16 and 26. See also Job 40: 15 and 41: 1.
11. Buren, 'Fish offerings', 102.
12. Anonymous, *The Fish*, 1–2.
13. Hemingway, *Old Man*, 38.
14. Hamilton, 'Hemingway', 148, 150.
15. Woolf, *Between the Acts*; Fox, 'Fish pond', 470.
16. Landuyt, 'Cain', 150.
17. The informal, draft-stage title of the episode is given by Joyce in a letter to Harriet Weaver dated 16 January 1924. See Joyce, *Letters*, I, 208. The editor of *Letters*, Stuart Gilbert, originally mistranscribed 'Esau' as 'Egan': see Landuyt, 'Tale told'. For further discussion of Genesis, see Landuyt's discussion (in 'Cain', 151–2) of Joyce's notes on Lamy's *Commentarium* (1883), a standard late nineteenth-century exegesis of the Latin Book of Genesis.
18. McHugh, *Sigla*, 29.
19. Tindall, *Reader's Guide*, 223.
20. Joyce, *Finnegans Wake* (2000), 124.10–11.
21. McHugh, *Sigla*, 29–36.
22. See Gilbert, 'Prolegomena'; Glasheen, *Third Census*, 115; Levin, *James Joyce*, 161; Tindall, *Reader's Guide*, 35, 123; Morley, 'Fish symbolism'; Beechold, 'Finn MacCool'. Marion W. Cumpiano offered the first sustained analysis of the salmon's appearance in the *Wake*, noting that it serves as a symbol for the work as a whole, as well as a traditional symbol for, among others, Ireland, Solomon, Finn MacCool, the

Fenians and the Divine Salmon of Norse mythology. See Cumpiano, 'Salmon', 257. For a connected analysis drawing on Sir James Frazer's work on primitive totemic fish, see Vickery, '*Finnegans Wake*', 218.
23. McHugh, *Annotations*, 169.19.
24. Joyce, 'Work in progress', 34–5; *Finnegans Wake* (2000), 169.11, 169.9–10, 169.14, 169.19. Robert H. Boyle has written (in a deliberate and jocular provocation) that the entirety of the *Wake* is 'about' fly fishing, angling, fish, rivers and fishy wordplay. He counts over 2,000 references and jokingly goads other Joyceans with 'Hey *Wake* watchers [. . .] wake up! [. . .] Have an epiphany on me.' Boyle, 'You spigotty anglease?', para. 5.
25. Joyce, 'Work in progress', 35; *Finnegans Wake* (2000), 170.25–6.
26. Joyce, 'Work in progress', 35–6; *Finnegans Wake* (2000), 170.26–9.
27. McHugh, *Annotations*, 170.28–9.
28. Joyce, 'Work in progress', 36; *Finnegans Wake* (2000), 170.32–171.1.
29. Joyce, *Finnegans Wake* (2000), 171.3.
30. Landuyt, 'Cain', 147–8.
31. Joyce, 'Work in progress', 34; *Finnegans Wake* (2000), 169.3.
32. Joyce, *Finnegans Wake* (2000), 189.8.
33. Larson, 'Biology', 169.
34. Huxley and Haddon, *We Europeans*; Turda, 'Race, science', 72.
35. Platt, *Joyce, Race*, 72.
36. Ibid. 69.
37. Lamarck, *Philosophie zoologique*. See also Bowler, *Eclipse of Darwinism*, 58.
38. Gould, *Ever Since Darwin*, 79–90.
39. Huxley, *Evolution*.
40. Bowler, *Evolution*, 224–5.
41. For a fuller history of this concept, from its creation by Theodor Eimer through to its eventual 'eclipse', see Bowler, *Eclipse of Darwinism*, 141–81.
42. Gould, *Ever Since Darwin*, 84–5.
43. Ruse, *Monad to Man*, 257.
44. Shideler, 'Paleontology and evolution', 183; Padian, '*Bone Sharp*', 245; Needham, 'Organicism in biology', 29; Bowler, *Eclipse of Darwinism*, 142, 148. It should be noted that the Bergsonian concept of the *élan vital* is only indirectly part of this history; by the early twentieth century even Cope, Osborn et al. regarded the idea with scepticism.
45. Bowler, *Eclipse of Darwinism*, 142, 148.
46. Ruse, *Monad to Man*, 113.
47. Bowler, 'Fins and limbs', 13.
48. Barrell, 'Influence'.
49. Rainger, *Agenda for Antiquity*, 229–41.
50. Gregory, 'Palaeomorphology, part I'. See also his 'Palaeomorphology, part II' and *Our Face*.
51. Alfred Sherwood Romer was one of Gregory's students. His 1930s vertebrate palaeontology remains highly influential, especially with regard to classifications between mammals and non-mammals. See his *Vertebrate Paleontology*.

52. Rainger, *Agenda for Antiquity*, 223.
53. Gregory, 'Two views', 602.
54. The scientific status of museum work ebbed away during this period to a more purely pedagogical and illustrative role. See Cain, 'Art of authority'.
55. Ruse, *Monad to Man*, 272.
56. Rainger, *Agenda for Antiquity*, 231 n.48.
57. Larson, 'Biology', 181–2, 184–5.
58. Quoted in Colbert, 'William King Gregory', 95.
59. Baron, 'Joyce, Darwin'; Bowers, 'Variability', 873.
60. Joyce, *Ulysses*, 49.31–6.
61. Joyce, *Finnegans Wake Notebooks*, scans VI. B. 172–3, pp. 208–10.
62. Osborn, *Men of the Old*. Scribner's published editions of Osborn's study almost every year between 1915 and 1930, with further reprints through the 1930s.
63. Ibid. xii.
64. Ibid. 452–3.
65. Thayer, 'James Joyce'; Anonymous, 'Scribner publications'.
66. Joyce, *Finnegans Wake*, 19.25–7.
67. Platt, 'Unfallable encycling'.
68. Mitchell, 'Evolution'.
69. Mitchell, 'Variation and selection'.
70. Ibid. 912.
71. Quoted in Wallace, *Beasts of Eden*, 118–19.
72. Hayes, 'Social forces'.
73. I am grateful to Jaya Savige for bringing this to my attention.
74. Joyce, *Finnegans Wake* (2000), 80.10–12.
75. Ibid. 179.1–5; Joyce, 'Work in progress', 43, emphasis added.
76. Baron, 'Joyce, Darwin', 187–8.
77. Joyce, 'Work in progress', 35.
78. Joyce, *Finnegans Wake* (2000), 169.20–1.
79. Joyce, *Letters*, I, 204.
80. Joyce, 'Work in progress', 48; *Finnegans Wake* (2000), 185.5–8.
81. Boyle, '*Finnegans Wake*', 6.
82. Joyce, *Finnegans Wake* (2000), 185.2.
83. Ibid. 185.8–13; Joyce, 'Work in progress', 49, emphasis added.
84. Joyce, *Finnegans Wake* (2000), 173.32–3.
85. Ibid. 173.34–6.
86. Joyce, 'Work in progress', 49; *Finnegans Wake* (2000), 184.14–26.
87. For a contemporary study outlining the classical basis of the male seed as conceptual matter, specifically in Plato's notion of the οὐσία (or *eidos*) as metaphysical substance, see Panofsky, *Idea*, 12. Panofsky's 1937 *transition* essay on cinema has become a classic text in film studies: 'Style and medium'.
88. Joyce, *Finnegans Wake* (2000), 185.18.
89. Boyle, '*Finnegans Wake*', 3, 10.
90. Joyce, *Ulysses*, 34.19.
91. Joyce, 'Work in progress', 49–50; *Finnegans Wake* (2000), 185.27–186.8.

92. McHugh, *Annotations*, 185.27.
93. Fordham, *Lots of Fun*, 47.
94. Ibid. 48.
95. Ruse, *Monad to Man*, especially 1–19. For four major studies in this field, see Childs, *Modernism and Eugenics*; English, *Unnatural Selections*; Turda, *Modernism and Eugenics*; Schulze, *Degenerate Muse*.
96. Fordham, *Lots of Fun*, 49.
97. The most famous scientists in this respect are James D. Watson and Francis Crick, whose 1953 publication is accepted as the first correct double helix model of deoxyribonucleic acid. See their 'Structure for deoxyribose', published in *Nature* in 1953.
98. Joyce, *Finnegans Wake* (2000), 118.21.
99. Fordham uses the term the 'chaosmologists' to refer to a group of critics who all focus on the 'chaosmos of Alle' as a pinnacle of the text. See Eco, *Aesthetics of Chaosmos*; Deleuze, *Spinoza*; Guattari, *Chaosmose*; Kuberski, *Chaosmos*. Fordham, *Lots of Fun*, 47 n.18.
100. Joyce derives his cosmological vision in the *Wake* from his reading of Giambattista Vico's *Scienza Nuova* (1725) as part of the cyclical understanding of history as recurrent threads of an epic narrative. For an introductory study of this intertext, see Verene, *Vico and Joyce*.
101. Joyce, 'Work in progress', 50; *Finnegans Wake* (2000), 186.6–8.
102. Joyce, *Finnegans Wake* (2000), 182.2–3.
103. Space does not permit a consideration of the major cultural influence of Max Nordau and his popular yet phobic study *Degeneration*. Joyce's parody is clearly responsive to this text, and this is a well-established connection in studies of modernist culture. See Nordau, *Degeneration*.
104. Joyce, *Finnegans Wake* (2000), 171.18.
105. Ibid. 190.22–3, 190.27–32.
106. Haldane quoted in Walsh, 'Teleology', 116, 118–19, 133.
107. Joyce, *Finnegans Wake* (2000), 190.34–5, emphasis added.
108. Ibid. 190.36, 191.2–4.
109. Ibid. 192.22–3.
110. Joyce, 'Work in progress', 56; *Finnegans Wake* (2000), 194.14–15.
111. Joyce, *Finnegans Wake* (2000), 191.7-8.
112. McHugh, *Annotations*, 191.
113. Joyce, 'Work in progress', 56; *Finnegans Wake* (2000), 194.22–3.
114. Joyce, 'Work in progress', 56; *Finnegans Wake* (2000), 194.34–195.4.
115. Darwin, letter to Joseph Dalton Hooker, 9 April 1849. *The Darwin Correspondence Project* at www.darwinproject.ac.uk/entry-1239 (last accessed 4 July 2018).
116. Joyce, 'Work in progress', 56; *Finnegans Wake* (2000), 195.5–6.
117. Joyce, *Finnegans Wake* (2000), 195.5.
118. Ibid. 193.29.
119. Whitworth, 'Late modernism', 280.
120. Wilde, *Horizons of Assent*, 106–9.
121. Miller, *Late Modernism*, 64.

122. Ibid. 62–4.
123. Ibid. 63.
124. See the revised text in Beckett, *Theatrical Notebooks*, I, 39. I am grateful to Laura Salisbury for making this point.
125. Joyce, 'Work in progress', 48; Joyce, *Finnegans Wake* (2000), 185.6; Boyle, '*Finnegans Wake*', 5.

3

LIZARD: GOTTFRIED BENN, 'THE "DARK" SIDE OF MODERNISM' AND *TRANSITION*'S 'PINEAL EYE'

In March 1932, after a two-year hiatus, Jolas published what was to become one of the most pivotal texts in *transition*'s eleven-year run. Gottfried Benn's essay 'The structure of the personality (outline of a geology of the "I")', translated from its 1930 publication in *Die neue Rundschau*, offered an ostensible overview of contemporary biology to explore human 'personality' in relation to 'primal unity', an imagined prehistory of the brain that supposedly underlaid the modern ego, much like a layer of rock in the fossil record.[1] A fervent piece of late Expressionist prose, Benn's text was, as Dougald McMillan states, 'one of the chief documents of *transition*'s development'.[2] It was also distinctly creaturely. Benn circles around a central image of the 'pineal' or 'parietal eye', a vestigial, pre-ocular organ found in phylogenetically 'low' creatures, principally lizards (and an altogether more modernist appendage than the Cartesian 'seat of the soul', which in any case refers to the little finger-shaped gland located in the centre of the brain[3]). Many other animals that are less evolved than lizards also possess a pineal eye. Frogs and toads, lampreys, some larger fish such as tuna and sharks, and a few species of salamander retain this evolutionary throwback, or pre-ocular 'vision'. In fact the pineal (or parietal) eye is not an eye at all, but a cluster of photoreceptive cells found beneath a thin membrane of skin on the top of the head, at the opening of a hole in the skull, and attached to the brain by a stem as part of the endocrine system. The pineal eye dates back to the earliest aquatic organisms or chordates (the first animals to develop dorsal nerve chords, a rudimentary tail and an endostyle, a mucus-producing precursor to the thyroid gland).⁴ The mechanism works very simply, triggering a motor reflex. The most basic of evolutionary mechanisms is at work in this appendage: to move away from danger, in the depths of the prehistoric sea.

Benn charges both the pineal eye and the pineal gland with an intoxicating power and an inhuman, distant past that dates back to the 'Sauria and their decline in the secondary epoch'. He implies that this 'eye' is a fulcrum of alogical thought, submerged yet 'unfolding itself limitlessly through the tattered psychological subject'.⁵ Benn also pictures the corrupted neocortex as having closed over the creative, primordial core of this 'small brain', implying that the gland is in need of revivification.

As the driving text in this, the third case of *transition*'s primordial modernism, Benn's non-mammalian, reptilian imagery came to influence Jolas's increasingly esoteric programme for the Revolution of the Word over the magazine's final six years. Until recently, Benn has been a consistently unpopular figure in anglophone criticism.⁶ Often compared to T. S. Eliot or Ezra Pound in terms of his stature in German literary culture, Benn was also a trained doctor, a First World War physician and, for a brief but significant period, a sympathiser with National Socialism. The case I present here thus highlights pressing political aspects of *transition*'s history. After Benn's appearance, the Revolution of the Word shifted considerably from the 'Proclamation' of 1929, through further manifestos, Jolas's editorials, *enquête* questionnaires, poetry, pamphleteering, and a body of critical and creative writing featuring variants of 'the third eye' and lizard imagery. The journal's pineal eye also focalises its most troubling legacy: its editorial proximity to a proto-fascist moment in the intellectual history of the Anglo-European 1930s avant-garde. This proximity was not lost on critics of the day. Writing for the *New Left Review* in July 1935, G. A. Hutt described 'a strong near-fascist flavour about Jolas's julep', accusing the editor of 'chuck[ing] reason and intellect overboard [to] line up with the very discreditable emotion-mongers of Nazi paganism'.⁷ Hutt was undoubtedly thinking of Benn, whose 1933–4 essays on aesthetics embraced the ideology of National Socialism 'unreservedly', as Andreas Kramer and Rainer Rumold put it: 'the "dark" side of modernism' to which Jolas was blinded by his own enthusiasms.⁸ As Hugh Haughton writes, Jolas displayed an 'inability to understand the force of his own parable – or the relationship between his utopian excitement about the Logos Unbound and the "nightmare of history" which overtook it' in the form of Nazi Germany.⁹ Although in retrospect Jolas realised that some of the authors he had cherished were prone to 'biological racism, anti-Semitism' and 'aggressive nationalism', as he wrote in 1940, his 1932–8 predilection for Bennian language was a vital characteristic of *transition*'s mission.¹⁰

One could find a measure here of the extent to which *transition* oxygenated Benn's ideological aesthetics, taking Hutt at his word and gauging other contributors, such as Bernard Faÿ or Pierre Drieu La Rochelle, for their extremist views. This would serve simply to point the finger at Jolas, however, and would produce a reductive analysis unaware of the shared fascination with the pineal eye and the myriad ways in which the reptilian organ inspired authors who were thinking outside a straightforwardly political framework. Yes, as E. B. Ashton puts it, Jolas was a 'rare devotee' of Benn, who in turn 'buried a kind of atavistic tribalism' under 'avalanches of genetic and anthropological terms'. But this is not all. Benn's animal imagery cannot be captured in a crude survey. In a letter to Johanna Gertrude Rottenberg, Benn wrote that the human mind 'originated as a killer', 'designed to fight the crocodiles of primal seas and the scaly giant sloths of the caves – not at a powder puff!'[11] The contrast between the archaic symbol of the reptile and the accoutrements of bourgeois modernity illuminates the journal's search for an answer to the perceived 'malady' of language, a quest that developed over the mid- to late 1930s. Although this potentially evokes the mystical notion of the 'third eye' found in populist versions such as Madame Blavatsky's nineteenth-century spiritualism, my focus here is on the critical fault lines between biologism in pineal cytology, the fable-like lizard as a modernist trope, and figurative reptiles as examples of primitivist discourse in anthropological and psychiatric texts that help us understand the nature of *transition*'s primordial modernism.[12] As Elazar Barkan and Ronald Bush have shown, primitivism in early twentieth-century Europe and North America was marked by the extreme 'disciplinary confusions' of ethnographic and colonial projects, and *transition* is no exception.[13] Rather than measure a political spectrum, then, this chapter takes such 'confusion' as a productive point of departure. Lizards, the parietal organ, and the saurian epoch offer interpretive lines whose stakes are high. We need to better understand *transition*'s inadvertent rehearsal of a dangerously apolitical fascination with the archetypal 'depths' of the Word, for which it drew on Benn's 'pseudo-anthropological valorisation of the archaic elements of creativity'; but we also need to isolate its editorial manoeuvres in the call for the 'verticality' of poetry that came to dominate its final years.[14]

This chapter's discussion of *transition*'s pineal eye is organised in five parts. First, by exploring 'The structure of the personality' in some detail, the chapter makes clear that the essay was not only pivotal to *transition*'s development, but also reflective of a shift in Benn's oeuvre. We are then left, as a second area of focus, with an unsettling ambiguity in the magazine – specifically in its emphasis on 'the primal personality' – that nonetheless orients a wider course through its project. Third, the most pertinent disciplinary 'confusion' Benn engendered exists in the overlaps between late nineteenth-century science and mysticism – the perfect ingredients for an articulation of the vestigial organ as a contradictory but definitive idea. This context illuminates distinctive francophone expressions of the pineal eye from the late 1920s and early 1930s, specifically in the writings of Georges Bataille and Roger Gilbert-Lecomte – an outline of which offers a fourth, comparative aspect of this history. Finally, I consider the various strands of lizard images running through the later period of the magazine: those that imply a fabled animal, and those that open broader articulations of modernist culture, whereby totemic lizards set the scene for a multitude of ideas around nationhood, zoological language and abject subjectivity. These reptilian metaphors constitute a series of primitivist concerns, from inhuman visions of the psychopath to exoticised Latin American stories, that are present in the work of a range of authors including Lothar Mundan, Édouard Roditi, Henry Miller and others – all of whom published in *transition*'s post-1932 issues, often with Bennian overtones. What emerges is a complex picture of the 'dark side' of *transition*'s intellectual legacy, made visible through the lizard. This is a far cry from late twentieth-century notions of the 'reptilian brain' from the likes of David Icke, conspiracy theorists and anti-Semites: in this story we confront the 'near-fascist flavour' of a magazine whose editor was, in fact, passionately anti-fascist. After all, his commitment was firm. 'The Apocalypse is in full swing', Jolas wrote to Blanche Matthias in 1941. 'It's the age of the Anti-Christ.'[15]

Degenerate Reptiles

Whence the 'personality'? How does one define the modern crisis of consciousness? These are the questions that Benn, a former young Expressionist poet now turned essayist (he was two years older than T. S. Eliot, seventeen younger than Else Lasker-Schüler), takes up. 'The structure of the personality (outline of a geology of the "I")' is a text of vertiginous proportions: an almost nauseating read for its roll call of scientific names, conceptually blurred hyperbole and eddying percolations of figurative beasts. It is a curious combination of the old and the new, of visions of distant dinosaurs 'consorting with' a deliberately pedagogical mode, as Michael Hamburger and Christopher Middleton put it: 'a phrasing so urbane and a diction so near-scientific' as to produce the effect of a full-blown lecture on the biological sciences.[16]

According to Benn, his generation was witnessing a great change in modern science. Elements of older and 'younger' discourses pertaining to evolution, the psyche, character, the glands and the degenerate were all at play in one single, elusive idea: the human personality. Benn enlists an enormous roster of scientists to shore up his claim. Among them are Hans Driesch, Ernst Haeckel's student and a proponent of the vitalist concept of 'entelechy' (or biological force); the sociologist Kurt Breysig; the contra-Darwinian botanist Wilhelm Johannsen (famous for coining the terms 'phenotype' and 'genotype'); the psychiatrist Karl Birnbaum (the first to use the term 'sociopath'); Alfred Storch, who worked on schizophrenia; the later Nazi sympathiser Ernst Kretschmer, who was also interested in schizoid 'types'; and Freud's student Paul Schilder, who developed group psychology. Other notable figures include the characterologist Arthur Kronfeld and the German palaeontologist Edgar Dacqué, who believed in a teleological model of evolution. Such disciplines were not Benn's primary concern, however.

He searches for the imagined location of that which 'unveil[s] the features of the growing of the "I"'. 'More than in the drama', he writes, 'more than in the novel', the 'I' is the site at which 'the human form struggles in its bases and in its abysses to renew itself intuitively and awesomely in the creative act.' His appeals to the work of authorities – unreferenced throughout – serve to reify his dramatic opening point. Benn positions modernity as a shift within psychiatric discourse. 'We stand at the end of an epoch for which the personality was only a scientific concept within its intellectual systems', he writes. 'The biological foundation, therefore, was up till recent times, nothing but a cerebral problem.' Cranial theory, Benn claims, was too rigid, too reliant on the neocortex as an emblem for modern civilised consciousness, lacking focus on affectivity and instinctual life.[17]

By 1900, however, Benn argues, a radical countercurrent began to emerge that was 'totalistic', 'age-old', 'rooted in Hellenic days' and animated by Immanuel Kant and Carl Gustav Carus. Benn champions this new energy in psychoanalytic and biological thought as moving towards a more somatic, more integrated theory of the personality. It hardly matters that Benn's evidence – principally Wilhelm Dilthey's work, which Benn says focused no longer on the 'dialectical, but the instinctive element of the "I"', and sociological studies that broke with the cerebral analysis of primitive 'peoples' – appears shaky, even out of date. The prose effects a grandeur as it builds: a vision of the modern subject drawn from new depths. Benn deploys branches of new science as further 'proof': the physician Friedrich Kraus's 'personalistic pathology', which was distinct from the work on pathology by Rudolf Virchow; endocrinology, according to which glands now determined aspects of the psyche, 'ineluctably in the organization of the personality'; and crucially, the 'big brain' model via Birnbaum's 'transvaluation' of different cerebral regions in favour of a new totality, 'directed only from the entire organism'. Beneath that neocortical 'big brain', Benn contends – the 'youngest part' of the human mind – lies a vital, powerful nub: the 'brain-kernel', as he terms it, which was closed over millennia ago, like a seed in the earth. Here lies the site of pure affect, the ancient yet modern conduit for the 'psychic personality': the pineal gland.[18]

At this point Benn's prose takes a distinctly literary turn. 'Here, it seems, lies the beginning of all things', he writes, as a refrain. The text unfurls a perplexing simultaneity of authorities, assembled in a virtually nonsensical argument that nonetheless draws power from the signifying animal. The imagined appearance of the 'kernel' now takes centre stage, with reference to dinosaurs. Referring to the Mesozoic – popularly known as 'the age of the reptiles', as the early nineteenth-century palaeontologist Gideon Mantell named it – Benn writes:

> Prehistory and geology shows us that this must have happened long before the last flood, long before the last ice age. For the memory of this cortex, realized in the primal cosmogonies, reaches back to the Sauria

and their decline in the secondary epoch, reaches back to the last world disasters and ends apparently only in the primary epoch.[19]

The lyricism of this image is met with a second refrain: 'the geological principle!' Despite the confusion here between the pineal gland and the pineal eye – of which more below – Benn continues to perform a sleight of hand among his neurologists, medics, psychologists and others – and to write rousing, emotive prose. The glandular blood system comprises the personality, for instance, 'the element of a disposition turned into the biological, which, when turned to the psychic, gives us the characterological facts'. John Hughlings Jackson, who saw the brain in terms of a geological model that was striated backwards to our origins, is called upon. So too is Théodule-Armand Ribot, as Benn now turns to regression. *Völkerpsychologie* founders Moritz Lazarus and Hermann Emminghaus come swiftly into view, for the manner in which they 'described the return of the mentally alienated to the imaginative world of the man of nature'. Pierre Janet's work is mentioned as evidence of a hierarchical 'organisation of the functions'.[20] A compelling roll call indeed.

The edifice of 'science' slips, however. Throughout his assertions, Benn jumps between registers, circling around an elusive, 'magical' idea:

> The old, the unconscious, in the magical transmutation and identification of the 'I', in the early experience of the everywhere and the eternal. The hereditary patrimony of the middle brain lies still deeper and is eager for expression: if the covering is destroyed in the psychosis there emerges, driven upward by the primal instincts, from out the primitive-schiszoid [*sic*] sub-structure, the gigantic archaic instinctive 'I'.[21]

'It is here!' 'It exists!' Such is the tone of Benn's presentation of the pineal gland, his elision of psychiatry and 'magic', of quasi-scientific discourse and an essentially symbolic idea, unmoored from the surface of 'fact'. Standing, signifying, and above all useful: the 'sauria' offer symbolic traction. As an inhuman, facilitating presence in the text, the 'pineal' is a primordial, nostalgic origin.

Benn here lards his lucubrations with yet more names: the pioneering psychologist Emil Kraepelin, and Benn's hero, Friedrich Nietzsche. Kraepelin was an ardent eugenicist who, together with Ernst Rudin, used Jewish people as an example of a group marked by nervous disorders; he was a social Darwinist who felt that 'undesirables' were obstructing the process of natural selection.[22] Yet for Benn's purposes, Kraepelin offers a revaluation of the 'primitive', here meaning the mentally unwell: Benn describes him as a scientist who 'saw quite distinctly the early forms of the psychic organism, to which belong the utterances of the degenerate insane'. This allows Benn to further expand on the archaic traces in the unconscious – *pace* Freud – and 'above all' on Nietzsche's insights regarding the 'close connection' between the dream and primitive mentality. 'From hereditary biology to phenomenology', Benn writes, reiterating several times the implicit value given to the biologically vestigial, 'we carry the remnants and traces of former evolutionary stages in our organism'; 'we observe how these traces are realized in the dream, in ecstasy and in certain conditions of the insane; we see these preliminary stages of the modern Ego appear, especially in the form of neuropathological symptoms'.[23] From a certain perspective, these ideas are nothing new. As early as 1918, in a piece entitled 'Diesterweg', Benn's narrator dreams of going back 'all the way to the pineal gland'; the self-named eponymous voice seeks the 'defence and preservation of a culture, whose identifying concept [. . .] was the personality [. . .] defined biologically as the unique and unrepeatable occurrence of organic synthesis'.[24] 'The structure of the personality' is a similar meditation on the 'age-old fragment of humanity'.[25] What is new in 'The structure of the personality', however, is Benn's tendency, from around this point in the essay to its end, to utilise animals, and to turn – almost accidentally – to the vestigial, reptilian eye.

Benn's Expressionist style underscores his science. He imagines the yawning gulf between modernity and prehistoric lands, where the functions of sight were formed in 'isolated' ways, each with 'its hour and its reign':

> Look[ing] perhaps into the moonless blue sky of the Tertiary epoch, work[ing], perhaps, together with the third eye, the parietal organ of the diluvian media, the electro-magnetic miracle of the mesozoan [*sic*]; sickened, decayed, or [. . .] assimilated into new strata, and now carr[ying] with it today, old and enriched, all the destinies of human vision from the first amorphous sensation of light, of the cellular-primitive eye-protrusion, to the splendour of the ultra-scope, split into prisms.[26]

These passages have a distinctly animal theme. 'The personality has performed mutation after mutation', Benn writes, appropriating Darwinian language, and 'it took part in the evolutions of the animal races, ever changing and bringing about new shades of evolution, at one time approximating the Marsupials, at another time the Sauri'. What we seek, Benn now writes in an almost intoxicated voice, is the 'primal word', perhaps through Goethe. The man with the primal word, or the primal nub: it no longer matters which, as Benn offers the same enjambment of reptilian and more human realms. 'We see him in the amphibian,' he writes, 'the reptilian, the marsupilian, the saurian, the simian: all these stigmata of his old decays and his new pleasure in the undulations of a great organic motif.' The saurian, the simian: a neatly summative image through which 'the germ of the species' moves. Here Benn reaches a climax: a vision of a definite point of origin. 'With the beginning of the Quaternary', he writes, going back two and a half million years, 'the big brain in all sauria began to grow.'[27] This is the wellspring of the text as a whole. It is a point, furthermore, where his lyricism turns on an unnerving revelation:

> This was the hour [. . .] a growth in the direction of man. Is the new truth, perhaps, that the body, which already contained more magnificent personality tensions than our own, certainly among the mesozoic and Tertiary peoples, among the geniuses of the races, those with the parietal organ, which ruled that epoch, the pineal eye, which conferred nature-intuition, the magical feeling, telepathy and telekinesis, which permitted them to move without effort their gigantic blocks of stone [. . .] [is] contained in the primal man, imitating apes and *degenerated reptiles*.[28]

Benn closes with three questions. Will we see the relegation of the big brain 'when new disasters have covered the planet'? Will we 'retrace' our path 'back to the brain-kernel' when the 'cries of distress' 'go on and on'? Will our 'Quaternary personality' 'reappear' in 'saga form', under 'the law of inconceivable mutation'?[29] It is impossible to read this ominous, evolutionary closing image of destruction without thinking of the lived reality of Germany in 1930, the year Benn's essay first appeared: Hitler's party had 178,000 members by January, it won 107 seats in the Reichstag in September, and unemployment reached four million by December. Of course, this is unlikely to have been on Benn's mind when he sought that 'primal unity'. His rhetorical reptiles belong to aesthetic theory rather than to Nazi rallying cries. But we ought to confront the essay in a broader context, in relation both to its precursors in the 1910s and 1920s and to its explicitly fascistic offshoots over the following few years. This context will illuminate Benn's place in Jolas's internationalist modernist programme: there was a dislocation between the two, and yet Benn was a constitutive element of *transition*'s own pineal eye.

The Primal Personality

The intellectual roots of Benn's essay were present as early as 1913. In 'Songs', published in the Expressionist magazine *Die Aktion* that year, the poetic voice harks even further back than the Quaternary, to 'restart our primal mission / and be a speck of slime in a tepid fen', rejecting the modern malaise as 'we gods are rotten with disease and sadness'.[30] A few years later, in a 1916 collection entitled *Gehirne (Brains)*, Benn's semi-autobiographical doctor narrator Rönne pauses to consider the foundational 'Cartesius' text, which posits the pineal gland as the 'seat of the soul' within the framework of mind–body dualism; but Rönne gives it a visceral tinge of corporeality and, again, the 'sounds' of science. In 'The island', for example, Rönne muses that the pineal gland resembles 'the finger of God': 'yellowish, elongated, mild but still threatening – the cerebral physiologists had found there was sugar in urine upon cutting into the brain-mass, when indigo occurred, yes, when spittle flowed'. 'The island' is an important piece, not only as a precursor to 'The structure of the personality', but also as the beginning of the partnership, instigated largely through Carl Einstein's influence, between Benn and the *transition* circle.[31]

Along with 'The birthday', another text from *Gehirne*, 'The island' was translated in the second and fifth issues (May and August 1927), the latter of which also featured an essay on the author. Astutely, Jolas saw in Benn 'a paralysing nihilism' born from 'the conscious will to disintegrate the structure which the intellectual mechanisation of our age has produced'. At this early stage in the journal, we can already see an editorially selective critique at work, emphasising the modern malaise of utilitarian language while still exhibiting a fascination with Benn's nihilistic themes. Locating the poet in a tradition of German writing from Nietzsche to Arno Holz, Jolas even diagnoses an incipient nationalism: 'it is excessively Nordic,' the editor writes, 'this brooding introspection, this preoccupation with the I, this hunger for "Southerliness"'. Jolas is highly intuitive here, in fact. Susan Ray has characterised Benn's demand for '"the southern world" as [a] "chiffre" or mantra throughout his creative years', an artistic *Südkomplex* that marks his cultural pessimism. 'The precocity that still is the current medium of the "beauty-haunted" minds is not for him', Jolas continues. 'Life is a hospital. There only remains his dream.' Despite such equivocations, however, *transition*'s editors were clearly enthralled. In March 1928, looking back on the first year of their magazine, Jolas and Paul refer to the poet directly, and in spiritual terms: 'With Dr Benn', they write, 'we persist in asking for the metaphysical man.'[32]

By 1929, however, this seeming unison between Benn and the editors began to change. Taking the 'intellectual mechanisation' referred to in his Benn essay to the heart of a summer 1928 questionnaire entitled 'Inquiry among European writers into the spirit of America', Jolas asked twenty-four respondents (including Benn, Tristan Tzara, Ivan Goll, Marcel Brion and Max Rychner) for their thoughts on the 'new conception of life' seen in America, and on how it was 'being felt in the old world' with regard to an attack on the Word. Although the answers were divided, responses tended towards thoughtful reflection and celebrations of multiculturalism. Joseph Delteil's response is characteristic, championing the 'melting pot' of nations: 'to discover America is to open your eyes, to become yourself, it is being'. But Benn is belligerent, anti-American and hostile. Not only Americanism, he writes, but also the German writers of his generation that 'wor[k] under the slogan of tempo, jazz, cinema, overseas, technical activity' present a problem that is analogous to various currents 'forming' the young writer today (including communism), whose attacks are 'directed against the individualistic and the metaphysical being'. Benn is Eurocentric rather than collectivist, favouring the supposedly 'pure' art of the 'Occidental' poet. His implicit appeal (in calling for a more Germanic body of art) to the *Volksgemeinschaft* or 'spirit of the people' was also partly in line with the National Socialist rhetoric of the late 1920s, as Germany faced a crippling financial crisis. It is conceivable that the editors delighted in some degree of anti-American sentiment in this, their 'American number'. Such mildly offensive material (to the magazine's domestic audience, at least) would doubtless have amused Jolas's circle.[33]

The following June saw Benn given more serious prominence, and with it a telling invocation of the signifying reptile. Malcolm Campbell translated Benn's essay 'Primal vision' directly from 'the German manuscript', and this is indicative of an unusually close relationship between Benn and the magazine, given the latter's normal practice of translating older published texts.[34] A passionate attack on the supposed decadence of Marxism, 'Primal vision' revivifies an earlier moment of Expressionist anti-rational writing. Reminiscent of works by Georg Heym or Alfred Döblin from the early 1910s, with their repeated calls for the heightened consciousness of a voice outside the forces of urbanisation, Benn combines images of evolution and extinction around an envisioned (and lost) organic holism of life.[35] Benn is nostalgic for a particular understanding of the modern self. 'I got hold of the idea that it was the unity of life that I was called upon to defend against attack', Benn's narrator declares, asserting that paradigmatic shifts in the biological sciences offered critiques of both socialism and capitalism. He moves from semi-scientific descriptions of the ego as an eyeball with a 'gaze' of 'primeval danger', to reptilian creaturely significance:

> Out of catastrophes that were latent, catastrophes that were born before the first word, gruesome memories of sex, something mongrel-like, animal form, sphinx-in-the-bag of the primeval face. [. . .] I rattled among runes, I entered into demons, sleep-tired and brutal, with the instincts of myth, in anteverbal impulsive threatenings of prehistoric neurones [. . .]. Once the green growth of anthracite forests, once the *vertebrates trailing the oceans for new conquests* before the existence of time – once again came all things.[36]

The text instates an animal image – here of early vertebrates – to stand in for a time before language: the exact same technique used in the later essay. The piece had form, furthermore. 'Primal vision' was essentially a more detailed rehearsal of Benn's 1927 prose work *Lyric Self*. Here the narrative voice starts with 'the lower zoological system covered with cilia', 'the animal sense organ before differentiation into separate sense energies'. Again, the non-human serves aesthetic reflection, here on corruptive language, on 'tendencies to regress with the aid of the word, heuristic states of weakness caused by nouns'.[37] Thinking across to the 'saga forms' Benn later conjures up as emerging after a great biological destruction in 'The structure of the personality', we can see a certain direction in the author's work, tending to a totalised view of the subject, with a 'lower' vertebrate adumbrating his fantasy of 'primal unity'.

A further turning point arose in another questionnaire, 'Crisis of Man', published in the same issue as 'The structure of the personality'. Heading up a segment titled 'The metanthropological crisis', the piece asked respondents to comment on individualism versus collectivism and the ways in which they desired – or rejected – a modern metaphysics. Ever the conservative, Benn states that it is not the ape of Darwinism but the metaphysical, psychological and intellectual individualism of our time that will be 'demolished'. Taking aim at the literary establishment, he castigates writers he deems to have failed to express the 'age-old', the 'eternal man! The human race!'[38] Again, the expression is cast as palaeontological, prehistoric: an image of life's origin. Benn's primordialism must have seemed to Jolas to be a synthesis of all he was trying to achieve. The 'mystic participation', the 'hallucination', the 'pre-logical' – all terms that echo throughout the journal – find form in Benn's prose for Jolas, whose 'stalwart belief in the universality of art' allowed him, in Rumold's words, to 'side with (and significantly misunderstand)' Benn's assessments.[39]

Benn's 'assessments' over the next few years took an explicitly fascistic turn, albeit a short-lived one. In 'After nihilism' (1932), Benn wrote of the Nietzschean superman as 'the new type, biologically more valuable, in racial terms advanced, vitalistically stronger, eugenically more complete, more justified by durability and maintenance of the species'. His speech to the Prussian Academy of Arts, given on 5 April 1932, extolled the virtues of eugenics and talked of transcendence as 'animal in nature'. The epigraph to 'Eugenics I' (1933) was nothing short of a clarion call for Hitler's ideology: 'he who wishes to rule a long time must apply eugenics widely'. The creative style of earlier works here gives way to a grave, prophetic tone. 'A new man will emerge from this transformation in Europe', he writes, 'half as a mutation and half as a result of eugenics: German man.' Benn ratchets up the rhetoric: '*brains* must be bred, great brains to defend Germany, brains with canine teeth, teeth of thunderbolts'. A piece entitled 'Expressionism', also from 1933, even talks of 'Germany's devout blood' at a time of crisis. 'Mind and body of future generations' (1933) takes things further, as Benn hails his nation as 'the last inheritance and the last grandeur of the white race', while in 'The people and the writer' (1933) he celebrates the state's activities and the search for 'the profound mysterious hieroglyph of the people's actual nature', a sentiment echoed in 'Writing needs inner latitude' (1934).[40] In thus embracing the new regime after 1933, Benn was 'one of the few distinguished German writers willing to play the game', as Francis Golffing puts it.[41] Benn's initial embrace of National Socialism was, for Rumold, a 'veritable salto mortale' that nonetheless offered 'an "inner" authority for an *aestheticization* of fascist politics'.[42] During 1933–4

Benn gave a talk welcoming F. T. Marinetti to Berlin, and he was for a time vice-president of Hitler's Union nationaler Schriftsteller (Union of National Writers).[43] Once he became aware of the thuggery of the 'brown battalion' of the Sturmabteilung (Storm Troopers), however, Benn was soon disillusioned with the Nazi Party; and not long after, in 1935, he was himself deemed a 'degenerate' and subjected to numerous smear campaigns, with accusations of Judaism, homosexuality and other alleged perversities in his poetic work. By 1938 this culminated in his complete ban from writing.[44] But despite an impassioned plea from Klaus Mann, who begged him to emigrate in protest at the new regime, Benn never left his native country, unlike many of his fellow artists and writers.[45] Nevertheless, he never formally joined the Nazi Party either, and he spent the majority of the war stationed at a venereal disease clinic in Hanover, which existed primarily for prostitutes.

It remains unclear to what extent Jolas was aware at the time of what Michael Hofmann calls Benn's 'drif[t] into the Nazi orbit' during the early 1930s, but from a hindsight perspective he certainly seems to have felt deep regret.[46] Hinting at the German poet's brush with Nazism, in the early 1970s Maria Jolas wrote to McMillan that 'Benn's evolution was a source of great distress to Gene', especially his 'inner emigration' and 'stubborn patriotism' – 'for [Benn] was as proud as Lucifer'.[47] Jolas also appears to have retrospectively expurgated Benn's influence. In his unfinished autobiography *Man from Babel*, the editor downplays Benn's significance across the *transition* project. Recounting their 1929–30 meeting in Berlin, he focuses instead on the brewing nationalism of those last years of the Weimar Republic and presents it as a force beyond understanding, as if retrospectively aware that all those ideas about primal unity did have real political implications after all.[48] Yet during the early 1930s, Jolas's obsession with the revival of the Word found fresh energy in the idea of the pineal eye, or as Rumold puts it, 'the mystical, visionary faculty of the "third eye", lost but to be recovered by the "Revolution of the Word"', the Word 'as "arche-logos," ur-name [. . .] as universal *nomos*'.[49] Benn was an ideal conduit.

In a text one cannot fail to read as a tragic misunderstanding of violence, published the very month the Nazis came to power, Jolas echoes Benn to the letter, announcing that 'the new man's chief characteristic will be a violent revolt of the intellect'.[50] Expounding the virtues of Heidegger alongside Ludwig Klages's panromanticism as dealing a 'death blow' to the 'naturalistic conception which saw in man primarily a being impelled by reason', Jolas's editorial essay 'The primal personality' supplemented Benn's text in both style and content. Jolas discusses the French ethnologist Lucien Lévy-Bruhl, then quotes from Dacqué's *Natur und Seele* (1928), extending Benn's quasi-neurological approach. Effectively endorsing 'The structure of the personality' from the previous issue, Jolas quotes

Dacqué: 'The anatomical properties of that primal man consisted most probably in the possession of brain-organs which we still find as remnants in us, but which the intellective great brain has overgrown.'[51] Jolas then enlists further evidence to support the atavistic notion of the 'primal personality' or 'unity' via Franz von Baader's writings on the 'inner eye', which he presents as a neo-metaphysical immediacy in modernity, science and the so-called new man. In taking up Benn's essay so directly, Jolas obtains a blueprint for much of his own subsequent programmatic content, as his lyrical prose anticipates further questionnaires and manifestos. 'An intuitive experience', he writes. 'A sinking into the stream of life. A hallucinated attitude before the object-world. The feeling of humility before the fundamentally irrational essence of being. *Wesensschau*. The inner eye. The third eye.'[52]

It would be easy to capitulate to Hutt's criticism at this point and write off Jolas's neologisms and editorial fanfares as merely an echo of proto-fascist Bennian aesthetics. Yet to do so would wildly miss the mark. Nevertheless, it is true that *transition* was culturally deaf in this regard. On the one hand, Kramer and Rumold are right to observe that Jolas's 'metaphysical temperament had long precluded any critical insight into the relation between culture and politics', and his continued inclusion of Benn is a troubling facet of the magazine's history.[53] In the subsequent issue, in July 1935, Jolas published Benn as part of a further questionnaire on the 'malady of language'. In this curious text, which also includes responses from *inter alia* Ivan Goll, Gorham Munson, C. K. Ogden and Laurence Vail, Benn postulates the holistic 'organic formal metamorphosis of words and language' as a crisis not simply of the romantically conceived 'human spirit', but specifically of the 'white man' and his modernity. 'Language is passing through a crisis', he writes, 'because the white man is passing through a crisis.'[54] Benn's racial panic goes uncommented. Without being fully cognisant of the fact, Jolas folds it into his editorial vision.

On the other hand, Jolas was mounting a crusade that was fiercely internationalist and ultimately opposed to any kind of racist ideology around the *Volk*. In a powerful comment in his 1932 pamphlet *The Language of Night*, under the subheading 'Depth and the chthonian image', Jolas's prose reveals key differences between his and Benn's sense of the 'malaise' of modernity:

> What is creative expression today other than cowardly genuflection before positivist dogmas and social idols? Progress and evolution as watch-words. Machine-mysticism as an illusion of progress. The hegemony of intellectualism, the dance around money, the principle of causality – all enemies of the absolute. *Biedermeier* orderliness. De-personalisation. Mass-man. Sport as a substitute for deep emotions. Fear of the symbol. Language as fordian [sic] standardisation. Literature in terms of honoraria. The urban feeling as anti-nature primitivism. Sobriety of photographic realism. Sexus

instead of Eros. Anonymity. Fear driving the I to mass-opium. Meliorístic world ideals. Aversion to facing the individual conflicts inherent in our irrational being. Utilitarian metaphors. Metaphors as substitutes for primal images. Onslaught against the subjective. [...] Normalisation. False Humanism.[55]

One can hear the journalist on the newswire here, yet without the lightness and irony found elsewhere in Jolas's editorials. In a departure from Benn's writing, Jolas looks to an absolute, to individualism, 'deep emotion' and symbolism, but expressed in an anti-hierarchical world. He calls for a utopian mode of thinking with the body and soul as collective identities: a multiplicity of all peoples and tongues, rather than a purified or singular consciousness rising from what he calls a 'Eur-America' too preoccupied with 'ephemeral reality'.[56] As Diana Rumrich observes, the reader should be wary here of 'a certain "sound" of the 1930s', which turned out to be 'a seductive siren's song of a new irrationalism'.[57] But Jolas goes on to critique Enlightenment rationalism in post-humanist terms. 'Only by recognizing the fact that the primordial background of life is characterized by enormous scissions can we recapture the lost qualities of our psyche', he writes. 'All cognition is anthropocentric.' Although directly influenced by Benn's idea of structured consciousness, then, Jolas departs from it by transposing the terms of the geological 'I' into what he calls 'the magical motif': a linguistic, narrative form cast beyond the human subject.[58]

The vestigial eye returned over the following few years, as both an offshoot of Benn's text and a distinct element of *transition* as a whole. For Jolas, impervious as he was to Benn's proto-fascist aesthetics, the 'third eye' became an idealist, 'inter-racial' idea, antithetical to the ideology of National Socialism, and part of a stream of writing that connected sites of vision with the reptile. Building on *transition*'s 'Poetry is vertical' manifesto of 1932, the February 1933 issue launched what the magazine came to call its 'Vertigral documents', introduced by a rousing statement of intent in a piece entitled 'Twilight of the horizontal age' (Figure 3.1).[59] Here the magazine announced a new era in which 'we stand in direct line with the primeval strata of life', 'rediscovering the mantic forces of pre-historic man' in search of a 'primitive grammar, the stammering that approaches the language of God'.[60] Later in the same issue, in a passage selected from Jolas's poetry collection *Secession in Astropolis* (1929), the reader encounters a surreal scene where the speaker confronts an unsettling reptile whose way of seeing is somehow sonorous:

> I raced around the place getting my feet entangled in a flaming heap of bindweed in which I noticed a lizard with a silk hat on its horny head. It stared at me with shillering eyes and whined. I ran away.[61]

TWILIGHT OF THE HORIZONTAL AGE

Nihilism is fighting its last stand.

On the flat plane of consciousness, man tried, in the past few decades, to see life with dreamless eyes, the stars were hidden behind the smoke of his machine-mind, his senses moved in the dull rotation of blind forces.

But in the face of the collapse of mechanistic utopias, man is beginning to revolt against the dogma of evolution, and turns again to the eternal elements of his being.

Man is beginning to think in cosmic terms again.

The Vertigral Age brings with it a recognition of the a-historic man, the religious man, the man who seeks a mystic union with the Logos.

The Vertigral Age sees modern philosophy turning deliberately to metaphysics after a long interregnum.

The Vertigral Age hails the cognition of a non-mechanical reality on the part of astronomy and physics.

The Vertigral Age believes that we stand in direct line with the primeval strata of life.

The Vertigral Age is re-discovering the mantic forces of pre-historic man.

The Vertigral Age wants to discover the supernatural reality through the dreams that lead to the transfiguration of life.

The Vertigral Age wants to give voice to the ineffable silence of the heart.

The Vertigral Age wants to create a primitive grammar, the stammering that approaches the language of God.

Eugene Jolas.

Figure 3.1 'Twilight of the horizontal age'. Editorial in *transition*, 22, February 1933. Reproduced by permission of Betsy Jolas

Over the page, in Jolas's 'Night is 3', one finds a creative expression of his editorial vision: 'Night is [. . .] the sea, the all-world, [. . .] the bridge from the I to the you. The pineal eye. Primal world. Meta-real logos. Mantic future. Hunger for the apex. Magna mater.'[62] A few pages on, Jolas's poetic voice offers a further polylingual meditation on our reptilian ancestors in a piece entitled 'Intrialogue' which is reminiscent of Benn's line about 'the saurian, the simian':

> Et la mère-terre?
>   C'est a shard of organvoices.
>   For the three-eyed Vorfahren still walk through the Champ de Mars, der Boden das Waldes crick-cracks noch immer von Saurien, le tremblement de peur psaume toujours devant le néant.
>
> (And mother earth?
>   It is a shard of organvoices.
>   For the three-eyed ancestors still walk through the Field March, the forest floor crick-cracks still of the Saurian, the trembling of fear always psalm before nothingness.)[63]

One cannot help but picture these 'three-eyed' ancestors as saurian reptiles with the vestigial organ, an image that is reversed in another Jolasian flourish entitled 'Verbirrupta of the mountainmen', where again one hears a form of sight: 'Faroff there is a rimblerumble', Jolas writes, 'like the voice of the hidden Cyclopmind'.[64] Towards the end of the issue, the editors incorporate programmatic statements as to the nature of this 'vertigral' awakening, printed in bold type at the foot of random pages. One reads simply: 'VERTIGRAL: Le Troisième Oeil'.[65]

Alongside such vivid animal writing there was a utopian pineal eye – starkly opposed to any racism in Benn's thought, yet devoted to a totalised view of the subject – and what Rumold has described as 'the "upward" mission of poetry', which I will survey in the next chapter.[66] The magazine was now running with the notion of 'vertigralism' with increasing alacrity. The July 1935 issue included an editorial written in French entitled 'Transmutation vertigraliste', in which Jolas laid out a mission for the future of the Word:

> Vertigral veut liquider l'époque du nihilism et du rationalisme en postulant une transmutation métanthropologique.
>   L'esprit vertigral cherche une synthèse créatrice à travers l'irrationalisme panromantique et le rêve individuel et collectif, afin de trouver la personnalité totale, l'homme surconscient, l'homme inter-racial, l'homme au troisième oeil.

(Vertigral wants to liquidate the epoch of nihilism and rationalism by postulating a metanthropological transmutation.

The vertigral spirit seeks a creative synthesis through the pan-romantic irrationalism and the individual and collective dream, in order to find the total personality, the superconscious man, the inter-racial man, the man of the third eye.)[67]

This marks the crucial difference between Jolasian idealism and Benn's quasi-scientific rhetoric. The 'inter-racial' is an exuberant celebration found throughout Jolas's texts – the mixing together of languages like so many colours on a palette, and an implicit, radical critique of the notion that miscegenation was coterminous with degeneration.[68] By 1937 – the year of the infamous German exhibition of so-called degenerate art (*entartete Kunst*) organised by the Nazis – this utopianism was to reach its apex. In a resounding piece of fiction entitled 'The third eye: ascension to the tremendum', Jolas opens with 'the time of death', of 'entranced grief', mourning a loss of faith through the trappings of Roman Catholicism, moving through nonsense words built from French, German, Spanish and English etymological roots. The text swells to a euphoric cry for 'the time when the texts of the ancient runes began to sing'. We are no longer in the imagination of the man with the pineal eye, or of Benn's Mesozoic, reptilian fantasies; now we are at an extremity of optimistic multiculturalism that, just two years before the onset of war, cannot but look naive in its 'vision' – 'a new race visionary with the logos of God'.[69] Jolas takes from Benn what he finds useful, but fails to see the urgency of acknowledging the emerging totalitarian state that would all but destroy European cultural life.

Involutional Dinosaurs

Transition's 'pineal eye' invites further analysis, since a range of authors also picked up on Jolas's zeal, often through distinctly reptilian imagery. Before we turn to such texts both in and beyond the magazine, it is important to contextualise Benn's initiating rhetoric as an interdiscursive and historically specific articulation that emerged from contemporary life sciences, much like Joyce's ichthyological play explored in the previous chapter. Benn's atavistic excitement coincided with a generation of pineal cytology dating back to the mid-nineteenth century, in which the genre of dry scientific prose approached the vestigial organ through the vitalist idea of 'involution', giving rise by the early 1930s to an extraordinary confession of scientific ignorance. If we outline this history, which was contemporary with the cultural, philosophical and political pineal eyes under discussion here, the reptilian image can be seen as a product of outmoded idealist thought across multiple disciplines. This in turn sheds light on the slippage between science and mysticism that was so characteristic of interwar 'third eye' writing in both *transition* and other avant-garde formations.

As is already evident from Benn's thinking, the pineal eye should not be confused with the pineal gland, which evolved in vertebrates from the glandular function of the cells-to-stem pineal mechanism. Similar to the parietal 'eye' in its singularity (as opposed to the duality of a pair of eyeballs), the pineal gland is a small outgrowth of the brain. In humans, it is situated behind the third ventricle, close to the optic thalamus, between the two hemispheres – almost in the very middle of the organ. It is a 'miniscule pedunculate bud', in David Krell's words, 'a gland soft in substance yet containing gritty particles'.[70] Also known as the epiphysis, epiphysis cerebri or conarium (because of its pine cone shape), the pineal gland forms the endocrinological headquarters for the body's production of melatonin, which in turn regulates sleep, sexual development and circadian rhythms. Whereas the pineal gland has been studied since antiquity (by Pythagoras especially), the pineal eye was defined experimentally in the 1910s, and it was explored by endocrinologists, palaeontologists and cytologists in the 1920s and early 1930s.

Readers of *transition* would not have known much about this particularly primordial organ, of course, despite being exposed to its avant-garde permutations. Even within the scientific community, the pineal eye's vestigial properties and the pineal gland's hormonal functions were far from clear, or even distinguished, during this period. Biologists investigating aspects of the pineal eye, however, were aware of a great question mark, and they used unusually emotive language. First named in 1828 after two separate anatomists – Antoine Dugès and M. H. Milne-Edwards – discovered a single protuberance on the head of certain lizards that was connected to the brain by a nerve, the pineal eye is very much a product of the nineteenth century.[71] In the 1880s, palaeontologists examining a range of dinosaurs and other prehistoric reptiles recorded the small hole in the skull of particular species as the 'pineal body'. One review of such work and observations elsewhere of the organ, which consisted of a cluster of retina-like cells, led J. Beard to question the pineal eye's evolutionary function. He saw it as indicative of a process of 'involution'. Physiologists most often used this term during that decade to denote a 'shrinking in the whole body which accompanies old age' (according to the 1887 issue of *The New Sydenham Society's Lexicon of Medicine and the Allied Sciences*) or 'cysts found in the shrivelled mammary glands of old women' (according to the *Oxford English Dictionary*). 'Involution', in its biological sense of degeneration or reversed evolution, would not be taken up fully in the discipline until 1896, when Thomas Clifford Allbutt described the 'involution forms [of bacilli] being pretty constantly developed'.[72] In a rare moment of embellishment in otherwise dry scientific prose, Beard writes that the organ suggests a kind of 'atavism' or reversed evolution. Coming from a biologist, such universal and loaded terms reveal an unusually unscientific excitement over the organ, indicating a lack of knowledge about its precise function.[73]

This gap in knowledge about the pineal eye extends to the first major cytological account, which was published the same year as Benn's essay. Spanning the pineal gland (epiphysis) in 'higher', mammalian creatures as well as the non-mammalian organ of the pineal eye, Pío del Río Hortega and Wilder Penfield's landmark 1932 study was hesitant as to whether the function of pineal cells was neuronal. They conclude: 'the prestige of the [pineal] organ undoubtedly rests largely on our defective knowledge'.[74] The period between the earlier palaeontological research into the pineal body and Hortega's consolidating efforts on glandular research – approximately 1887 to 1932 – was therefore important with regard to the emergent field of neuroendocrinology. In 1905, F. K. Studnička offered an extensive description of pineal cytology in non-mammalian vertebrates, resulting in the first postulation of the gland's evolution from a purely photosensory organ (Figure 3.2). In 1911, Karl Von Frisch began the earliest experiments into the connection between light perception and the pineal with his laboratory studies of minnows. Carey Pratt McCord and Floyd P. Allen's

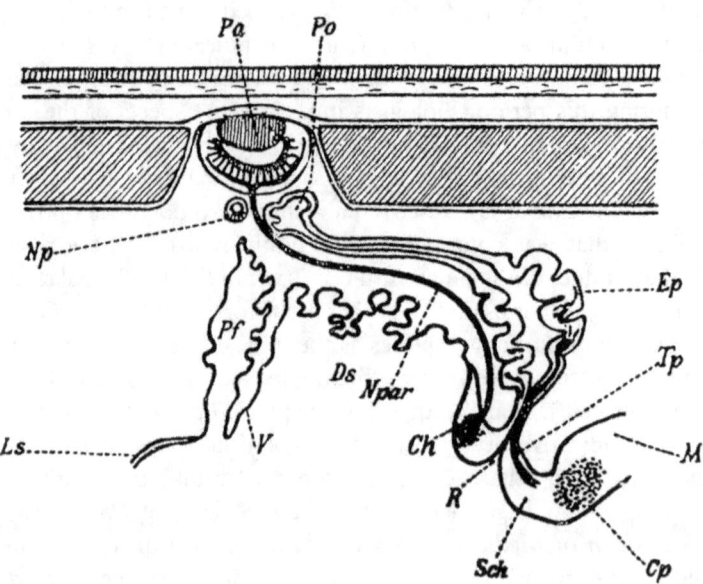

Ls., lamina terminalis; *V.*, velum transversum; *Pf.*, paraphysis; *Ds*, dorsal sac; *Ch.*, commissura habenularis; *Pa.*, parapineal organ; *Npar.*, nervus parapinealis; *Po*, pineal organ; *Ep.*, proximal portion pineal organ; *Tp.*, tractus pinealis; *Sch.*, pars intercalaris posterior; *Cp.*, commissura posterior; *M.*, midbrain, *Np.*, accessory parapineal organ; *R.*, Recessus pinealis.

Figure 3.2 F. K. Studnička, 'Schematization of the pineal region in Sphenodon' (1905). Reproduced in Frederick Tilney and Luther Fiske Warren, *The Morphology and Evolutional Significance of the Pineal Body*, 1919

1917 work on tadpoles raised a query about skin pigmentation, which led to Aaron Lerner and his research group's discovery of melatonin in 1958.[75] Harvey Cushing's work on intracranial tumours on the pituitary gland (hypophysis), the pineal's 'topographical antipode' (to quote science historian Francis Schiller), led to the investigation of biochemical factors in sexual development around the turn of the twentieth century, although again throughout this period the precise glandular function remained unknown.[76] As in Benn's text, there is an elision between the 'higher' gland in mammals and the pineal system (including the so-called median eye) in reptiles and other primitive vertebrates. On the one hand, there is the 'eye' that senses changes in light, pre-dating the camera eye; on the other, the pineal gland appears to be somehow connected to sexual development.[77] This is of no small significance when we assess the history of this biological work: a writer exposed to the latest thinking in various life science discourses would have been presented with the excitingly new 'fact' of atavism, lodged inside the brain. Benn was not alone, therefore, in making a semi-logical association between the pineal eye as a vestigial reptilian organ and a more metaphysical notion of involution.

Effluent Eyeballs

Although the writings and collaborations of the dissident Surrealist Georges Bataille did not appear in *transition* until its 1948 incarnation under the editorship of Georges Duthuit, his ideas around the pineal eye developed during this same period of scientific discovery, and they offer a vital counterpoint, adding a philosophical dimension to the animal contours of Jolas's milieu. Jolas and Bataille evidently knew each other: *transition* 15 was advertised in Bataille's first issue of *Documents*; some of the latter's intellectual circle appeared in both journals (chiefly Michel Leiris and Carl Einstein); and Jolas himself published a piece on Picasso in *Documents*' first issue.[78] Yet Bataille is significantly absent from *transition* due to his radically subversive thinking: he produced an altogether different body of work from Jolas's more conservative yet idealist visions, as Rumold has amply demonstrated.[79] Bataille's pineal texts date from his early period, at the height of his controversy with André Breton. One of his chief objectives during this time was to articulate a subversion of the 'bourgeois prison', as he foregrounds in a 1929–30 essay about Surrealism and its perilous proximity to 'pretentious idealistic aberrations'. In a direct attack on Surrealists as revolutionaries detached from the class struggle, Bataille describes the guilty bourgeois conscience as expressing itself 'with a disgusting idealistic verbal outpouring that gives free rein to a craving for cheap utopian blindness'. Elevation of humanity's 'spirit' is 'imbecilic', he writes: we must excavate the 'fetid ditch of bourgeois culture' and perhaps unearth yet more 'sinister caves where force and human liberty will establish themselves, sheltered from the call to order of a heaven'.[80]

Such 'excavation' is thus Bataille's praxis. Much like his pseudonymous and most famous work *L'histoire de l'oeil* (Story of the Eye, 1928), texts such as 'The solar anus' (written in 1927, published in 1931), 'Eye' and 'The big toe' (September and November 1929) offer the reader images of a masturbatory sea, the enucleated eyeball of Salvador Dalí and Luis Buñuel's avant-garde film *Un chien andalou* (1929), and the ejaculatory, excremental, vaginal and scatological shocks of a human subject confronting the 'ignoble shaft' of an eruptive, destructive, anal sun.[81] Bataille's is a poesis of corporeal baseness, of a body shorn of its Western, post-Enlightenment head, indeed the acephalous or headless body that would become integral to his later work. Along with Georges Ambrosino, Pierre Klossowski, Jean Wahl and others, Bataille founded a journal entitled *Acéphale*, which ran from June 1936 to June 1939.

Around the same time that Benn was drafting 'The structure of the personality', Bataille was composing 'The Jesuve', the essay where the reader first encounters his implementation of the pineal eye. Written in 1930, the text refers back to 1927 to recount a vision: 'I imagined the eye at the summit of the skull like a horrible erupting volcano, precisely with the shady and comical character associated with the rear end and its excretions.' Bataille is evidently writing in the wake of the same biological discourse as Benn, albeit indirectly, with a palaeontological air – 'this extraordinary eye would finally really come to light through the bony roof of the head' – and a quasi-neurological aspect – 'I had read [the eye's] embryo existed, like the seed of a tree, in the interior of the skull.'[82] Yet in 'The pineal eye', a text unpublished until 1967 but dating from around the same time, Bataille goes to great lengths to ridicule almost all branches of biological science, especially anthropology ('empty terms and impotent paralogisms'), before restating his notion of the vestigial organ:

> The eye, at the summit of the skull, opening on the incandescent sun in order to contemplate it in a sinister solitude, is not a product of the understanding, but is instead an immediate existence; it opens and blinds itself like a conflagration, or like a fever that eats the being, or more exactly, the head. [. . .] This great burning head is the image and the disagreeable light of the *notion of expenditure*.[83]

For Martin Jay, Bataille was an unparalleled figure in French avant-garde culture whose commitment to the 'dethronement of the eye' – in the wake of the visual shocks of the First World War – comprised a sustained, subversive engagement with traditional ocularcentrism, a 'rational heliocentrism' that ignored what Bataille saw as the destroying sun. Jay identifies Bataille's pineal eye texts as attempts to 'concoc[t] a phantasmatic anthropology' that was turned against the Cartesian 'seat of the soul' – the coherent, unified, rational intellect – and transferred the focus from the pineal gland to the eruptive, ejaculatory, effluent 'eye'.[84] The pineal texts also mark a shift in Bataille's thought towards expenditure as a key component of his political theory, upon which a vast array of critics including Roland Barthes, Julia Kristeva, Michel Foucault, Gilles Deleuze, Jean-Luc Nancy, Susan Sontag and many others have reflected in their own philosophies.[85]

In some ways, then, Bataille and Benn shared a combative relationship with bourgeois modernity, and each attributed the relatively contemporary concept of the pineal eye with explosive power. For Benn it represented the lost holism of primal unity, submerged beneath a corrupted neocortex; for Bataille it offered a volcanic escape from what he considered humanity's 'horizontal axis of vision', into a violent discharge of Icarian verticality that was just as rotten, stinking, indecent and base as the sight of the anal protuberance of an ape.[86] But whatever Benn and Bataille shared in their subversive deployment of the vestigial organ, their work was to take almost polar opposite directions. As we have seen, Benn went into his 'Nazi orbit', while from 1930 onwards Bataille entered his most Marxist phase, going on to write at length about the totalitarian regime under Hitler's dictatorship.[87]

Another francophone writer from the period who engaged with the pineal eye was the poet Roger Gilbert-Lecomte. Along with René Daumal, Gilbert-Lecomte edited the Marseille dissident Surrealist journal *Le grand jeu*, a literary project devoted to what Claudine Frank calls 'metaphysical Dadaism or morbid *pataphysique*'. Jolas translated an excerpt in *transition* as 'The big game'.[88] Not only was Gilbert-Lecomte textually closer to Jolas's circle than Bataille (albeit, as Frank observes, with an 'ambivalent attraction' to the latter's work), but he was also more conceptually zoological: he was explicitly concerned with the reptilian organ, and with the folkloric, semi-occultist mysticism of the broader 'third eye' that so dominated *transition*'s later years.[89] In a letter to Daumal and Roger Vailland dated 13 March 1926, Gilbert-Lecomte articulates a recent vision:

> I had an intuition (and the experimental verification of witnesses who know about anatomy) that this line from the North Pole crosses the pineal gland or epiphysis (which in lizards is a *third eye*) whose role in human intellect, until yesterday night, remained obscure. A discovery that is Unique since the creation of the world. Vast expanses advanced in the direction of Socrates's *gnoti seauton* [know thyself], I, Cyclopean hyper-lizard, I know, I know I KNOW because I knew to annihilate every link in my intellect to ideas born from my frontal eyes' view (of all the senses, the most intellectualised view, as Uncle Marcel would say).
>
> The great BUBU – navel of the cosmos – has allowed the immediate, intuitive, total vision of this third eye to be revealed to me (thus I shall

soon have omniscience, which is fatal). When I'm dead, drill my skull and you will see, you WILL SEE what's there in my brain instead of the epiphysis (that atrophied eye of the common mortal).[90]

Pre-dating both Bataille and Benn, this letter is a forerunner to Gilbert-Lecomte's later investment in the distinctly reptilian aspect of his visions, as his 1928 essay 'La force des renoncements' (The power of renunciation) would go on to explore. The destructive force of a third eye, which is capable of 'annihila[ting]' the frontal or post-Enlightenment ocular system of rational perception (as articulated above), is modulated in the later essay into a reflection on other lizard organs. 'The reptile has tirelessly devoured its anterior limbs', he muses, 'which in primitive eras where there was a great zeal for life, always grew back.'[91] Two years later Gilbert-Lecomte went so far as to herald *'the Three-Eyed Man'* whose birth *'will surpass the individual and truly be the cosmic consciousness'*.[92]

Although further discussion of this avant-garde formation exceeds the case at hand, it is clear that the *Grand jeu* circle were an unacknowledged influence, not least in the fact that both they and Jolas closely read the anthropology of Lévy-Bruhl and Claude Lévi-Strauss, and articulated a totalised view of the subject, as discussed above.[93] Bataille was a major influence, too: in 1936–8, *transition*'s final years, the magazine took structural cues from *Documents* directly with segments such as 'The eye' and 'The ear', incorporating 'the evolution and function of the senses in perception processes' as well as an overriding fascination with insights from contemporary ethnology and primitivism.[94] Yet *transition*'s preoccupation with the pineal eye must also be read as an overwhelmingly naive aspect of its mission, albeit one born of the shared intellectual climate of interwar France. In what can be read as a desperate attempt to look from Europe to what he called 'America Mystica', Jolas still held to the notion of 'Chimera-Words from Sleep and Half-Sleep', as one subheading in 'The third eye: ascension to the tremendum' rhapsodised. Unwittingly close to 'the "dark" side of modernism', Jolas's reverie now seems utterly unaware of the imminent threat of totalitarianism, something that was far more obvious to Bataille by the early 1930s. What remains to be done is an assessment of just how pervasive these conceptual third eyes and metaphorical lizards really were across the magazine, in order to better understand the journal's 'pineal eye', its Bennian influence, and modernism's 'dark side'.

'Monsterlizards', 'Marble Lizards' and 'the Cosmological Eye'

A broad overview of *transition*'s many reptilian images and invocations of the third eye reveals an array of writing distinct from Bataille's and Gilbert-Lecomte's visions, and with it an insight into the journal's primordial modernism.

Contributors linked the pineal eye's air of biological discourse, so forcibly evinced by Benn, to expressions of the modern subject and the power of the Word. Lizard imagery offered specific signifying power in articulations of primitivist narrative, nationalised postmodernity and abject subjectivity in psychiatric discourse. In addition, Benn's influence spawned numerous anglophone iterations of this semi-scientific third eye as conjoined to a transformative aesthetic, most notably by Henry Miller. Not only was the magazine's 'pineal eye' and 'lizard' writing a major dimension of its history, but it was also part of a current of thought that ran counter to the racialised symbology of Benn's fascist phase. Although Jolas was demonstrably impervious to the 'dark side' of Benn's thought in the early 1930s, by the end of the magazine's run and into the early 1940s he was on a crusade to fight Nazi barbarism.

The most explicit example of a *transition* author linking the pineal eye to the magazine's modernist project appeared in 1935, when Lothar Mundan (an alias of Jacques Fourmann) published an appraisal of the journal entitled 'Vertigral poetry: the third eye', reprinted from *La voix de Lorraine*. Giving a detailed description of Jolas's project in markedly animal terms, Mundan links the vestigial organ to the structure of a fable. The mysterious 'parietal or pineal eye' is a vision of 'metaphysical being' which Mundan posits as the most 'extreme' mystery of 'our modern times'. He then turns to the authority of zoology and anatomy, where the pineal is well known. He focuses on it as an explicitly reptilian organ, moreover, when he describes one species in particular, the tuatara lizard:

> In New Zealand there exists a curious lizard, of very primitive form, called Hatteria punctata, with a bright spot on its skull, underneath which there is a rudimentary parietal eye. The same observation has been made in the cases of several other species of lizard, and it is most likely that it existed originally with all the lower vertebrate animals. [. . .] With many vertebrate animals (petromyzon, saurian), the epiphesis (a growth on the back of the mid-brain) is found in the form of an uneven parietal eye which probably still functions as a sense organ. This is the more interesting in that the embryonic mid-brain also forms the mother-soil from which the retinae of the two eyes evolve.[95]

This vividly anatomical account is then used to bolster Mundan's understanding of Jolas's poetry and magazine. The manifestos are 'belligerent', he writes, 'against the philistine, reportorial, horizontal quality of a superficial lyricism, in favour of a vertigral poetry that is directed towards the zenith, not a poetry of the brain, but of the parietal eye'. This statement leads to Mundan's conclusion: the reptilian 'magic' of this vision is an 'intuitive apperception of the cosmos'. The excitement behind Mundan's description of the tuatara indicates a confusion as to whether the pineal eye works like a fountain or – in that use of the word 'apperception' – like a black hole in the brain. Directly opposing Bataille's volcanic and ejaculatory anti-humanist image, Mundan's alignment of the 'apperceptive' eye with Jolas's vision of poetic verticality is a signal example of a *transition* contributor garnering support for its mission by deploying the sign of the lizard. Mundan calls for irrationalism 'based on magical laws, like the universe itself'. We must 'destroy the logical, old-fashioned old language' and 'speak the language of the twentieth century', he writes, 'which has now become a necessity, and which will constitute a bridge to the age of the parietal eye' (Figures 3.3 and 3.4).[96]

Jolas's creative writing in the same issue extends this call, celebrating a realm of hybrid animals through his signature neologisms and his fascination with a chthonic world from which this 'age of the parietal eye' might appear. In his 'Paramyths from a dreambook', in a segment called 'Subhuman pilgrimage', the narrative voice seeks solace in the company of animals: 'I knew that I was in the domain of the subhuman. I knew that this was the refuge of stonebirds and chimerapes and monsterlizards.' The speaker enters a 'tropical forest' after

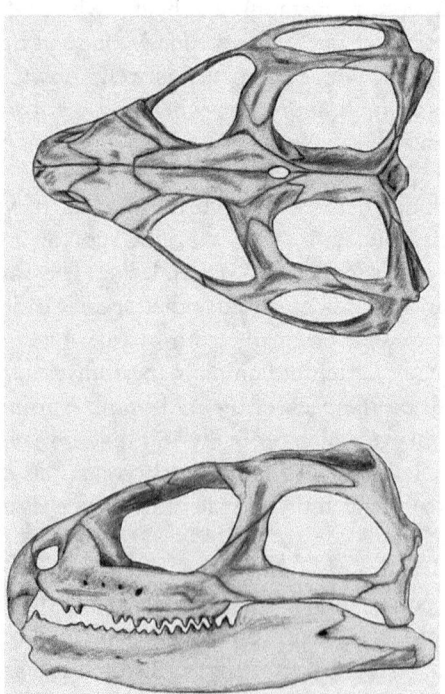

Figure 3.3 Nobumichi Tamura, 'Tuatara skull' (2007). Illustration.
© Nobumichi Tamura

Figure 3.4 Tuatara (*Sphenodon; Hatteria punctata*). Photograph by Andrew McMillan (undated). Reproduced under Creative Commons Licence CC0 1.0 Universal

finding 'fascist and marxist symbols in tangleconfusion' in a little cottage. The dream sequence suggests the speaker is more than aware of a profound change in the world, which is cast in Bennian language, but that he is confused and overwhelmed:

> I knew that a geological revolution had occurred, the rind of the earth had begun to burst, there was a firesparklecrepitation. The houses were collapsing. [. . .] I ran in circles [. . .]. [A] faroff rumblebellow was heard, it was a night of forebodings.[97]

If we compare this with Mundan's explicit endorsement of the magazine's 'age of the parietal eye', here we see a far more circumspect voice, a transposition of editorial pomp into vulnerable, haunted expression. The 'monsterlizards'' land is but a temporary escape.

Earlier instances of lizard images reveal primitivist leanings. Published in the same issue as Benn's essay, Whit Burnett's 'Balkan journey' – an exoticised story set in San Francisco but referring to the south-eastern European region – deploys the familiar trope of a lizard on a sunny wall, but here with direct emphasis on vision:

> So inspecting near me too something incommensurably queer. And quiet. The monster like a marble lizard lazy in the sun sloped gently on a slate wiping with a paw the tabula rasa. Blinking he was too with one eye friendly open.[98]

Burnett's prose is distinctly Jolasian, and its 'marble lizard' with its open eye has agency in the story. A similarly primitivist tale from the Aymara people of Bolivia, recounted to the author in Lucurmata, Wendell Bennett's 'A visit to the witch of darkness' tells of a witch who prepares lizards that she will take to a child and then slice open to retrieve the child's soul. Jolas likely included the piece as part of his 'inter-racial' drive during *transition*'s post-1932 phase, and the reptile occupies another familiar narrative trope, this time linked to supernatural practices.[99]

Parallel to this thread of ethnographic writing, the lizard also offered a signifying power for futuristic scenes in which the reptilian appears in nationalised visions of the soullessness of American capitalism. Édouard Roditi's 'Mirages' talks in vivid hyperbole of an ultramodern metropolis that nonetheless recalls the ancient dinosaur. 'The city of the Americans of the Future brandishes in the sky its phallic ten-thousand-floored buildings. The lower thousand floors are occupied by the inferior races of animals and men, and by other such machinery.' Intricate bridges mean the Americans of the Future 'need never touch the vulgar earth'; by 'living on such altitudes of the mind they have forgotten their bodies and only use them automatically and unconsciously in the natural acts of life such as the bringing in and letting out of money'. Roditi's critique of capitalism goes on:

> They have also forgotten their souls which are in the hands of the devils of comfort, wealth, and efficiency, and only exist in an entirely dead and mummified form; and the more abstract limbs of their minds are slowly dropping off them like the useless legs of certain prehistoric lizards.[100]

The vestigial, reptilian appendage comes into play in a dystopian vision of the modern that arrives alongside Jolas's more idealist pronouncements, yet it should be read as part of the story.

Another instance of a textual reptile appeared in July 1935, in a text largely in keeping with Benn's fascination with psychiatric discourse and abject subjectivity. F. M. Huebner describes the phenomena of psychopathic possession, focusing on a patient's encounter with animal forms:

> When the swarm of human beings which congregate for personification, are exhausted, as it were, there comes a moment when the aura is filled with phenomena from the world of animals. At first there come the milder creatures, representatives of a safe and tamed variety; these are followed by the heads and maws of animals from virgin forests and deserts; finally the reptiles and the larvae appear, loathsome and fearful.[101]

Huebner quotes the psychiatrist Karl Jaspers regarding cases of dementia in which the patient creates caricatures of beasts of prey, and again he mentions the reptilian. Deeper into Hades, he writes, 'satanic demons' are 'formations which, when examined at close range, reveal themselves as apparitions from prehistoric days. The similarity of these grinning, horned, mongrel demons with the creatures of the saurian age is obvious'.[102] As in the primitivist narrative, the saurian occupies an originating position, or is that which remains when the psyche is stripped down. In each of these instances, the signifying lizard is an agent – of horror, ritual, crushing capitalism, and a single blinking eye.

Again, Jolas's creative and critical writing encapsulates this trend. In a poem entitled 'Ergriffenheit' (the German for 'emotion'), the speaker summons polylingual neologisms in a scene with a reptile:

> You are still far away yet I hear your steps come softflying on the leaf-rug the hedges of the forest-edge protect your shadow from the mountain fumes the thistles lie in ruins a lizard creep-waits praying for a miracle in the verklaerung of the glutkosmos.[103]

'Verklaerung' comes from both the Dutch for 'declare' and the German 'Verklärung' or 'transfiguration'; the Joycean portmanteau 'glutkosmos' invokes the glut or gulp of a greedy world. A lizard awaiting this change or declaration is thus more than a mere metaphor: it seeks a 'miracle', much as the 'man with the pineal eye' that Jolas so frequently invoked might reconnect with the 'participation mystique' in search of a new mythos. In Jolas's rapturous praise of Joyce in his 'Homage to the mythmaker', published in *transition*'s final issue, he turns directly to this idea. Elucidating some of the 'Work in progress' and Joyce's 'larval and anthropological transmigrations', Jolas returns to his theme of the previous six years. 'Legend tells us that prehistoric man possessed a third eye', he writes, which was 'said to have given ancestral man the natural intuitive faculties which modern man has lost.' In a joint celebration of Joyce, his own mission and that implicitly reptilian concept, Jolas suggests that the 'man with the third eye may come back again, according to certain modern palaeontologists, who foresee the eventual re-development of that anatomical organ'.[104] By 1938, then, Jolas had departed significantly from Benn's initiating text, with the pineal eye now capable of answering a deep malaise in the 'glutkosmos' where impending totalitarianism could be sensed. Jolas and his authors' many lizards help us read this trajectory.

At the same time, Benn's presence can be felt across a range of writers' works during the 1930s, in a number of distinctive ways. The German poet's influence was as creative as it was editorial. In his *Whoroscope* notebook of 1932–7, Samuel Beckett, whose earliest prose and poems appear in *transition*, draws up a table of geological time periods that is reminiscent of Benn's piece, and in early drafts of *Watt* he seems to echo (with detectably ironic mockery) the desire to plummet 'deep down in those Palaeozoic profounds'.[105] Dylan Thomas, another *transition* author, was also directly influenced by Benn's logic of the totalised Word.[106] In striving for an eternally creative poetic language, some of Thomas's early poetry and prose bears the hallmarks of Jolasian 'paramyths'. Thomas's notebooks, especially from around 1932–3, frequently call upon 'mythic' landscapes of prehistoric earth, dust and animal symbols. 'We see rise the secret wind behind the brain', begins one poem from September 1933, for instance:

> The sphinx of light sit on the eyes,
> The code of stars translate in heaven.
> A secret night descends between
> The skull, the cells, the cabinned ears
> Holding forever the dead moon.[107]

During the period when he is most closely reading *transition*, Thomas's artistic vision is strongly reminiscent of the Bennian 'geological principle' with its refrains of stone, of 'ageing rock' and a chorus of 'in the beginning was the word'.[108]

William Carlos Williams was another author who took Benn seriously. He incorporated parts of 'The structure of the personality' into a 1936 text entitled 'How to write', published in 1936 as part of James Laughlin's first anthology of verse and prose for his newly inaugurated New Directions Press.[109] Printed alongside 'A face of stone', one of Williams's doctor stories, in which the dry, misanthropic narrator deals with (racially profiled) patients, 'How to write' reveals a synergy between the two physician-poets.[110] Every page of Williams's text makes implicit reference to Benn. 'Today we know the meaning of depth', he writes. 'It is a primitive profundity of the personality.' Williams echoes Benn exactly, stating that such depth is located in the 'deeper' 'portions', the 'middle brain, the nerves, the glands, the very muscles and bones of the body itself speaking' from 'the deeper strata'. At the end he gestures to Joyce and Stein (and presumably to his own work, as a fellow *transition* contributor) as 'the birth of a new language' – 'the cracking up of phrases which have stopped the mind'.[111]

Williams's vision of the modern may be more utopian than Benn's, but the influence is striking. In a letter to Louis Zukofsky in November 1932, Williams writes:

> I have read with interest a short thesis by Gottfried Benn in the last Transition (the new T. #21) on the nature of the ego – sounds rough but it's well done. I've known vaguely much of what he writes but never had it so well systematised for me before. It's curious, too, in the world how one's intimate thoughts have foretold all the discoveries and dilemmas of science. [. . .] It is great to read of the stratification of the consciousness – the self – down through the middle brain into the nerves and the very glands. It is the basic stuff of poetry, the 'depth' which peaople [sic] speak of in a writer is really more of a depth than anyone has heretofore realised. Lautreamont [sic] and the others become more valuable in this light. Prose, most prose, becomes as we have always known it to be – just the patter of the intelligence, the almost negligible forebrain.[112]

Much like Jolas, Williams does not question Benn's science, and he allows it to inform his entire concept of artistic creation, borrowing the 'big brain' idea and importing it as 'the almost negligible forebrain'. Yet also like Jolas and his utopianism, Williams transposes the pessimism of Benn's essay into a more whimsical, more humorous key, much in the manner in which he and other American writers responded to Surrealist avant-gardist art and literature, as discussed in the opening chapter.

A similarly humorous yet Bennian text appeared in *transition*'s final issue. A short work of first-person reportage, Henry Miller's 'The cosmological eye' invokes its titular concept through the author's encounters with the German artist Hans Reichel.[113] Reichel's canvases offer the author an artistic mode of seeing, a direct vision of the pineal eye that was so prominent in earlier issues. We know Miller read *transition* very closely: he subscribed to and followed the magazine even before his move to Paris in 1930.[114] He also adopts a similar objective to Jolas, writing that 'my friend Reichel is just a pretext to enable me to talk about the world, the world of art and the world of men, and the confusion and eternal misunderstanding between the two'. The text spans ten pages of fluid prose, loosely written in the mode of the *Künstlerroman* or artist's novel. Miller hails Reichel as the struggling artist par excellence, 'alone, ignored, unappreciated', and he describes his visits to Reichel's grotto-like studio in a cheap hotel that is 'not quite a hovel, his little den, but [. . .] perilously close to one' – a place completely lined with the artist's paintings, which 'themselves are holy'. Reichel's sorrow becomes central, repeatedly surfacing as his 'gnawing black pain'. Only Miller can see this. It is, he says, 'the reverse of his great love: it was the black unending curtain against which his gleaming pictures stand out and glow with a holy phosphorescence'. This reflection propels Reichel to disclose what an unnamed observer had recently told him: 'in all his pictures there was an eye, *the cosmological eye*, this person said'.[115] 'Perhaps', Miller writes,

> the ubiquitous eye was the vestigial organ of his love so deeply implanted into everything [. . .]. This eye had to be there in order to gnaw into men's vitals, to get hold of them like a crab, and make them realise that Hans Reichel exists.[116]

'Gnawing men's vitals' is an apt phrase from the author that George Orwell famously described as 'a mere Jonah, a passive acceptor of evil, a sort of Whitman among the corpses'.[117] The image is structurally similar to the depth model of the brain that Benn evinced, and to his refrain that 'here lies the beginning of all things':

> This cosmological eye is sunk deep within his body. Everything he looks at and seizes must be brought below the threshold of consciousness, brought deep into the entrails where there reigns an absolute night and where also the tender little mouths with which he absorbs his vision eat away until only the quintessence remains. Here, in the warm bowels, the metamorphosis takes place.[118]

In 1955 Alfred Perlès highlighted Miller's 'eye' in an account of the friendship between the author and artist. 'There was no need for [Reichel] to explain [his paintings] to Henry', he wrote in his memoir, 'who recognised them for what they were – messages from tree, flower, stone, fish, moon: prototypical messages, all of them, staring back at him with their "cosmological eyes".'[119] This sense of the 'prototypical' runs throughout the story. Reichel 'seems to be floating up from the paleozoic ooze'; he creates pictures of 'anarchic moons which swim in the latent protoplasm of the race'; he is an artist who can only 'stutte[r] and stamme[r]' while Miller, the great interpreter, 'hear[s] the music playing'.[120] The echoes of Benn and Jolas need hardly be spelled out: Miller, the infamous 'pornographer' of twentieth-century literature, writes a direct response to the pineal eye of those earlier *transition* issues.[121]

Although not concerned with the reptilian directly, Miller was expressly engaged with broader issues of race and the dangerous use of symbols so essential to Nazi ideology, and his admiration of Jolas and his circle was a major part of his thinking. As he described in a 1961 *Paris Review* interview, Miller was 'infatuated, intoxicated' with *transition*'s 'bizarre artists' that 'nobody had ever heard of'.[122] *Plexus* (1953) leaves a 1927 issue of *transition* 'lying around' and quotes large swathes of Benn's essay.[123] Miller's 1930s correspondence offers further clues in this regard, especially in his letters to fellow *transition* contributor Michael

Fraenkel. Miller repeats Jolas's very phrasing when in November 1935 he insists that 'a sense of mystic participation with the universe, a religious awareness, is the all-important'.[124] Miller even writes to Jolas directly in July 1950 of the artists who had so profoundly affected him, asking about their fate: 'Kurt Schwitters, Gottfried Benn, Hugo Ball – are they all dead now?'[125] Such seemingly complete admiration of Benn was in fact more complicated, however, since Miller was well aware in the mid-1930s of the proximity of the 'third eye' to a racist world view. In an extended exchange in which Miller and Fraenkel considered the structure of Shakespeare's *Hamlet*, Miller understood the play as a schema for an idea that was developing between him and Fraenkel about the current anti-Semitic groundswell. Miller describes 'the third eye' as that which *Hamlet* 'springs out of'; Fraenkel then reiterates this to Miller on the basis of a previous discussion 'of this Hamlet conspiracy which has its dragnet round the world'. With virulent anti-Semitism engulfing Germany during the time of this correspondence, a letter from Fraenkel to Miller dated 7 November 1935 shows the two authors situating the notion of the mystical 'third eye' in terms of racist logic:

> Hamlet – The Third Eye
> Horatio – The First Eye
> Ophelia – The Second Eye
> Rosenkrantz, Jew
> Gildenstern, Jew[126]

At first glance, the schematic rigidity of Fraenkel and Miller's 'third eye' renders it somewhat prosaic: the third eye could simply be a version of the hubris of Shakespeare's tragic hero. But the ordering suggests the two writers were instead interested in a racist impulse inherent to the nature of drama: one can celebrate the mysterious principle of inner vision, but one does so at the risk of a singularising logic that requires a demonised other. It is possible that the writers were thinking of the Nuremberg Laws, created the same month, when they referred to the 'dragnet' of conspiracy in *Hamlet* in terms of monolithic ideological forces. Whether or not Miller was aware of Benn's sympathies with the National Socialist movement, his dialogue with Fraenkel draws pineal vision into a cultural engagement with ideas of race.

Given this broad spectrum of influence, in which the signifying lizard and the conceptual pineal eye gave rise to both Benn's proto-fascism and Miller and Fraenkel's anti-fascist sentiment, I turn finally to wartime writing by both the *transition* editor and his once beloved German poet. While Jolas became all too aware of the threat of Hitler's power, writing in his memoir that 'the poet had not the right to remain entirely aloof', Benn languished in obscurity, his Expressionist lyricism and biological vocabulary turned gloomy and disquieting.[127] In 1941, Benn wrote 'Monologue', a mournful meditation on sinister power that is replete with grotesque animal imagery, visceral brains and a revisited scene of the reptile as an originating transformation. In one passage, here translated by Christopher Middleton, the reader is invited to consider 'history's monument' as itself reptilian, corrupt – a sorrowful reflection on the war:

> The puddle plums the source, the worm the ell,
> toad squirts his liquid in the violet's mouth,
> and – hallelujah! – whets his pot on stones:
> The reptile horde as history's monument!
> The Ptolemaic line as tic-tac language,
> the rat arrives as balm against the plague.
> Most foul sings murder. Gossips wheedle
> obscenity from psalms.
>
> [. . .] these spicy pickles of the protoplasm,
> Here transformation starts: the beasts' base form
> shall so decay the very word corruption
> will smell for it too much of heaven – the vultures
> are gathering now and famished hawks are poised![128]

Benn's doleful voice appears in another text written that year, entitled 'Poems' and equally mournful as 'Monologue': the speaker describes 'the rubble of the World's cadaver', where 'the oath of verse' 'bans reality with mystic word'. In both poems it is clear that, as Rumold observes, 'no other "dark" writer of the age lapsed into such a disturbing mentality of anger and denial'. Benn's 'darkness' was the reason why, as McMillan shows, Jolas ultimately broke off contact, even though Benn attempted to send him greetings through a third party after the war. 'Monologue' reveals a poet clinging to the same aesthetic as over a decade before, with a sense that the 'protoplasm' or primordial creaturely force is now a harbinger of doom rather than of the lost primal unity of 'The structure of the personality'.[129]

While Benn was in 'anger and denial', that same year Jolas published *Vertical: A Year-Book for Romantic-Mystic Ascensions*. Released just a few years after *transition*'s final issue, which McMillan describes as its 'anti-Nazi' number, this volume was intended as a successor to the magazine. It was written in defiance of German totalitarian rule: an implicit response to the Nazis burning a copy of *transition* in Munich during one of their infamous book-burning campaigns and also, as Jolas writes in the preface, to their 'invasion of Paris, which has engulfed, along with so much else, my entire library'.[130] As Rumold observes, Jolas's mission was essentially 'to fight Hitler's barbarism with modernist primitivism, and Hitler's racist myth with universal myths'. The romanticism and utopian idealism of Jolas's earlier project was still paramount: he wanted to 'take a stand on a grand geopolitical, transatlantic linguistic scale'. His pursuit was dedicated to mythologies of elevation, uplift, of Icarian flight, and to a poetry capable of reaching what he called the 'heavenly apex'.[131] The extent – and precarity – of Jolas's many images of elevation and verticality in their own distinctly animal, avian expressions will form the subject of the next chapter, but it is clear that what Jolas described in his memoir as an 'anti-Nazi, anti-totalitarian orientation' did come to 'dominate [his] life for years to come'.[132]

To conclude, the idea of a reptilian, pineal 'eye' enables a reading of *transition* that reveals the prominence given to one particular voice: Gottfried Benn. A pre-logical, pre-human mode of 'seeing' without eyes was a powerful concept. From the reptiles of Benn's lyrical biologism, through to Mundan's mystical tuatara, Jolas's 'man with the pineal eye' and Miller's 'cosmological eye' of the artist, one encounters a shared interest in metaphysical transcendence through the power of art, or indeed in the supposed purity of a lost origin or 'primal unity' of humanity. The 'dark side' of these iterations is integral to *transition*'s history, as this chapter makes clear. But the reptilian lines of imagery and aesthetic expression also gave rise to distinctly anti-fascist writing and thought, as with Miller and Fraenkel, and with Jolas's own later editorial work. In this case, finally, we must confront the simultaneity of editorial blindness, a shared fascination with primordial modes of 'seeing', and the ultimate rise of Nazi Germany that extinguished the magazine's fantasies of 'Logos unbound'. Yet despite such editorial blindness, the animal – here the lizard – helps us see.

Notes

1. Benn, 'Structure', originally published as 'Der Aufbau'.
2. McMillan, *transition*, 65.
3. Descartes, *Treatise of Man*; Descartes, 'Passions' in *Selected Philosophical Writings*, 218–38.
4. Schwab and O'Connor, 'Lonely eye'.
5. Benn, 'Structure', 197, 199–200.
6. See Frank, *Responses to Modernity*, 116–19; Hamburger, *Reason and Energy*; Travers, *Poetry*; Leeder, 'Nihilismus und Musik'. For two recent English editions of Benn's work, see Benn, *Impromptus* and *Selected Poems*.
7. Cited in Cunningham, *British Writers*, 5.
8. Jolas, *Man from Babel*, xxvi.
9. Haughton, 'Sorry', 18.
10. Jolas, 'Romanticism and metapolitics', 215. Kiefer and Rumold, in *Critical Writings*, suggest that this is an unpublished article from after 1949, and quote from a corrected typescript held in Box 5, Folder 125, Maria and Eugene Jolas Papers, Beinecke Rare Books and Manuscripts Library, Yale University (subsequent references to this archive will be indicated by the Box and Folder numbers followed by an indication

of the collection as the Jolas Papers). However, in an inventory of Jolas's publications likely compiled by Maria Jolas, the text is cited as '"Romanticism and metapolitics", *Cahiers du Sud*, Marseilles, 1940'. It would appear that the article was originally written in 1940, but never reached publication. See Box 1, Folder 1, Jolas Papers.
11. Quoted in Ashton's introduction to Benn, *Primal Vision*, viii, xii–xiii.
12. For introductory sources concerning the 'third eye' in late nineteenth- and early twentieth-century culture, see Blavatsky, *Secret Doctrine*; Mead, *Pistis Sophia*; Adler, *Findings*.
13. Barkan and Bush (eds), *Prehistories*, 12.
14. Jolas, *Man from Babel*, xxvi.
15. Letter from Jolas to Blanche Matthias, 6 January 1941. Box 3, Folder 54, Jolas Papers.
16. Hamburger and Middleton (eds), *Modern German Poetry*, xxxvi.
17. Benn, 'Structure', 195–6.
18. Ibid. 196–7.
19. Ibid. 197.
20. Ibid. 197, 199, 201. For an analysis of Benn's engagement with neurology, see Salisbury, 'Linguistic trepanation'.
21. Benn, 'Structure', 200.
22. Engstrom et al., 'Kraepelin'.
23. Benn, 'Structure', 201.
24. Benn, 'Diesterweg (1918)', in *Selected Poems* 350–7, 352, 350.
25. Benn, 'Structure', 201.
26. Ibid. 201–2.
27. Ibid. 203–4.
28. Ibid. 204, emphasis added.
29. Ibid. 204–5.
30. Benn, *Selected Poems*, 21. Originally published as 'Gesänge' (1913).
31. Rumold, 'Archeo-logies', 50.
32. Benn, 'The island', 67; Benn, 'The birthday', originally published in Benn, *Gehirne*; E. Jolas, 'Gottfried Benn', 146–8; Ray, *Beyond Nihilism*, 12; Jolas, 'Gottfried Benn', 149; Jolas and Paul, 'A review', 142.
33. Jolas et al., 'Inquiry among European writers', 266, 248, 251–2.
34. Benn, 'Primal vision', 304, 306. On *transition*'s practice of publishing older texts, see Setz, 'Transocean'.
35. For a discussion of such 'primal visions' in earlier Expressionist literature, see R. W. Williams, 'Prosaic intensities' and 'Primitivism'.
36. Benn, 'Primal vision', 308, emphasis added.
37. Benn, 'Extracts from *Lyric Self*' in *Selected Poems*, 370–1.
38. Jolas et al., 'Crisis of Man', 107–12.
39. Rumold, 'Archeo-logies', 52.
40. Benn, *Selected Poems*, 390, 394, 396–7, 400 (emphasis original), 408, 410, 412, 436.
41. Golffing, 'A note', 274.
42. Rumold, *Janus Face*, 96, emphasis original.
43. Hofmann's introduction to Benn, *Impromptus*, xvii.

44. Ritchie, *Gottfried Benn*, 20.
45. Cuomo, 'Purging'.
46. Hofmann's introduction to Benn, *Impromptus*, xvii.
47. M. Jolas, notebook of corrections to McMillan's draft typescript of his *transition*, n. d, likely 1973. Box 42, Folder 955, Jolas Papers.
48. Jolas, *Man from Babel*, 124–8.
49. Rumold, *Archaeologies*, 135, emphasis original.
50. Jolas, 'Primal personality', 82. For a full account of Jolas's conceptual and biographical relationship with Benn, see Rumold, *Gottfried Benn*.
51. Dacqué, *Natur und Seele*, quoted in Jolas, 'Primal personality', 81–2. See also Lévy-Bruhl, *La mentalité primitive*.
52. Jolas, 'Primal personality', 82. Jolas refers to Franz von Baader's 'Ueber den innern Sinn im Gegensatz zu den auessern Sinnen' (On the inner meaning as opposed to the external senses) in Baader, *Schriften*.
53. Jolas, *Man from Babel*, xxvi.
54. Jolas et al., 'Inquiry about the malady', 145–6.
55. Jolas, *Language of Night*, 40.
56. Ibid. 40.
57. Rumrich, 'Introduction', 130.
58. Jolas, *Language of Night*, 42–3.
59. Jolas et al., 'Poetry is vertical'. For further discussion of this text, see Monk, 'Modernism in *transition*'; North, 'Words in motion'; Boyle and McAlmon, *Being Geniuses Together*, 265–6.
60. Jolas, 'Twilight'.
61. Jolas, 'Lillitoo's voyage', 18; Jolas, *Secession in Astropolis*.
62. Jolas, 'Night is 3'.
63. Jolas, 'Intrialogue', my translation.
64. Jolas, 'Verbirrupta', 22.
65. *Transition*, 22 (February 1933), 135.
66. Rumold, 'Archeo-logies', 53.
67. Jolas, 'Transmutation vertigraliste', my translation.
68. Other editorials that demonstrate Jolas's post-Benn vision include: 'Confession about grammar', 'What is the revolution', 'Paramyths', 'Dreamers', 'Notes for a lexicon' and 'Vertigral'.
69. Jolas, 'Third eye', 154, 156, 158.
70. Krell, 'Paradoxes', 215.
71. For the first scientific study of the Lacertidæ lizard family, see Milne-Edwards, 'Recherches zoologiques'. This appeared at the same time as the first discovery of the parietal organ or pineal eye: Dugès, 'Espèces indigènes'. For a biological study focused directly on the pineal eye, see Tilney and Warren, *Morphology*.
72. Allbutt, *System of Medicine*, I, 761.
73. Beard, 'Parietal eye'; Cope, 'Pineal eye'; Graaf, *Bijdrage*. See Leydig, *Die in Deutschland* and Eakin, *Third Eye*, 32.
74. Hortega and Penfield, *Cytology*. Cited in Adams and Haymaker, *Histology and Histopathology*, 1801.

75. See Studnička, 'Die Parietalorgane'; Frisch, 'Beiträge zur Physiologie'; McCord and Allen, 'Evidences'; Lerner et al., 'Isolation of melatonin'. For a useful account of this history, see Kappers, 'Evolution'.
76. Cushing, 'Partial hypophysectomy'. See also Schiller, 'Pineal gland', 156.
77. For a full account of pineal histology, see Hansen and Karasek, 'Neuron'.
78. *Documents* 1: 1 (1929), iv; Jolas, 'Pablo Picasso'. See also Bataille, *Oeuvres Complètes*.
79. As Rumold writes: 'the constellation of Benn, Jolas, Einstein, and Bataille, tells us that Jolas was a *conservative* avant-gardist, to coin a contradiction in terms'. Rumold, 'Archeo-logies', 60.
80. Bataille, *Visions of Excess*, 32–44.
81. Bataille, *Visions of Excess*, 5–9.
82. Bataille, *Visions of Excess*, 73–8.
83. Bataille, *Visions of Excess*, 79–90, 81, 82, emphasis original.
84. Jay, *Downcast Eyes*, 216, 227, 226.
85. See Surya, *Georges Bataille*.
86. Bataille, *Visions of Excess*, 83, 77.
87. Jay, *Downcast Eyes*, 227; Bataille, 'Psychological structure', reprinted in *Visions of Excess*, 137–60.
88. Frank's introduction to Caillois, *Edge of Surrealism*, 9; Gilbert-Lecomte, 'Big game'.
89. Frank's introduction to Caillois, *Edge of Surrealism*, 9.
90. Gilbert-Lecomte to René Daumal and Roger Vailland, 13 March 1926, in Gilbert-Lecomte et al., *Correspondance*, 108–10. 'Bubu' was the God figure of their invented cult. I am grateful to Dennis Duncan for this translation.
91. Gilbert-Lecomte, 'Power of renunciation', 46, emphasis original. Originally published as Gilbert-Lecomte, 'La force'.
92. Gilbert-Lecomte, 'Horrible revelation', 129, emphasis original. Originally published as Gilbert-Lecomte, 'L'horrible revelation'.
93. Caillois, *Edge of Surrealism*, 48–9.
94. Rumold, *Archaeologies*, 135.
95. Mundan, 'Vertigral poetry'.
96. Ibid. 61.
97. Jolas, 'Paramyths from a dreambook', 19–20.
98. Burnett, 'Balkan journey', 39.
99. Ibid. 39; Bennett, transcriber, 'Visit'.
100. Roditi, 'Mirages', 95–6.
101. Huebner, 'Possession', 57–8.
102. Ibid. 58.
103. Jolas, 'Ergriffenheit', 17.
104. Jolas, 'Homage to the mythmaker', 171–2.
105. Beckett's potential reading of Benn is hinted at in Rodriguez, 'Everywhere', 105. Extract from the *Watt* notebook quoted in Ackerley, 'Fatigue and disgust', 179.
106. See Thomas, 'Poem' and 'The mouse'.
107. 'Eight' dated 8 September 1933 in Thomas, *Poet in the Making*, 233.
108. See, for example, 'Fifteen' dated 18 September 1933 in Thomas, *Poet in the Making*, 240–1, later published as 'In the beginning' in *Collected Poems*, 22–3.

109. Williams, 'How to write'.
110. Mansanti, 'William Carlos Williams' *A Novelette*', 35. It is worth noting that, like Benn, Williams also worked with prostitutes and soldiers during the First World War.
111. Williams, 'How to write', 45–6, 48.
112. Williams, letter to Louis Zukofsky, 14 November 1932, in Ahearn (ed.), *Correspondence*, 143.
113. Miller, 'Cosmological eye'.
114. Anderson, 'Henry Miller', para. 3.
115. Miller, 'Cosmological eye', 322–3, original emphasis.
116. Ibid. 322–3.
117. Orwell, *Inside the Whale*, 50.
118. Miller, 'Cosmological eye', 322.
119. Perlès, *My Friend*, 140.
120. Miller, 'Cosmological eye', 327, 329.
121. Blinder, *Self-Made Surrealist*, 156.
122. Wickes, 'Henry Miller'.
123. As pointed out in Hofmann, 'Notorious ever after', 39.
124. Miller, letter to Michael Fraenkel, 26 November 1935, in Miller and Fraenkel, *Fraenkel–Miller Correspondence*, 79.
125. Miller, postscript to a letter to Jolas, 14 July 1950. Box 3, Folder 56, Jolas Papers.
126. Miller and Fraenkel, *Fraenkel–Miller Correspondence*, 16.
127. Jolas, *Man from Babel*, 149.
128. Benn, 'Monologue' in *Primal Vision*, 220–5, 223, 225.
129. Benn, 'Poems' in *Primal Vision*, 218–19; Rumold, *Janus Face*, 166; McMillan, *transition*, 95–6.
130. McMillan, *transition*, 95, 71; Jolas, *Vertical*, 1.
131. Rumold, *Archaeologies*, 136; Jolas, *Vertical*, 99.
132. Jolas, *Man from Babel*, 149.

4

BIRD: EDITORIAL FLIGHTS WITH EUGENE JOLAS

There's a genial young poetriarch Euge
Who hollers with heartiness huge:
Let sick souls sob for solace
So the *jeunes* joy with Jolas!
Book your berths! *Après mot le déluge*!

James Joyce, 1933[1]

The curious racket-tailed Motmots have what I call the most velvety of all bird notes. [. . .] The Maya Indians of Yucatan call the brilliant little Eumomota 'Toh', and as an appreciation of their interest, he has come to nest and roost familiarly in the age-long deserted ruins of their former glory.

Louis Agassiz Fuertes, 'Impressions of the voices of tropical birds' 1914

Throughout history, across cultures, and in a diversity of forms, the bird has been invoked as a totem of the soul. In the Western tradition it is a winged soul, a soul on the move – a messenger of the gods, or of the grave. In some cultures the bird is a shamanic spirit helper implicated in two types of creation myth, the 'earth diver' and the 'cosmic egg'. Birds are central to the figure of the trickster, commonly issuing warnings or knowledge from the animal to the human kingdom. The thunderbird is a Native American emblem of the eagle, which in turn is the symbol of the United States. In the Christian tradition birds have come to emblematise aspects of the Holy Trinity: the goldfinch's association with thorns and hence with Jesus's crown; St John's eagle; the dove of the Holy Spirit.[2] The human-headed bird or *ba* was the emblem of the soul in ancient Egyptian mythology, evoked in the acephalous bodies of Georges Bataille's writing or in the many bird-headed hybrid figures in Max Ernst's collages. In medieval literature, the blackbird in particular often symbolises a form of religious despair; in more modern contexts, it symbolises Europe.[3] The bird is lofty (of the soul), emblematic (of a populace), a messenger (of peace), or a harbinger (of death). It is hard to pin down. In *transition*, birds are one of the most dominant animal symbols. This was largely driven by Jolas, 'the impresario of the avant-garde', as Marjorie Perloff has named him.[4] Birds enable us to reflect on Jean-Michel Rabaté's comment: 'thanks to Jolas, one will learn a lot about modernism, and also unlearn a lot, which is useful'.[5]

Because of the immensity of its species genera and tropological uses, the symbolic bird is not the first creature one thinks of with regard to the literary experimentation and innovations in language that critics have come to call modernism. The songbirds of love are often no more than mindless, edifying symbols – too much of a Keatsian 'drowsy numbness' to be meaningful in the early twentieth century. Yet when one turns to *transition*, it is striking that the editor frequently selected texts which featured a songbird, a bird messenger, or an avian figure for the spirit. This metaphysical quality became essential to Jolas in his quest for 'verticality' in poetry, but this was not the case for all his contributing authors. The editor strove for 'cherubic ascension', but at times he was alone – his voice that of an isolated optimist. Yet this lone editorial voice is, I wish to suggest, definitive of the magazine, and demands examination.

Over its eleven years, the arrangement, translation, and explication of *transition*'s project came primarily through Jolas's stewardship. The magazine's preference for poetic birds, especially in its first year, is thus a question of editorial ethos and vision. Jolas's contributions as editor and poet demonstrate how closely he aligned the Revolution of the Word to a desired ideal: a collective mythos which humanity should be forging anew. This ideal was first and foremost a desired change in language: an answer to the 'smugness' that dominated the ossified uses of utilitarian language in contemporary American journalism.[6] Jolas continually sought spiritual humility transported into literature. Critics might turn away from him here: his faith in continuity, and in the possibility of spiritual revolution emerging from new linguistic production, does not readily fit into a canon of literary modernism that includes *BLAST* or *Documents*.

As explored in the previous chapter, recent scholarship on Jolas has questioned his idealism, which he retained even after the war, and has tended to focus on his predilection for Germanic romanticism. Jolas was moved by the early strain of this history of thought and writing, which is distinguished as

Frühromantik or 'first' romanticism and exemplified by the Jena romantics of the turn of the nineteenth century. For Philippe Lacoue-Labarthe and Jean-Luc Nancy, definitions of romanticism are problematic. One of their formulations, which underlines the essentially illusory nature of the category, is useful. 'As it is usually understood', they write, 'or not understood',

> this name [romanticism] is quite inaccurate, both in what it evokes as an aesthetic category (which often amounts to an *evocation of evocation*, so to speak, to an evocation of flowing sentimentality or foggy nostalgia for the faraway), and in what it pretends to offer as a historical category (in a double opposition to classicism and to realism or naturalism).[7]

This notion of the 'evocation of evocation', capacious an idea as it is, is helpful when we approach Jolas's circle of poets and authors. Totemic birds that promise 'the faraway' often come at the price of vagueness. Michael Ferber's definition is also enlightening. He regards romanticism as, among other things, a cultural movement that 'sought solace in or reconciliation with the natural world'; he suggests that it '"detranscendentalized" religion by taking God or the divine as inherent in nature or in the soul', and that it replaced doctrine with 'metaphor and feeling', honouring 'poetry [. . .] as the highest [of] human creations', and rebelling against received social norms in favour of the 'more individual, inward, and emotional'.[8] One finds these qualities in Jolas's many bird texts, the most characteristic of which appeared in *transition*'s final issue in 'Frontier-poem', written in Strasbourg in 1935, excerpted here:

> a bird flutters over the wellen and zwitschert in the rhythms
> der verborgenen silben
> between tag und nacht ist die einsamkeit wie eine liebe freundin
> and I believe in the silence of angels [. . .]
>
> for the language of man is tired and sick
> for the grammar of man is soaked in disease
> in the nightmare of his nothingness [. . .]
>
> we shall build the mantic bridge
> we shall sing in all the languages of the continents
> we shall discover les langues de l'atlantide
> we shall find *the first and last word*[9]

As a symbol of so many ideals outside or above the human – divinity, transcendence, the absolute or fate – the signifying bird was an utterly essential element of what Stuart Gilbert called the 'subliminal uprush' that *transition* came to proclaim, and of what Jolas called the 'intuitive reaching towards the *above*'. Gilbert describes the poet's inspiration: 'the poet's "escape" is no craven flight from reality, but a bold evasion from the "shades of the prison-house," a quest of perilous adventure on uncharted shores'.[10] Jolas's undying commitment to a 'new romanticism' (both during the interwar period and after 1945) was an unusual position, as Christopher Reid has emphasised; but if we view it alongside Ferber's focus on the secular divine and the individual, it goes some way to explaining why his 'new romantics' were in fact avant-gardist trailblazers of modernism, and were not necessarily wedded to his views.[11] However one takes Jolas's plaintive cry here for the 'first and last word' – as misguided reverie, intoxicated irrationalism, or serious modernist commitment – his birds enable an understanding of his creative and critical endeavours.

It is in this sense that Jolas's mode of cultural production is 'atypical', in Rabaté's words; and this is why the bird is the odd one out, necessitating a focus not on art history, as in the first chapter, nor on biological discourse, as in the second and third, but on the iterations of symbolic birds that move through the journal. Jolas was unique in the period for positing the force of art as an 'offshoot' of German romanticism.[12] If he was too idealistic, that says more about the critical desire to align modernism with a cohesive sensibility broadly defined as post-humanist than it does about his practice. The 'paramyths', 'hypnologues', 'polyvocables', 'vertigralist' and 'mantic' creations of his many editorials may now appear ephemeral – as opposed to Yeats's gyres or Eliot's objective correlatives, for instance – but it is beyond doubt that Jolas played a vital role in American modernist literature. As they appear in *transition*, birds invite a consideration of Jolas's translations, his avian aesthetic, and *transition*'s reception, which often tapped into that aesthetic, for better or worse. Hence this chapter will consider three interrelated topics. First, I introduce several early poems published in 1927 – a series of bird texts from avant-garde artists – that Jolas translated and arranged, synthesising and absorbing certain images in the process. Second, I explore how Jolas's birds could be said to lead the project named in later issues as his 'verticalist' or 'vertigral' programme. Between *transition*'s comeback issue of March 1932 and the publication of his 1941 anthology *Vertical: A Year-Book for Romantic-Mystic Ascensions*, Jolas extended his metaphoric language of elevation and flight. Avian imagery becomes integral, I suggest, to the nationalised transactions between America and Europe that *transition* sought to enable.[13] Third, I consider *transition*'s diverse reception in both anglophone and francophone contexts. A sharp division between repudiation and high praise exists in this material, along the very European–American line that Jolas sought to bridge. In this reading, however, metaphors of flight and avian transportation, in derision and encomium alike, can mobilise critical understandings of both the modernism at stake and the winged creature as a textual and paratextual entity.

Although numerous critics were enraptured by the journal's artistic message, not all of its readers embraced its mission. On the contrary, Jolas's irrepressible optimism must have seemed jarring by the mid- to late 1930s. Readers who were prepared to listen closely to the editor, however, often picked up on his avian tropes. Jolas's totemic birds, I suggest, were constitutive of his belief in the possibility of forward motion in literature, and were emblems of an imagined variant of religious hope. In his own words:

> The new style began in the twenties:
> word extasis
> Icarian principle.[14]

If, as Rabaté has written, this 'extasis' in Jolas's sense was the end of the 'happy avant-garde' in Europe, how can we read the birds etched into so many of *transition*'s texts?[15] What do we learn – and *unlearn* – about modernism?

BLACKBIRDS AND WORD BIRDS

In the following unpublished text, undated but probably written in the late 1920s, we find the poet Jolas searching for a suitable image:

> Wir ersticken in dieser atomischen Zeit. Nirgends finden wir
> Licht. ich habe eine vertikalistische Sehnsucht: das Meer, das
> fliessen und das fliegen aufwaerts. die sternensehnsucht. unbewusste
> urgrund
> wie kann das alles dargestellt werden?
> durch worte?
> ~~die sprach ist wie das wasser~~
>
>   ich leide die sprache –
> mein hass gegen die standardisierung der [xxx] worte – denn die sprache
> ist im fliessen – im flux permanent – in transition
> wir mussen die worte martern –
>
> We suffocate in this atomic time. Nowhere do we find
> Light. I have a verticalist longing: the sea, the
> flow and fly upward. The star-yearning. unconscious
> original ground
> how can all this be shown?
> through words?
> ~~language is like water~~
> I suffer from language –
> My hate towards the standardization of the Word – because language
> is in flux – permanent flow – in transition
> we have to torture the Word – [16]

Jolas hopes for modern art to 'flow and fly', like a bird: to make language fly, to swoop and soar, but also (as this sketch intimates) to press upon or 'torture' it – to strain away from the centre of a received Logos. We can see the scrubbed-out line likening language to water, another flowing element, but it is not enough. Jolas replaces it with the subsequent line denoting an immoveable state of pain: 'I suffer from language', he writes, as if it were a virus.

If we turn to his early translations in the journal, it becomes clear that Jolas synthesised a number of bird texts which directly informed his subsequent thinking. Between April 1927 and April 1928, Jolas translated a series of Expressionist and Surrealist poets' works which drew on a tradition of bird symbolism. In the first issue, Robert Desnos's poem 'The dove of the ark' makes a surprising juxtaposition between the allusive title and a compact curse against familial generation. I quote the poem in full:

> Cursed
> Be the father of the wife
> of the blacksmith who forged the iron of the hatchet
> with which the wood-cutter hewed down the oak
> in which someone carved the bed
> where the great-grandfather was engendered
> of the man who drove the wagon
> in which your mother met your father![17]

The poem attacks a patrilineal series of craftsmen in a layered depiction of tools and meeting places (the hatchet, the hewing, the carving, the bed, the wagon), a lineage of fathers culminating in the addressee (who is defined as neither male nor female), and their implicit conception. It is a tight, forcible curse on 'the father' at the start, which, taken simply as 'Cursed / Be the father', is an iconoclastic blasphemy that reverses the opening of the First Epistle of Peter (1 Peter 1: 3): 'Blessed be the God and Father of our Lord Jesus Christ, who according to his great mercy hath regenerated us unto a lively hope, by the resurrection of Jesus Christ from the dead.' The eponymous dove, implicitly from Noah's ark and the symbolic bringer of peace, is so at odds with the content that the effect is both secular and sacrilegious, vitriolic and comical.

Else Lasker-Schüler's contribution, translated by Jolas as 'A song', evinces a more emphatic, more yearning stance. The poetic voice 'long[s] to fly away / With the migratory birds' – a repeated couplet that acts as a refrain. In a short verse we find the poetic voice turning the colours and objects of love into pathos:

> The blackbirds like mourning roses
> Fell from the high blue bushes.[18]

All 'their muted twittering', the poet hopefully declaims, 'wants to exult again'.[19] Drawing on the traditional association between bird flight and freedom, Lasker-Schüler and Desnos move between diverse sentiments. Both create textual birds that bring together the dissonant registers of the reverential or hopeful and the despairing or bleak. The two poets' proximity on this issue suggests that Jolas was drawn to such modulated romanticism: poetic birds that both give and take from expected forms and contents. A similar quality appears in the second issue with Paul Éluard's poem 'Georges Braque'. With the artist's bird motifs clearly in mind, Éluard takes a romantic set of associations around the bird and lays them bare, yielding a plaintive quality:

> A bird flies away,
> It throws off the clouds like a useless veil [. . .]
>
> All the leaves in the woods say yes,
> They only know how to say yes,
> Each question, each answer,
> And the dew flows in the depths of this yes.[20]

That 'yes' denotes a resignation in the verse, as if the accoutrements of the muse-like, angelic, feminine, predictable reverie were sighed out – the obligatory stock material of a love poem transposed into a vision of the poet beholding the modern artist's work. Éluard's closing similes for a man 'with soft eyes' who 'describes the sky of love' work to redouble the repeated 'yes' left in the path of the departed bird. He

> gathers its wonders
> Like leaves in a wood,
> Like birds in their wings,
> And men in their slumber.[21]

'Slumber' carries two senses here: the blissful, healing act of sleep, and the unthinking adjective 'slumbering', which the *Oxford English Dictionary* defines as 'dormant, inoperative, quiescent; torpid'. Again, the reader encounters an ambivalence. Do the slumbering men invoke mindless acquiescence to a harmonious vision of nature? Does the bird offer comfort, or does its exit disrupt the gaze of the Petrarchan lover, or indeed of the speaker beholding the canvas? The uncertainty is rich in possibility, both here and with Desnos and Lasker-Schüler. The birds reveal a thwarted, weary, husked-out idealism.

Where Surrealist poems featuring birds push against the harmonising impulse of a romantic vision of flight or song, Expressionist instances preserve the sentiment in a different, though equally anguished form. The late nineteenth-century naturalist German poet Arno Holz, included in the May 1927 issue, is a good example, with an extract Jolas translates from 'Phantasus'. Here a bird on a ledge sings of something that the speaker sees as childhood and other forgotten things:

> Forget! Forget!
> From a far-off valley, hark, there pipes a bird . . .
> It sings its song.
> [. . .] Red roses
> wind themselves about my gloomy lance.
> [. . .] my stallion sniffs.[22]

In Georg Trakl's poem 'To the lad, Elis', published the following month, such wistfulness is more ominous, especially in the first three stanzas:

> Elis, when the black-bird calls in the dark forest,
> This is your end.
> Your lips drink the coolness of the blue spring in the rock.
>
> When softly your brow is bleeding
> Leave age-old legends,
> And dark augury of bird-flight.
>
> But you go with gentle tread into the night,
> Which hangs full of purple grapes,
> And you move your arms more beautifully in the blue.[23]

Trakl invokes the paradoxes and parallels of bird flight and omens, blackness and futurity. The 'dark augury of bird-flight' comes directly from Jolas, rather than from the poet. The original German reads 'Und dunkle Deutung des Vogelflugs', which is translated by Alexander Stillmark as 'dark deciphering of birdflight' and by Margitt Lehbert as 'dark readings of the flight of birds'.[24] Jolas takes *Deutung* and merges the connotations of reading and deciphering into the logical next step – the ancient art of augury. That which Elis is both drawn into and compelled to overcome is left uncertain: the performative noun *Deutung* as Jolas has it is altogether more portentous and ominous. Stillmark points out that, as a more inflected language, German allows transpositions in word order that do not necessarily work well in English. Trakl uses a wide range of bird symbolism to denote various forms of ambivalence, blackness and movement.[25] By taking a word that that denotes the reading of bird flight and translating it into an act of divination – of writing, effectively – Jolas fundamentally connects the translated bird to textual practice. This bird-as-inscription image is Jolas's addition, and it drives his aesthetic sensibility.[26]

The influence of the German romantic poet and philosopher Novalis (Georg Philipp Friedrich von Hardenberg) is also of central significance. The lad Elis drinks the cool water; his arms move beautifully in blue. This is a strong invocation of Novalis's blue flower, a touchstone of the tradition by which Jolas was so affected. Looking back at his youth in an essay entitled 'White romanticism', Jolas mentions this image directly, describing himself as drunk on the vision of the all-rescuing, all-seeing, all-saving symbol of the blue flower found by Novalis's blond boy hero. Remembering his European roots, his boyhood days as a 'youthful visionar[y] [. . .] talk[ing] pretentiously of our "romantic souls"', Jolas mocks his old obsession with the blue flower. 'The words *Nacht* and *Sehnsucht* became almost sacred', he writes, remembering the blue flower as an occult symbol. More mindful of this sentiment as an impossible nostalgia, the older Jolas seems to recognise that the grand annunciation of a 'new' form of romanticism was 'an absurdity', despite his willingness to stake claims on contemporary and powerful writing in its name.[27]

Taken paratextually, Trakl's poem is not without humour. Reading 'To the lad, Elis' alongside its neighbours in the June 1927 issue reveals a playful editorial juxtaposition. Jolas places the poem immediately before an untitled work by the French poet Georges Ribemont-Dessaignes, so that the two appear on facing pages as single-page texts – a pair. Ribemont-Dessaignes's poem employs another usage of the bird, incorporating a bleak humour into its own vision of omens and darkness. Trakl's solemn art of augury is almost entirely offset by Ribemont-Dessaignes's nonsense verse. Here is the translation in full:

> And the pregnant woman through the skin of her womb
> Showed the child the crescent of a still-born moon
> Put on his head the hat imported from Germany
> The woman had a miscarriage by Mozart
> While in an armoured car there passed
> A harpist
> And amid the sky of doves
> Tender Mexican doves ate Spanish flies.[28]

The Surrealist jumble of entities and organisms overturns the familiar tradition of the signifying bird. The white doves filling the sky frame a neat succession of associations ordinarily wedded to the bird: woman, becoming, the femininity of the moon, even its Symbolist status as an omen. Yet these associations are confronted with a jarring national dimension. Why are they 'tender Mexican' doves? What of the idea of 'Spanish flies'? If much is lost in translation, the absurdity remains. As with Desnos's verse, a foundational romantic bird of peace or the muse appears, but it is a muse that has been tampered with through iconoclasm, ambivalence and humour.[29]

The June and July 1927 issues also contain Jolas's first authored poems in the magazine. They reveal the unmistakable influence of these early translations, but also a misrecognition of that tampered-with romanticism. In 'Nocturnes', Jolas mixes in the tone of his translated Surrealist and Expressionist verses. The poem opens with the image of a cold, barren landscape and 'carrion shrill with laughter'. Following a line where 'lonely birds wait for / the end of day', Jolas has several stanzas that echo his translated European poets:

> and minds are darkened by an eclipse of luminousness
> and voices sicken into heat of summer afternoons
>
> and words loose crows owls parrots down corridors of faintness down phantom racks down cruel laughter of pity
>
> [. . .]
> sometimes a bird sings blood red songs heavy with rain heavy with scent of forgotten hair heavy with ghosts of smiles[30]

Jolas traces the sounds of Desnos, Trakl and Laske-Schüler especially, with his emphasis on light, on waiting for the roost, and the 'cruel laughter of pity' evoking the curse in 'Dove of the ark'. He also combines the bird omen with an act of human expression, both verbal and textual. The line 'words loose crows owls parrots down corridors' is an incantatory image, bringing along its own opposite with its focus on birds that talk. It is as if the speaker is casting a spell that can unleash a cacophonous mass of birds, flapping and squawking in a condensed space. Between the presence of the other writers and the strange effect of birds and words here, Jolas is demonstrably synthesising an aesthetic. With that 'cruel laughter' in the verse, and Jolas's pairings of 'bird sings' and 'blood red songs', the poem's ambivalence complicates its romanticism. Through these unsettling birds, the editor produces an encomium to his translated authors.

Such loose quotation is also evident in Jolas's creative prose, such as his piece 'Landscapes', published in July 1927. Two months previously, Jolas had translated an extract from Éluard's latest novel under the title 'In company' (discussed in my introduction). A visceral comment on a breakdown in communication, articulated through a consciousness that is clearly suffering shell shock after the First World War, the text uses animal imagery to evoke incomprehension. Here is Jolas's translation again:

> All this lives: this patient insect body, this loving bird body, this loyal mammiferous body, and this lean and vain body of the beast of my childhood,

all this lives. Only its head has died. I had to kill it. My face understands me no longer. And there are no others.[31]

Two issues on, this is Jolas:

> I have not forgotten that they lived. They flew silver in the brain that was rotting in a dusk, in a planet swimming through fairy-tale forests.
>
> Now they pass trailling [sic] blood and laughter and time weeping in a Sunday garden, where the child echoes a blackbird in the afternoon bushes. Faces cry against my shadows and wintering eyes sink into my towers.[32]

Jolas's admiration for Éluard is clear in the phrasing of an entity that lives ('this lives', 'they lived') but does so post-traumatically. Where Éluard divorces his head and face from his 'loving bird body', Jolas hears a blackbird amid repeated images of bloodshed, suffering and murder. The narrator hears 'the rutilant magic of bird-song', but 'a little bird vomits death'.[33] Yet where Éluard's image signifies a dire implosion of consciousness, Jolas's is pastiche, a kind of magpie writing. He solidifies his style along the way. During this formative period, Jolas readably copies styles in order to reach towards the 'fairy-tale forests' of symbols – to escape into his 'Logos Unbound'.[34]

Subsequent issues contain more birds, and with them more Jolasian pastiche. 'Monologue', also in the September 1927 issue, ponders 'magical space and sinister time' – the object of an unknown love:

> I sleepwalk through the city and plunge into a golden smoke. What is my love for you, magical space and sinister time, when the dusk settles into marble and the owl is a categorical imperative? I left dream-staring puppets in a room, where the Ethiopian trembles at a blasphemy, and the sketch-book holds the contours of an atlas. The mother had a child in the dust and the lonely woman cried in a café. Then came a girl from out the autumnal solitude of her rooms, where she had stared at mirrors, and her silence was the dream of a midnight. Cool waters flowed under bridges and electric wires brought decay of flowers, tempests, portraits of nightmares, broken violins. Comrades walked tired into hurricanes. When the philosophies panted, and the symphonies ended in a shriek, stallions ground fire, and the bandits swilled brandy in an hallucinated den. The organ at the fair whimpered love-songs, but the funeral of the poor went past us with memories of a loam. The trees became brass shining in the sun. My waiting gulped busses, tears, dust, drinks, sparrows.[35]

With its associations of wisdom, omens, Athena and the nocturnal, the owl turns into a 'categorical imperative', a Kantian invocation to moral action.

Jolas hangs the 'panted' philosophies, 'ended' symphonies, and 'ground' stallions upon the earthy word 'swilled'. The two birds are connected to a sense of marking out, of bringing out epochal change, and the desired ascent of cultural renewal carried over from the earlier translations. An awaited flock of sparrows indicate an awareness that the blue flower is but a boyish dream. They also express the grounding tawdriness of an impasse – of the impossibility of such spiritual transformation. Where the 'swilling' of this piece undercuts any profession of illumination, conversely almost all the poets Jolas selected and translated for this issue offered representations of light or of spiritual travail towards something better, especially in works by Pierre Minet, Henri Solveen and Hans Arp.[36] It is a process the editor came to consciously embrace, as part of an ascensionist ideal of the Word.

By the end of *transition*'s first year, this ascensionism extended to Jolas's editorials. 'On the quest', published towards the end of the December 1927 issue, reveals an attempt to address *transition*'s detractors (significantly, this was the first 'special' issue, and was named 'the American number').

> We are struggling for a new faith which may help us create the mythos for which every true artist is waiting today. We hope for an aesthetic synthetism in which not only Europe and Asia will coalesce into a new flowering, but to which the two Americas will bring their vision.[37]

Over the journal's first nine months, then, Jolas moves from his initial translations of poetic birds to an explicit theorisation of 'aesthetic synthetism' – a term he used to describe his wish for a new spirit in the Word, but that is also indicative of the ways in which his poetry drew from his translations. 'Aesthetic synthetism' is an apposite name for his editorial practice: his desire to convey what he would later call the 'polysynthetic quality' of language.[38] For Jolas, America was at once the colossus, the vacuity and the space of new creation. Next to the bird, it was the most emphatic of his emblems – sometimes expressed as 'atlantide' – for a reconfigured Word. Jolas's idealism may have been of the Western, humanist, unfeasibly optimistic variety, but as the above examples show, there is an openness in his writing which is too easily lost when not read alongside its creative neighbours. Birds as omens are deliberately ambivalent, drawing on a romantic impulse towards transcendence, yet also indicative of a fraught poetics that disallows any easy aesthetic harmony. Jolas's emphasis on America was always integral to his embrace of as many languages and nationalities as possible in his vision of the collective mythos.

'Glintbirds' and 'Gleambirds'

Neo-romantic though he was, Jolas was highly consistent. In 'Almanach', from *transition*'s summer 1928 issue (the first issue released as a quarterly), Jolas repeatedly included the entwinement of birds and visions in his prose. As he entered the magazine's second year, the editor actively escalated those inaugural intertexts, as if leaving the European blackbird behind in search of something more exotic. With less sophistication and subtlety than Éluard or Trakl, perhaps, Jolas pressed on in this direction nonetheless:

> *But the axes hiss among the vespers of the lightning crashing into doves that whirl white among trees. [. . .]*
>
> *Only my evening-bells still mingle with the sing-song of the visionary birds floating in the sky. [. . .]*
>
> *With tom-tom rhythms down the singing rivers of a beatitude, down the hollow words, down the throats of birds*
>   *That hold the balm for the lonely trapper in the malady for the infinite.*[39]

As before, Jolas couples his birds to the act of speech, here with the violence of words thrust into beaks – a reversal of the singing nightingale, to put it mildly. In 'Daily graphic', also published in summer 1928, word and bird are conjoined in an image of flight metaphorically linked to reading and the printed page: 'night falls into day, and the desert stares at me from the height of the towering buildings. The swallow brushes against the white architecture that is the last verb in a book of fairy tales'.[40] The swallow emblematises an end point, not of the act of speech but as part of a system of stories. Where Jolas's source poets twisted the totemic birds of love or peace, Jolas is more transparent, repeating his vision over and over again. The avian becomes a movement within language, sealing off an impossible romanticism, yet also offering a sense of passage, much like the idea of the cultural bridge between nations and tongues so foundational to *transition*.

This technique returns in Jolas's 'Construction of the enigma', published the following winter (and included in his 1929 collection of poems *Secession in Astropolis*). Where before there was the visual swoop of the swallow against the white of buildings, Jolas here plays on metal, machinery and the architecture of industry:

> I met you, when the night was steel. The metallic birds fluttered over the steam of the roofs, and the city was a litany of endless marvels. Immense was the darkness in me, when you came, and the bitter root was in my mouth. But you changed the day into night, and the night into day, and the shadows whirled about us astrally. The gates of the fable crashed open, o you, my glistening companion, imagination, my last hope in judgement days.[41]

With this metallic imagery Jolas strongly alludes to 'Un soir', a 1911 poem by Guillaume Apollinaire, the second stanza of which reads:

> La ville est métallique et c'est la seule étoile
> Noyée dans tes yeux bleus
> Quand les tramways roulaient jaillissaient des feux pales
> Sur des oiseaux galeux
>
> (The city is metallic and it's the only star
> Drowned in your blue eyes
> When trolley cars rumbled pale sparks flew upward
> Over mangy birds)[42]

'Mangy' birds denotes a firm tradition in modernist bird imagery that moves between urban scenes and the artificiality of human-made metals. One also thinks of the entirely smooth burnished gold and bronze bird sculptures by Constantin Brâncuşi, which were also highly influential during the period. 'Construction of the enigma' also strongly anticipates a poem published in Jolas's 1941 pamphlet *Words from the Deluge*. 'Migration' echoes and intensifies the same image, again with a trace of Apollinaire:

> Metallic parrots chattered odes to a dark age
> Travailing stickfuls danced on the city editor's desk
> The mergenthalers roared a dirge from the composing room
> And the strike of the alien laborers was a battle
> Nous étions tous ensemble dans le creuset des races
> We were in the wild melting pot of the fekterjas[43]

The combination of the feathered and the galvanised – textures of organic and artificial forms – creates an unsettling scene. Like the birds 'loosed' as words down a corridor in the earlier poem, here the avian offers a counterpoint to the city scene. The literal image of welding is joined by both a heavenward stare and a hesitant reflection upon how or why this faith appears.

Jolas is committed in these creative works to a more nuanced presentation of the 'crisis' of modern language than his editorial texts suggest, announced as they were in something more like a shout than the tremulous voice of spiritual uncertainty found here. The poems indicate an artist-editor drawn to ways of expressing not simply the pronouncements of a manifesto, but the enjambment of gritty modernity and airy creatures of flight. Metropolitan life, newspaper offices, the factory and other industrialised modes of being are often contrasted with the swoop or flutter or brush of a bird. The 'first and last word' of 'Frontier-poem' arrives, through the symbolic bird, not as the declaration or proclamation of a 'revolution', but as a profound articulation of the need to regain lost faith in a secular world.

Indeed, Jolas's figurative birds frequently testify to a crisis of faith. In a line in an unpublished poem, for example, Jolas moves between literal description (as before) and literal forgetting: 'in the brambleword the stems sheen the birds fluttertwitter in an oubli du temps what I am waiting for'. The switch to the French verb *oublier* ('to forget') instates Jolas's 'Babelist' ideal of polyglot literature (with an obvious reverence for Joyce). But it is equally significant that Jolas often utilises a language change when the poem itself forgets: a textual gap filled by the movement from one tongue to another. This is a literal search, a need for action, the 'what am I waiting for'. Similarly, in the line 'gleambirds flutter into a rubia torre the mariposas are drunk with pollen and solar incantations', the birds shine and drift into the verse. Another line, 'the glintbirds qui tremblemt dans les branches en s'unissant a mes psaumes dans une transe de petite creatures en ivresse', develops this theme, echoing again that sense of light on metal, of birds 'united with my psalms' in a 'trance of little drunken creatures' – linked, categorically now, to the Word in its biblical sense.[44]

Jolas's play upon polylingual and nonsense words alongside avian imagery is a constant feature of his work. In a corrected typescript for 'Strophades', an extract from his *Epivocables of 3* pamphlet (1932), 'a blish of wings is hooshing through the air. They flittersheen on plumes of down'. In another piece, 'Three cities', the poetic voice searches for spiritual fulfilment: 'and the boulevards will sing a luminous bird'.[45] 'Choirprair', also from *Epivocables of 3*, offers a signal example of Jolas's 'word birds' and his search for faith. Here too one finds a distinctly primordial scene, referencing the protozoic ooze:

> Nightling we singlaud mountainous idyla, martens, skyrooted trees.
> Thingsyntax in stone, flower, bird, tree, clouds, stars, grows with us high.
> Grows first law, originslime, primamater.
> Time conceives wonderweed and bears hearts in firecircles.
> Comets floosh overhead from hour into no-hour.
> We stand listening to village-rounds, paradise-animals, gleam and glast of nighthymns[46]

This giddy, almost tribal incantation at first appears devoid of any critical stance. The reverie is an end unto itself. If we return to 'Migration 1' in light of Jolas's many birds, however, a marked self-awareness comes to light:

> My alien comrades of the darkling milltown
> Hungering still for the thunderbird of wonders
> Still in the embrace of the drunken *delirium* of ascent
> We fly planet-glistering into the forests of crystal.[47]

Jolas is here invested in a symbolic bird that draws attention to a desire for transcendence, even as the impossibility of realisation is built into that desire, here in an image of labour. The workers are detached and yearning 'still'. This anchors the 'thunderbird' as an emblem of nostalgia, of that which cannot be recaptured. The single word 'delirium' summons the workers' desire for intoxication, an escape from drudgery, but in a way that acknowledges the 'ascent' as a mental disorder. Viewed politically, however, the idea of flight, or 'wonders' in the 'dark', takes on an irksome quality. Manual labour rarely sits well with the stargazer's 'forests of crystal'. By the early 1940s, then, Jolas is arguably more aware that his 'delirium' is a far-off dream.

This subtlety – Jolas's self-awareness – did not always come through to contemporary critics. Reviewing Jolas's *Vertical* anthology in the *New York Times* in 1942, Peter Monro Jack homes in on the editor's avian rhetoric directly. Although valuing Jolas's generosity and importance as an editor, Jack cannot take the collection seriously. He sees confusion on Jolas's part between the sensation of flying (the ontological bird side) and the desire for transcendence (the ethical side), or rather between 'the real sense of flying higher to the sky' and 'the ideal sense of getting nearer to heaven'.[48] Jack makes a valid point: Jolas produces – deliberately, and as part of his self-avowed 'aesthetic synthetism' – a combination of these two elements. Rather than a dualistic confusion of body and spirit, however, it might be more accurate to describe this as a conflation of the bird and the Word. A more generous reading would bring out Jolas's nuanced vision of a transcendence that is desired but whose impossibility is bleakly acknowledged.

This subtlety is evident in Jolas's 1929 'Document' (also published in *Astropolis*):

> My mother is an old woman with snow in her hair. She bore me under Gemini shadowed by skyscrapers. I grew into the day amid the spawn of strangers and listened to the first rumblings of the industrial revolution. On the cliffs of the Indian river, my parents dreamed anarchic dreams, and crossed the ocean again in search of the ancient loam. My childhood blossomed in the shadow of a cathedral. Hunger for the absolute gnawed me, when blackbirds brought marvellous words of dusk, folksongs sank out of star-dew, a gothic wind blew over aryan strings. I bit my teeth into the steaming soil, I dreamed over almanachs summer-heavy with litanies, I drank the swelling silences before the chemical sleep. But wolves crept around the border-acres. Steel clinked in midnight watches. Temples burst with panic.[49]

That familiar image of the European blackbird returns: a bringer of language, a companion to that youthful romantic spirit and, more ominously, a presence in the 'gothic wind' blowing over 'aryan strings'. Hope is tempered with its inverse: that 'chemical' sleep, the stealth of oncoming predators, and the sound of change running counter to any promise of a communal mythos. The blackbird, then, does not simply repeat the romantic gesture. It is the creature of flight and song that brings a promise of the reconfigured Word. Its appearance marks the spots where the author feels the need for his quest most keenly.

This ties in with Jolas's most direct writings on romanticism. In an undated handwritten notebook entitled 'Romanticism', Jolas discusses Ernst, perhaps the most avian of all interwar artists, whose visual alter ego on the canvas was a variously specied bird named Loplop. Admiring Ernst's method of cutting and pasting together old science illustrations into new forms, Jolas sees something akin to his own belief in the splicing of language. What we see in Ernst's art, Jolas writes, is a *'naked*, a disintegrating reality' and 'a side issue of the romantic movement'.[50] Although hesitant to think about what 'these practices of naked and disintegrating beauty [might] lead to', Jolas locates Ernst in an artistic collective caught between the romantic impulse and specific fears for modernity. He finds 'an immense renunciation':

> as compared with the time when people still believed in works 'well done' according to a highly developed technique, in the problems of the 'métier', [and] in the quest for means of creation which had nothing to do with what the romantic doctrine contains in the way of de-compositional ferments.[51]

Jolas searches for a way to describe Ernst's bird artistry, landing on a place between divinity and decay. It is the avian that inhabits this 'ferment' that is emblematic of a textuality, as *transition* itself will bear out. In writing on romanticism, therefore, Jolas unwittingly sums up the paradox inherent in much of his magazine: a 'side issue' of romanticism, wedged between a desire for a transcendental Logos and the abject impossibility of such a dream.

Later issues testify to this desired yet impossible transcendence. 'Poetry is vertical', the manifesto printed in the March 1932 issue, is a pertinent example. Although critical attention has focused on the text as a single document, assessing the extent of the signatories' involvement and agreement, when read as a foreword to the subsequent texts it appears as more of a provocative preface than a credo. If we read it in this light, it is less pressing to gauge Beckett's conflicted involvement, for instance, than to regard the work as a collaborative pamphlet.[52] In order, Jolas publishes 'Das Tages Gerippe' by Hans Arp, 'Reine de mon silence' by Joë Bousquet, 'Glad day for L. V.' by Kay Boyle, 'The shepherd's vision' and 'The vision' by Emily Holmes Coleman, 'Spring' by Charles Henri Ford, Jolas's translations of Hölderlin's later poetry, Jolas's own prose ('Night through night'), and works by Thomas McGreevy, Georges Pelorson, Paul Scheerbart and James Johnson Sweeney.[53] Read together as they were clearly intended to be, the texts intensify the need understand the deeper uncertainty beneath Jolas's befuddled romanticism.

This is especially true of the opening text, Hans Arp's 'Das Tages Gerippe'. The poem appears in its original German – a rare moment when the editor's zeal for translation is less important than the native tongue – and the title could be translated as 'Skeleton days', or perhaps 'Skeleton daily'. It is composed of ten stanzas, the fifth of which introduces a direct bird image, cast in a familiar romantic scene:

> die flammen schlafen unter den blättern ein
> das blatt des himmels ist blau
> grüne vögel wiegen sich in den zweigen
> du wurst sie singen hören den ganzen mai
> aus den fluren der lippen steigen die blumen ohne augen
> der grund füllt sich den die stimme naht
> das blatt meines herzens wird schwarz
> meine augen warden zu schwarzen früchten
> die brust des lichtes stürtz ein
> aber im sommer wachsen den toten wieder flügel
>
> (the flames fall asleep under leaves
> the leaf of the sky is blue
> green birds sway in the branches
> you'll hear her singing all morning
> out of lips' hallways eyeless flowers rise
> the reason fills the vote
> the leaf of my heart turns black
> my eyes are black fruits
> the chest of light crashes
> but in summer the dead grow wings again)[54]

A poem as much of sounds as of playful images, Arp's text uses words such as *flammen*, *himmel*, and *blättern* ('flame', 'sky', and 'wings') in unpunctuated, circulating verses, loosening and forming around the repeated images of flames as waves, lips and words, waves and heaven, bells and kisses – lightening and darkening by turns. Alongside the heavenly angels of the poem, Arp repeats the word *nester*, moving his lines between places of flight and nested repose. This allows him to transport the reader between an imagined flying consciousness and its deadening groundedness. 'Die spuren der flügel führen ins leere' ('the traces of lead in the empty wing') indicates an emptiness in flight, leaden – perhaps lead-poisoned. This clashes with an element of hope that flickers in and out but by the end is a soaring proclamation: 'und auch die nester läuten in der höhe des himmels' ('and the nests are ringing in the height of the sky').[55] Arp's poem exemplifies the quality Jolas so often picked out and translated: a movement through a romantic terrain that also blocks itself off from any easy identification as such.

'A FLOCK OF OWLS'

Bird imagery is so prevalent across *transition* that it even informs Jolas's later attempts to formulate a school of thought around his 'Icarian principle', which were partly a response to the magazine's reception. The magazine's sharply differing critics on either side of the Atlantic offer further insight, especially towards the end of its interwar existence, and they often touch upon the implicit flying creature. In a 1942 letter to Kay Boyle with regard to a potential review of the *Vertical* anthology for the *New Republic*, for instance, Jolas's earnest sincerity shines through. 'That's one review where the mention of the mystic, the sacred, the romantic is practically taboo', he writes, nudging Boyle's review with quotable lines:

> I conceived 'Vertical' as a cohesive manifestation, and everything in it has reference to an *organic idea*, which I think I explained in my manifestoes: continuous ascension, belief in a cosmic and seraphic universe, expansion of consciousness in a continual spiritual migration. The road is upwards.[56]

This is Jolas's rationale for regarding 'Vertical' as the 'antithesis' of a more diabolic, downwards-looking Surrealism, which by 1942 was well past its early phase in France and was more active elsewhere in Europe, the United States and Latin America. Boyle's review never appeared, but the letter indicates just how closely Jolas's 'organic idea' ran to the permutations of the textual bird at the heart of his project.

By July 1935, the author's familiar narrative voice floats into a landscape of airy fantasy. Again one finds birds, and again they are skewed. 'A flock of owls stood on the roofs of a house lazyblinking into the sky', runs one line in Jolas's 'Paramyths from a dreambook', an image that interrupts the text's reverie. Owls do not come in flocks. If their stare could be humanised at all, it could not be called lazy; and if staring were their pursuit, it would be downwards on their prey, not up. Jolas thus forces an oddly artificial metaphor, and with it a misuse of the totemic impulse. The scene he describes is one of ancient life forms: the 'mammothworld', the 'stoneworld' he has to leave behind as he travels through life. The owls offer a pathetic fallacy, framing the appearance of the speaker's mother with a 'heart in her hand'. Mother and son walk through the landscape, through the 'huddlepark along poplarlined paths'. They are accompanied by the detail of 'lotsoflowers [. . .] easeshimmering' – a wholesome vision of beauty undercut by the flock of owls. The 'blue flower' paradigm within which Jolas had previously operated cannot quite exist here, where easy symbolism is upturned.⁵⁷ Jolas's flock of owls signal a later version of the earlier translated birds. Although delivered in English, the text repeats the same language shifts as the unpublished poems: an unsteady metaphor, or literal *oublier*, again occurs with a metaphoric bird. The oddly incorrect bird symbol appears at moments where Jolas is literally lost for words. In his editorials and promotions, such uncertainty is off limits, replaced by the self-assuredness of a 'message'.

If we turn to these more declamatory editorials, we see his conviction growing in *transition* year by year. In the late 1930s, Jolas held all the more firmly to his ideals of expression, deliberately aligning himself with intellectual networks. His conviction and belief in 'Verticalism', with all the swooping, singing, tweeting moments its bird-shaped manifestations entailed, extended to his sending *Vertigralist Pamphlet* to friends and teachers. A letter from Dallas Kenmore explains that a classics lecturer at Exeter University was 'very interested [in the text]; he mentions especially the idea of the sky-ladder'. Kenmore sent copies of the pamphlet to William F. Jackson Knight, the spiritualist, academic and author of *Cumaean Gates* (1936), and to fellow classicist Maud Bodkin, author of *Archetypal Patterns in Poetry* (1934). When he reflected on his work during the late 1930s and onwards, Jolas styled his calls for the 'upward toward illumination' as pedagogical – part of a body of literary criticism of the period, rooted in the romantic canon.⁵⁸

Such pedagogical intent extended to Jolas's post-war writing, when he retrospectively attempted to build an intellectual movement out of his 'Verticalist' schema as *transition*'s popularity grew during the 1940s. At the same time as he was describing the 'mushrooming' of literary magazines during this period in his 'Across frontiers' column for the *New York Herald Tribune* European edition in 1949–50, Jolas witnessed *transition*'s earliest appearances on university syllabi and American literature survey courses.⁵⁹ In 1941, Chester H. Cable at the University of Chicago placed a series of Jolas's editorials on a short story English module. Jolas also received requests to participate in various surveys of contemporary literary culture, including a proposed article on the return of the exile for the University of Minnesota's *American Quarterly* in 1948, although it appears this project never came to fruition.⁶⁰ Jolas was also admired at Yale. In 1942, Norman Holmes Pearson invited the editor to talk to a group of students at Jonathan Edwards College, as an informal speaker:

> [They] are keen about writing, and reaching out in their writing. What I wish they could do is to have you give them your Verticalist slant some night at dinner and after dinner. Say sixteen or twenty of them, not more – and less, as you would wish, to dine together and sit around the table afterwards. No members of the faculty present, including myself, so that the direction could be between you and them. Nothing especially prepared

on your part: they get enough of slick lecturing on the platform. What with the war, etc., and the immediate prospect of quitting college for the draft, they need a renewed emphasis on communication and what communication can communicate, and all your thinking would be immensely useful to them.[61]

Buoyed by this belated appreciation, Jolas's post-war writing reveals an augmented confidence regarding his 'Verticalist slant'. He reads the critical disdain with which his writing on Novalis was met as a distaste for 'all metaphysical or metaphysic manifestations' – a shortcoming of the critical scene of the 1930s. This was only rectified, he claims, with the publication of Mary Colum's 1937 study *From These Roots*.[62] Had Jolas lived into the 1950s and early 1960s, he might well have extended Colum's approach to literary criticism with a more American focus, albeit one equally committed to the legacies of romantic thought in literature from the first few decades of the twentieth century. Colum's study underlined the stylistic connections and influences that existed between European Symbolism and subsequent American writing. In a section entitled 'The revolt', for instance, on late nineteenth-century reactions against realist writing, Colum positions 1890s Europe alongside 1930s Chicago and New York (a triangulation of Jolas's life, coincidentally), pointing to a shared spirit of escapism that was criticised in its time but which put the Symbolists into synergy with American writing, with Poe's style, or Whitman's form.[63]

Jolas's efforts to find critical purchase for his project pre-dated his appreciation of Colum, however. In 1938 he translated the Swiss editor and academic Albert Béguin: *transition*'s final issue featured an excerpt from Béguin's 1937 work on German romanticism, *L'âme romantique et le rêve*.[64] The attempt to produce a school of thought around *transition* was a driving force in 'Prolegomenon', where to this growing roster of scholarly works Jolas added (somewhat oddly, since he was an arch-positivist) G. T. Fechner, included for his apparent belief in star dwellers. Jolas even called upon Gaston Bachelard's *L'air et les songes* (1943) as a study of the theory of ascensionism, and on the Swiss psychologist Robert Desoille's *Le rêve éveillé en la psychothérapie* (1943) as using 'the dialectics of rise and fall in the waking dream as an active form of therapy in neuropathic patients'. Looking back after the war, Jolas maintained that he was searching for 'a four-dimensional consciousness having cosmological perspectives'. This ascensionism, he writes,

> is still the quintessence of the philosophical quest of today; the struggle between Lucifer and the angelic forces is still in progress. And poetry is more than ever the logomantic art of the word which tries to incite the human being to take wing to spiritual summits. It also seeks to exorcise the lower, or daemonic, powers.[65]

The awkwardness of Jolas's bird symbolism has a particular resonance here. It is a symbolic line that wavers between a humanist, liberal assumption of progress, and the outright denial of any such edifying narrative.

Jolas's combination of idealism and awkwardness, gathered round the many bird metaphors throughout *transition*, is reflected in the magazine's reception. Commentators highlighted its provocations. Waverley Root, in the Paris edition of the *Chicago Tribune*, characteristically described *transition* as a series of 'embattled theories [. . .] flung defiantly at the reader'.[66] Such resistance was common in anglophone criticism of *transition*'s early to mid-1930s phase. Some reviewers simply must not have read the material, and resorted to typewritten versions of tossing it against the wall. 'B. K. H.' in the *Providence, RI Journal*, for instance, issued a typically damning jibe: 'its garbled and weird contents' are just 'three hundred pages of cheaply printed paper'. Harvey C. Webster in the *Louisville KY Times* was similarly unimpressed. 'It is easier to ridicule "Transition" than to appraise it', he writes. 'To ridicule all one needs to do is quote.' Such mockery on the part of these largely American reviewers often extended to placing Jolas, 'artistically speaking', on the 'extreme left', as one piece in the *New York Herald* in 1937 had it, attacking the journal by positioning it as a barometer of 'leftist' experimentation.[67] But an even more vehement dislike existed on the political left. Writing in August 1932 for *New Masses*, Philip Rahv denounced Jolas and his associate editors as promoters of decadent 'bourgeois illuminati' taking 'refuge in a flight from consciousness'. He concludes:

> [These] experiments with word-dismembering are of no more value than the well-known experiments of children with flies, yet the bourgeois illuminati take these word-revolutionists quite seriously. [. . .] The Revolution of the Word is a pretext for indulging in psychopathological orgies; it represents a deep-seated craving for the prenatal stage, for non-being. The vagaries of Jolas & Co. and the necromantic method of producing literature through the immaculate conception of automatic writing are quite proper end-phenomena of a dying class, and of a crumbling hegemony.[68]

Rahv's demolition may come from the desire to find the political truth or socioeconomic driver behind art in a culture of polarised systems of governance, both communist and fascist; but in rejecting Jolas so squarely, he misses the point of any position that seeks, as Jolas still maintained, an apolitical designation for art. Rahv fails to grasp the fact that, as Kramer and Rumold point out, Jolas's 'aesthetic utopianism, like that of all avant-gardists', is never really such.[69] Rahv's inflammatory response, with the implication that the 'psychopathological orgy' was a nihilistic leaning towards Thanatos, emerges as even more nonsensical than the automatic writing from which Jolas had in fact moved on, following his 1930 break from the Surrealism, and the movement's experiments that Rahv unknowingly paraphrased. The cruelty of a child stripping an insect of its wings suggests permanent damage done to language in an irrevocably destructive process. Rahv's position is important, however. It is a reminder of the growing need felt through the 1930s to acknowledge the external forces of political reality.

This need was expressed by one of Jolas's most insightful critics, Babette Deutsch, in a 1942 piece for the *New York Herald Tribune* entitled 'The pilot's confusion'. Reviewing the *Vertical* anthology, Deutsch echoes Rahv's position – all the more pressing during the war years – that Jolas did not articulate a satisfactory position against fascism, or indeed any point on the political spectrum. His 'lofty' aims, she writes, lose sight of the democratic world from which to launch upwards: 'the voyagers who enter his aerobus for the heavenward excursion are a varied company. [. . .] Some are dead, [. . .] most are French, but few of the latter represent Gallic clarity and wit'. She goes on: 'very little is clear except the fact of the editor's confusion'. Where Rahv rejects Jolas as bourgeois, Deutsch rejects him as naive, and she closes by reminding her readers of Antaeus, son of the Greek gods Poseidon and Gaea, whose strength lay in keeping his feet on the ground.[70]

Responses to *transition* written in French, however, reveal a far more sympathetic readership. Writing for the Romanian cultural journal *Le moment* in 1938, for instance, Jacques Mercanton was more receptive to the idea of the 'aircraft symbol' as the implicit bird emblem of 'Vertigral' poetics. He writes in harmony with Jolas's exaltations, yet maintains a critical distance:

> Ce n'est pas un hasard si le symbole de l'avion se propose à l'esprit de l'animateur de ce courageux mouvement esthétique: il s'agit de compléter cette belle conquête du génie humain dans l'ordre technique par une conquête analogue dans l'ordre spirituel. *Mais cette ascension ne va pas sans une descente* au plus profond de la nature et de l'âme, et les enquêtes sur la préhistoire et l'art primitif si plein de symboles l'exploration des vieux mythes et de la vie inconsciente et nocturne, sont les sources mêmes de cette récréation de l'art.
>
> (It is no coincidence that the aircraft symbol suggests the essence of the brave animator of this aesthetic movement: it completes this beautiful conquest of human genius within the technological order by an analogous conquest within the spiritual order. *But this rise does not come without a descent* more profound than nature of the soul, and enquiries on prehistoric and primitive art are full of the symbols of exploration of the old myths and unconscious life and night, these are the very sources of this recreation of art.)[71]

Unlike the more condemnatory anglophone voices, Mercanton's approach reflects a sensitive acknowledgement of the value of the project, cognisant of the directional emphasis of the aesthetic quest in the same animalised terms as Jolas. He is unencumbered by the need to demystify or debunk; his recognition of the primitivism and 'prehistoric' gestures in the magazine indicate a more insightful European readership.

Mercanton's response was far from unique. An anonymous reviewer in *Les nouvelles littéraires* in 1932 was similarly supportive, and keenly aware of Jolas's intent. Reviewing the pamphlet *The Language of Night*, he or she praises the author's talent and acuity, quoting his sentiments on the normalisation of language through its modern usages. If Jolas desires a return to the romantic *Weltanschauung*, they write, it is not a return to romanticism in any straightforward sense:

> [I]l préconise le retour à une *weltanschauung* romantique celle-ci n'étant pas, bien entendu, le retour à des formes extérieures périmées, mais une philosophie cohérente, valable pour tous les temps, en ce qu'elle affirme avant tout "la croyance fondamentale que les forces de la vie sont des forces irrationnelles avant de devenir des entités créatrices." Il ne s'agit pas là d'un *retour au romantisme*, et encore moins d'un *néo-romantisme* mais d'un moyen de connaissance qui retrouve le sens du miracle, du phénomène onirique.
>
> ([H]e advocates a return to a romantic *Weltanschauung* that was not, of course, the return to previous, external eras, but a coherent philosophy, valid for all time, one that says above all that 'the fundamental belief that the forces of life are irrational forces before becoming creative entities'. This is not a *return to romanticism*, much less a *neo-romanticism* but a means of knowledge that finds the meaning of the miracle, the phenomenon of dreams.)[72]

The anonymous reviewer clearly read *transition* carefully, and shared its beliefs. That she or he differentiates Jolas's project from both romanticism and neo-romanticism reflects a nuanced reading simply not encountered in anglophone criticism until much later, with the advent of the early 1940s American journals that appeared in *transition*'s wake, such as *View* or *Arson*.[73]

The most significant example of a francophone reading of Jolas's avian aesthetic appears in *transition* itself. In the February 1933 issue – the month when the Nazi Party in Germany instated the so-called Law for the Protection of the People and the State, just days after Hitler's appointment as chancellor – the inward-looking nature of *transition*'s content is unnerving. 'À Eugene Jolas' by Georges Pelorson is an elegy to his 'literary godfather', using imagery that reflects the themes and concerns of Jolas's editorials and poetry.[74] Georges Pelorson was a significant figure in *transition*, who went from journalist and regular contributor to highly active collaborator with France's Vichy regime. Between December 1937 and August 1939, Pelorson was also the main editor of the monthly periodical *Volontés*, the editorial board of which included fellow *transition* contributors Henry Miller, Raymond Queneau, Camille Schuwer and Jolas himself. As Vincent Giroud has shown, *Volontés* carried an uneasy number of texts promoting nationalist and racist ideas, largely due to Pelorson's increasingly fascist politics during the period. In February 1941 Pelorson became 'Chef de la propaganda des jeunes', and by August 1942 he was instrumental in creating a French equivalent of the Hitler Youth. Before his 'collaborationist zeal' had endeared him to the most pro-Nazi activists within the regime, however, Pelorson had been highly astute. 'À Eugene Jolas', excerpted below, explicitly rejects the harmonised humanist subject in its mention of insects and its desire for the oblivion of sleep, and it gives an extraordinary description of the content of the journal:

> Il y a des poèmes (à défaut d'autres mots) de lumière
> Il y a des poèmes de bruit et de son
> Il y en a qui sont surfaces, d'autres des cubes ou des sphères rotatives dont le bourdonnement menace d'arracher la tête, d'autres font mal au cou soulèvent les omoplates pénètrent lentement les côtes ou saisissent les cuisses.
>
> (There are poems (in lieu of other words) of light
> There are poems of noise and being
> There are surfaces, other cubes or rotating spheres with a buzz that threatens to tear the head, others a pain in the neck slowly lift the shoulder blades penetrate slowly grasp the ratings, grab or thighs.)[75]

This description of *transition*'s pages moves from the abstract to the corporeal. That 'buzz' of texts is evocative of Éluard's 'mammiferous body', the insect body that meets with the acephalous figure of the split subject. It continues with a visceral splay of fleshy parts, urging the reader to release the 'giblets of humanity', yet with a declaration of letting go:

> Quittez depuis le temps etc . . .
> Quittez l'homme
>
> (Exit the times
> Exit the human)[76]

Pelorson's language veers towards the corporeal realm, taking the bodily matter of physicality into a more fractured space. The 'giblets of humanity' emerge as the text's central image:

> Trop longtemps nous nous sommes cramponnés de la nuque et des reins à notre humanité, fiers de nos connaissances (le bel esprit la belle jambe) fiers des substances grises qui nous permettaient de comprendre et d'imiter à l'aise les fous les Etrangers [sic] et les esprits du Noir
>
> (For too long do we cling to the giblets of our humanity, taking pride in our knowledge (the good and pretty spirit and stride), that grey matter that leads to awareness, to imitation ... the easy insanity of the strange spirit of the Night)[77]

The 'giblets' of humanity are devoid of any semblance of the emblematic bird here. Pelorson is interpreting the meaning of Jolas's idealist quest – a strange reversal of the editor's own 1927 translations of European avant-garde writers into English. As the piece nears its end, there is a striking image of a primordial animal, an answer perhaps to the verticality of Jolas's programme, as Pelorson writes of a thwarted point of contact between the human and its furthest living reaches:

> Ayez des mains qui sauront prendre les insectes Et d'autres mains qui savent se fermer la nuit Des paupières qui aiment la pesanteur Un corps qui peut bien choir Il ya loin du nyctalope vigilant qui s'arme d'un crayon contre son être et le sommeil au nyctalope naturel amant des flammes de la nuit
>
> Et, les ténèbres déchaînées, les démondes sauront bien trouver seuls le chemin de vos rêves
>
> (Have hands that will take insects, and others that know how to close the night, with eyelids that like gravity A body that, in chorus, falls far from the vigilant nyctalopic who arms against his being with a pencil – the sleep of the natural nyctalopic loves the flames of the night
>
> And, with darkness unleashed, the demons find only the way of your dreams)[78]

The urgency of Pelorson's writing, which combines a sense of ripped flesh with an entomological swarm replacing that which might stand for 'truth', is gathered here under the rubric of the 'night'. The text offers an extraordinary understanding of the primordial contours of the journal, and Pelorson's subsequent fascism is itself an uneasy dimension of *transition*'s history, as discussed in the previous chapter. He arrives at such insight through the juxtaposition with the 'poems of light' that sing of verticalism or ascensionist belief, of that which is 'in lieu of other words'. Pelorson's text produces the same syntactical placing of the emblematic bird in which Jolas is engaged. The avian symbol – translated, twisted, called upon, implicit, and in lieu of other words – emerges as a critical point of entry into the proper relational place of Jolas's pronouncements within the arranged content of the journal.

By the time of *transition*'s final issue in 1938, Jolas was firmly attached to the ideal of a non-political house of literary production, despite the very real need to acknowledge historical events. As Dougald McMillan points out, *transition* 'had held on for nearly a decade after the first wave of expatriates had left Europe to return to America and write their memoirs, but the war was too great an obstacle even for [the journal]'. By allowing *transition* to come to an end, Jolas upheld the founding principle of an apolitical space for writing, even as he himself 'felt that he must adopt a more active political attitude' in his working life.[79]

Jolas's astonishing post-war work should not be underestimated, and it is diametrically opposed to the flight and mythos desired throughout *transition*. Following on from his work as editor-in-chief at the Deutsche Allgemeine Nachrichten-Agentur in Bad Nauheim (later to become the Deutsche Presse-Agentur) and the German Allied Press, Jolas became responsible for the denazification process in German newspapers, a purging of the effects on news language of an entire era of propaganda. He identified and gathered anti-Nazi printers, editors and assistants, and he trained young German journalists from scratch. He founded *Die Wandlung* (Transformation), a magazine focused on democracy that ran from October 1945 to December 1949, and organised a thorough debunking of euphemistic terms such as *Führer* and *Betreuung* ('taking care of', 'a perverse euphemism for "finishing off"', as Kramer and Rumold put it). In April 1946 Jolas was awarded the Medal of Freedom by the Military Government of Germany.[80] For all the vertical heights of the preceding era in his literary avant-garde world, Jolas's work for German culture was about clarity of expression: a grounding, rather than an ascension.[81]

'Sweet as a nightingale' and Its 'grotesque hymn'

To turn back to *transition* and Jolas's editorial flights, an assessment remains to be made of some of the bird imagery employed by contributors, and of the ways it interrupted or 'grounded' the editor's mission. The emblematic bird in the final issues sometimes dethroned the Jolasian 'extasis' of 'the Icarian principle', transforming avian images into expressions of an untenable romantic spirit. 'Your love song' by Kay Boyle, for example, contains two of the most totemic birds in all literature: the nightingale – romantic icon of the muse, of Keats's ode, of beauteous song – and the peacock, the strutting green and preening symbol of *fin de siècle* decadence. Here is the opening of the text, which was laid out as an indented stanza, then as prose, and then a second stanza to close:

> Here or in any public place you may begin to sing
> The violent serenade that rises with the tide of drink's
> Green icy rising that once plunged in thaws to flesh
> And melts the veins to music, turns your tongue
> To harp or cello weeping notes of love.[82]

Boyle couples a true serenade with a false one, via the 'tide of drink'. Drunkenness as a 'green icy rising' invokes images of bottle glass and clinking in a scene of empty sentimentality. The addressee's intoxication, which 'turns your tongue / To harp or cello weeping notes of love', underlines the play of the sonorous and the maudlin. The musical harp is undercut by the equally available meaning of 'to harp', as in to harp on about something. The addressee is an alcohol-soaked figure of redundant romanticism.

The speaker then describes the sound of the addressee's love song, repeating the opening image of bottle-green decadence as containing something uglier than the ostensible declaration of love:

> I have heard you sing
>   sweet as a nightingale at the articulation of that grotesque hymn which lies in necks of bottles springing for escape from silence. The pitiless eye on you over the unlifted glass, you, peacock-headed, do burst into song and, sheeny-throated, marvellously sing such words of beauty that his nights and days swoon with delight, slumber in glamor, leap like winds at morning straight into the sun.[83]

The doubled image of the bird is telling. There is Keats's nightingale – an encounter between sleep and waking, with a pang for 'a draught of vintage' or a 'beaker' of wine.[84] In the 'peacock-headed' vanity of this singer, there is also an echo of Oscar Wilde. The two birds create a botched romanticism and a deluded dandy: 'this symphony that whirls and hurls venom through anguish into purity transforms shit, whore, patroness, bitch and parasite to declaration tender enough for children's ears to hear'. Rearranged backwards, this list of gendered identities is a meditation on the hypocrisy that pretends the contrary but reads women precisely as parasites, bitches, patronesses or whores, then as formless waste or faeces:

> The sweet high declaration that it has
> Impugns the air unlike the sound of what
> Is recognised as it: (as if the speech of it
> Could lie at rest upon the tongue
> As soft as arms around the neck, or weave
> From mouth to ear or mouth to mouth as kisses weave.)

> It may be sung without rehearsal any night
> At bars or café tables: it may suddenly rise
> The way a statue in the falling dark
> Discards its marble and its classic eyes.[85]

The second indented stanza then rounds back upon the speaker, indicating that it is the love song belonging to the addressee that is the object: 'the sweet high declaration that it has / Impugns the air'; it is not 'the sound of what / Is recognised as it'. This is what the poem 'does with birds', half anticipating the Robert Frost sonnet of 1942.[86] Birds here are clear allusions to previous forms. Much like Jolas's translation practice in the early issues, Boyle syntheses diverse and experimental imagery. But where Jolas's idealism held the journal together, here Boyle writes with a genuine distance from her fragments. The nightingale ultimately signifies waste, the peacock a brittle ego. Boyle's deliberate commingling of exhausted romantic bird symbols presents the poetic gesture as an untenable dead end. Even though her deployment of the bird symbol here is sharply distinct from Jolas's, Boyle was a major figure in the magazine, and was part of a community that was well aware of the threat of National Socialism. Her 1936 novel *Death of a Man* focuses on an Austrian medical doctor and his clandestine support for the Nazi Party in 1934, offering a powerful reflection upon questions of political engagement in the years prior to the Second World War. The book is dedicated to Eugene Jolas.[87]

A final example of the avian in *transition* illustrates contributors' invocations of idealism as a dead end. In his sole contribution to the journal, the otherwise unknown author Thomas Good's prose piece 'Carrion' weaves together various origin images and mythological figures, from the pagan gods of Rome to Clovis, king of the Franks. Like vultures picking at dead carcasses, birds feature as indicators of something hidden in the story, bound up with a sense of rotting flesh, yet part of a biblical parable. The words indicate barrenness, drought and winter, as opposed to the apparent declaration of fertile vitality, with two bird words pushed into the configuration:

> Dry lanes he came through without sugar in stomach and temptation in coldness. He looked and called and no answer. He spoke and said: 'You yellow cuckoo, only touch my bellysprings and you'll find I'm randy enough. I'll pink straight if they don't leave me now, or when they hear my body crackle.' Not to speak of the apple-orchard and blossom to cover her. Firm loins broke his goose-step, and there were crazy children singing into his ears, asking him to murder them, because the priest withheld absolution.[88]

The piece unravels into an unnerving voice of ages, with biblical fragments echoed through incantatory language: 'only the anchorite had any salt to his pie and left no sting in the serpent's mouth. The acrostic was numerical and eleven bases of brimstone led to the gossamer pavement'.[89] The two birds are ominous harbingers of death. Good's text is not Surrealist in the sense of excitement over dissociated psychosexual iconography unmoored from any familiar narrative: instead it borders on gibberish, albeit with a knowing quality that nods to earlier writing practices, and to the 'goose-step' of Nazi Germany. There is a note of Bataille's *Story of the Eye*, for instance, as the narration flickers with horror-genre imagery:

> Now the twin-monster is harnessed to a star, and the bite of a tooth in her left breast. [. . .] A day is two halves and few women have goat's milk, but when two angry girls stripped the priest, he shaved his bones to sawdust. [. . .]
> 'O, lapwing in heaven of time carry a countenance of grim odour through the bays.'[90]

With a possible allusion to Bataille's 1928 novella, Good's prose condenses fragments into a seemingly coherent whole. 'Carrion' appears immediately before the final Kafka text in *transition*, which, itself a fragment, considers the origin and form of the word 'Odradek'. Kafka's narrator gives an image in this text that refuses to name the concept or thing behind the word. The two passages' proximity may be deliberate – another editorial pleasure – as with the positioning of the texts considered earlier by Trakl and Ribemont-Dessaignes. Kafka's text similarly recalls the many signifying birds, now on a spectrum from the fragile European blackbird to Good's vulturous imagery. 'We might be tempted to believe this form had once a functional significance of some kind', writes Kafka's narrator,

> and now we see it in a damaged state. This, however, does not seem to be the case [. . .] No-where can we discern any appendages or fragments that might point to that conclusion; the whole thing seems senseless, yet quite complete in its peculiar way.[91]

Kafka's fragment is a challenge to the interpretive gesture, pointing to the word as a thing that seems full of meaning and yet is poised on the edge of meaninglessness. Jolas's editorial presence is palpable in this final issue: he urges his readers towards a consideration of the texts together, alongside the exhausted sense of the symbolic. It carries with it the putrefaction of an avian symbol, and a statement of encounter with a kind of linguistic carcass.

Good's closing line is significant, finally: 'The Waste Land and Joseph is stripping the muddle by the oak beams and clover.'[92] Like Boyle, Good is drawn to fragments of earlier writing – both the avant-gardist ideas of a figure such as Bataille and the high modernism of Eliot – and turns them into a glistening, sickly expression, here likened to carrion. At the closing of the largest American expatriate magazine of the interwar period, Jolas's birds legibly take their exit, lending his earlier invocation of the 'first and last' Word a strangely prescient quality. Although often at odds with the content of his authors' works, Jolas's verve is written into this proliferation of birds, even when the reader is aware of its absence, as these later examples attest. Boyle and Good's aesthetic insists upon the irrevocably broken symbolism of the signifying bird, angled now towards a representation of death.

It is essential to register the nature of Jolas's belief in his artistic project, even amid tragedy. Writing about the 1942 suicide of the novelist Stefan Zweig, Jolas again employs a soaring bird figure, here in answer to the horrific realities of the destruction of European cultural life.[93] After paraphrasing Zweig's suicide note, Jolas calls for a 'means of synthesis' against a 'Babelist' language pitched upwards to on high. He is irrepressible to the last:

> We live in the darkest period of history.
>
> The peoples of the world live in fear and anguish. After the most titanic war in history, the huge questions continue to obsess us. Nobody understands each other anymore. Words are used by different persons and each puts a different concept into them.
>
> We need a universal consciousness. An awareness of ecumenical associations. The historic nexus of humanity which the machine seemed to reinforce for a while is again broken by the machine. The barbarism of a civilization in decay spreads its stench. Misery, famine, hate and fear are the monstrous emotions under which mankind suffers. The frontiers are at once closed.
>
> Mankind needs an intercontinental language, a means of synthesis. We must return to the eternal. We must transform the human personality with words taken from all the languages, with words that will reconquer their sacred and liturgic character.
>
> *Transition Word* will attempt in these pages to occasionally to [*sic*] make us see the universal problem of the word.[94]

This is the position Jolas maintained throughout *transition*. As this late passage shows, he was more than aware of the bleakness of the times through which he was living. In a letter to Blanche Matthias the year before, Jolas writes about this in no uncertain terms. He feels the threat of an apocalypse, an end of days in Europe, 'in full swing'. 'The only thing we can clearly perceive is that a revolution is preparing which will sweep all our little ideas of art and letters into the dustheap. Will there be a revolution of the angels? A seraphic revolt?'[95] Could the next question here turn towards the actual societal, political change in modern Europe – towards an era of totalitarian oppression towards which

Jolas perhaps nods the word 'dustheap' – and the ways in which the editor's generation might respond? Yet in this letter, and in the *Transition Word* statement, Jolas's despair turns back towards his faith.

It comes as no surprise to read Philippe Soupault's tribute to Jolas, which is written in terms of an intensity of vision, belief and hope. For Soupault, Jolas was 'the most honest – I would say the most hopelessly honest – human being who has lived in our age. [. . .] His revolt was pure and genuine. [. . .] He wanted to be the liberator of language.'[96] In light of the ways symbolic birds functioned for Jolas and the *transition* project, Soupault's words could not be more apt. Although the end of the journal was marked by a turn towards the deathly and exhausted categories of romantic symbolism, it was Jolas's irrepressible optimism in the face of the ongoing crisis that bound its creative content together.

In threading his faith and hope for art through so many poetic birds, the editor of *transition* left his readers not with a confused emblem of death, but with an emblem of life. Contrasting with the other primordial creatures in this study – the amoeba of abstraction, the parody of the degenerate fish, the lizard of pre-human vision – Jolas's birds reveal an opposing energy that is no less central to our understanding of the magazine and its primordial modernism. Theirs is a consistent voice amid so much heterogeneous, anti-romantic and modernist experimental writing. They are often, as Deutsch puts it, a 'flight into the intense inane', yet they are essential.[97] What would the journal have been without this fixity, without Jolas's hope and vision? If Jolas's editorial predecessor at the helm of the *transatlantic review*, Ford Madox Ford, is 'the stormy petrel of modern literature', as Jolas described him in 1924, then the *transition* editor is a magnificent frigate bird: romanticist to the core, yet at the helm of an important document of late modernist literary production.[98] Jolas's stewardship and paratextual choices reveal a swiftly collating hand running over the magazine. The early translated birds – as black and white, and as symbols for Europe and America – help us understand the editor's role as a synthesiser, a provocateur of artistic styles and movements.

Jolas was a powerful force. He inspired a whole generation who followed him, like Henry Miller, to the tail end of the Parisian avant-garde. To judge from his efforts to disseminate the 'Verticalist slant', it seems likely that, had Jolas lived longer, he would have produced retrospectives that aimed to arrange experimental poetry in a didactic mode similar to that of Charles Olson, for example.[99] As Hugh Haughton has written of Jolas, we might conclude that 'one of the most moving things about [him] is his obstinate innocence in the face of the horrific confusion he witnesses'. Jolas even goes so far in his memoir as to describe the interwar period as a 'golden age of the logos'.[100] As Pelorson's elegiac words and André Masson's insightful sketch (Figure 4.1) reveal, this is an 'obstinate innocence' of which the artists and collaborators around Jolas

Figure 4.1 André Masson, *Portrait d'Eugene Jolas* (1942). Reproduced by permission. © ADAGP, Paris and DACS, London 2018

were aware. Masson's sketch even includes a flock of birds that appear to fly from the editor's brain. Impossible though it was, Jolas remained steadfast to his vision of the exalted, seraphic language of expression in which the bird, for all its textual contortions, is perpetually volant. 'A new cycle in history is about to open', he writes in the very last words of the epilogue to *Man from Babel*. 'The huge urban collectivities that are arising will forge the migratory and universal tongue in an exaltation of sacred and communal vocables, in a voyage without end.'[101]

Notes

1. Joyce, MS typescript entitled 'Versailles, 1933'. Box 13, Folder 259, Maria and Eugene Jolas Papers, Beinecke Rare Books and Manuscripts Library, Yale University. Subsequent references to this archive will be indicated by the Box and Folder numbers followed by an indication of the collection as the Jolas Papers. Jolas published a collection of poems entitled *Mots-déluge* the same year.

2. Werness, 'Bird', in *The Continuum Encyclopedia of Animal Symbolism in Art*, 44–6.
3. Bataille, *Prehistoric Painting*; Ernst, *Une semaine de bonté*; Ernst, *La femme 100 têtes*; Ernst, *Rêve*; Sachs, 'Religious despair'.
4. Perloff, 'Logocinéma', para. 2.
5. Rabaté, '*Eugene Jolas*', 458.
6. Hoffman et al., *Little Magazine*, 170.
7. Lacoue-Labarthe and Nancy, *Literary Absolute*, 1, emphasis added.
8. Ferber, *Romanticism*, 10–11.
9. Jolas, 'Frontier-poem', 220, 224, emphasis added.
10. Gilbert, 'Subliminal tongue', 141; Jolas, 'Vertigralist pamphlet', in Kiefer and Rumold, *Eugene Jolas*, 291, emphasis original; Gilbert, 'Subliminal tongue', 152.
11. Reid, 'Introduction'.
12. Rabaté, '*Eugene Jolas*', 455.
13. Jolas (ed.), *Vertical*.
14. Jolas, 'Atlantica poem', unpublished typescript, n. d, c. 1938. Box 12, Folder 241, Jolas Papers.
15. Rabaté, 'Joyce and Jolas', 246.
16. Jolas, 'The word', unpublished poem typescript, my translation. Box 12, Folder 243, Jolas Papers.
17. Desnos, 'Dove'.
18. Lasker-Schüler, 'A song'.
19. Ibid.
20. Éluard, 'Georges Braque'.
21. Ibid.
22. Holz, 'From Phantasus', 147, 146.
23. Trakl, 'To the lad, Elis'.
24. See Trakl, *Poems and Prose*, translated by Stillmark, 43, and *Poems*, translated by Lehbert, 42.
25. Stillmark, 'Problems and principles', 185. See also Hermans, *Structure*, 203. For a broader discussion of Trakl's bird imagery in relation to earlier German literary traditions, see Stinchcombe, 'Trakl's "Elis"'.
26. For more on the ancient art of augury and its appearance in literature, see Lutwack, *Birds in Literature*, 78–9, 117–19.
27. Jolas, 'Prolegomenon, or white romanticism and the mythos of ascension' (n. d.) in Kiefer and Rumold (eds), *Eugene Jolas*, 222–3. See also Jolas, 'Georg Trakl'. For Jolas's critique of both romanticism (which he saw as definitively over) and the desire for a 'new imagination', see his 'Workshop'.
28. Ribemont-Dessaignes, untitled text.
29. Georges Ribemont-Dessaignes was a dissident Surrealist who wrote searing critiques of both André Breton and Georges Bataille. Although Jolas's translation predates the 'crisis years' of Surrealism, it is very likely that the *transition* circle was aware of factional tensions within the movement. For a detailed account of Ribemont-Dessaignes in this context, see Spiteri, 'Surrealism'.
30. Jolas, 'From "Nocturnes"'.
31. Éluard, 'In company', 113.

32. Jolas, 'From "Landscapes"', 134.
33. Ibid. 135–6.
34. Haughton, 'Sorry', 18.
35. Jolas, 'Monologue', 133.
36. Minet, 'Poem'; Solveen, 'Psalm'; Arp, 'Light-shunning paradise'.
37. Jolas, 'On the quest', 191.
38. Jolas, *Man from Babel*, 89.
39. Jolas, 'Almanach', 71–5, pp. 71, 72, 74, italics original.
40. Jolas, 'Daily graphic', 174.
41. Jolas, 'Construction', 56.
42. Apollinaire, 'Un soir', in *Alcools*, 166–7.
43. Jolas, 'Migration 1', in *Words from the Deluge*. Preserved in Box 17, Folder 327, Jolas Papers.
44. Unpublished typescripts, n. d. Box 12, Folder 243, Jolas Papers.
45. Extracts from Jolas, *Epivocables of 3*, and 'Three cities', n.d. Preserved in Box 17, Folder 319, Jolas Papers.
46. Jolas, corrected typescript of 'Choirprair', dated 1932, from *Epivocables of 3*. Box 15 Folder 279, Jolas Papers.
47. Jolas, 'Migration 1', in *Words from the Deluge*, emphasis added. Preserved in Box 17, Folder 327, Jolas Papers.
48. Jack, Untitled, *New York Times* book review, 15 March 1942, 9. Preserved in 'Transition scrapbook I, 1927–1952'. Box 60, Folder 1400, Jolas Papers.
49. Jolas, 'Document', in *Secession in Astropolis*, 79–84.
50. Jolas, 'Romanticism notebook', n. d., emphasis original. Box 5, Folder 124, Jolas Papers.
51. Ibid.
52. For further discussion of Beckett's role here, see Hatch, 'Beckett in *transition*', 43–9.
53. Arp, 'Das Tages Gerippe'; Bousquet, 'Reine'; K. Boyle, 'Glad day'; Coleman, 'Shepherd's vision' and 'Vision'; Ford, 'Spring'; Hölderlin, 'Homeland', 'To Heinse', 'As birds . . .', 'Greece', 'To know little', 'The eagle', 'Yet from self-inflicted wounds . . .', 'New world', 'To the Madonna', 'Fate', 'On fallow leaf', 'Vineyard and bees', 'Klopstock' and 'From the abyss'; Jolas, 'Night through night'; McGreevy, 'Treason of Saint Laurence O'Toole' and 'Elsa'; Pelorson, 'Isocele' and 'Plans'; Scheerbart, 'Gesang der Walfische'; Sweeney, 'Mole'.
54. Arp, 'Das Tages Gerippe', 151, my translation.
55. Ibid. 150–2, my translation. Jolas republished this poem in English in *transition* five years later, using his own translation as 'The skeleton of the day' (1937).
56. Jolas to Kay Boyle, 31 January 1942, original emphasis. Box 2, Folder 8, Jolas Papers.
57. Jolas, 'Paramyths', 19.
58. Dallas Kenmore, letter to Jolas, 19 May 1939 (Box 3, Folder 43, Jolas Papers); Knight, *Cumaean Gates*; Bodkin, *Archetypal*.
59. Jolas reports on the 'mushrooming' of literary titles in post-war France, such as *Arcadia, Escales, Flammes, K-Revue* (Jolas defines this as 'an echo of Kafka and

certain neo-Dada tendencies'), *Le messager boiteux de Paris*, *Osmose*, *Traits* and *Transit*. Jolas, 'Across frontiers', clipping preserved in Box 4, Folder 85, Jolas Papers.
60. Course syllabus from Chester H. Cable's course 'The short story in English and American literature from 1800 to 1940' (University of Chicago, 1941). Box 26, Folder 502, Jolas Papers. William Van O'Connor, letter to Jolas, 8 July 1948. Box 3, Folder 60, Jolas Papers.
61. Norman Holmes Pearson, letter to Jolas, 21 September 1942. Box 3, Folder 62, Jolas Papers.
62. Jolas, 'Prolegomenon' (n. d.) in Kiefer and Rumold (eds), *Eugene Jolas*, 224. Jolas cites Colum, *From These Roots*. Colum's importance as a critic of literary modernism has gained recognition in recent years. See Ayo, 'Mary Colum'.
63. Colum, *From These Roots*, 313. Colum was friends with Joyce and part of Jolas's social circle. See Colum and Colum, *Our Friend*.
64. Béguin, *L'âme romantique*. Béguin brought a raft of *transition* authors out in print (among them Louis Aragon, Charles Péguy and Paul Éluard) during the Second World War. His efforts were part of a resistance movement in Switzerland and France. See also Béguin, 'Night side', 218.
65. Jolas, 'Prolegomenon' (n. d.) in Kiefer and Rumold (eds), *Eugene Jolas*, 225. Bachelard, *L'air* (1943); Desoille, *Le rêve* (1943).
66. Quoted in Anonymous, *'Transition'*, 204.
67. B. K. H., 'Sideshow'. See also Turnell, 'Malady of language', a review of *transition*, 23; Webster, 'Review, *Transition* 26'; Anonymous, 'Review, *Transition* 26'. Preserved in 'Transition scrapbook I, 1927–1952'. Box 60, Folder 1400, Jolas Papers.
68. Rahv, 'Literary class war', 8.
69. Jolas, *Man from Babel*, xviii.
70. Deutsch, 'The pilot's confusion'. Preserved in 'Transition scrapbook I, 1927–1952'. Box 60, Folder 1400, Jolas Papers.
71. Mercanton, 'Le X-ème anniversaire', my translation, emphasis added. Preserved in 'Transition scrapbook I, 1927–1952'. Box 60, Folder 1400, Jolas Papers.
72. Anonymous, 'L'actualité littéraire', emphasis original. Preserved in 'Transition scrapbook I, 1927–1952'. Box 60, Folder 1400, Jolas Papers.
73. See Hoffman et al., *Little Magazine*, 181–8.
74. Giroud, 'Transition to Vichy', 227–37.
75. Pelorson, 'À Eugene Jolas', 24, my translation.
76. Ibid. 27.
77. Ibid. 27.
78. Ibid. 27.
79. McMillan, *transition*, 72.
80. See Jolas, *Man from Babel*, xxiii–xxv, 179–273.
81. Deissler, 'Introduction', 465.
82. Boyle, 'Your love song', 39.
83. Ibid. 39.
84. Keats, 'Ode to a nightingale' (1819), in *Complete Poems*, 346.
85. Boyle, 'Your love song', 39–40.

86. 'Never again would birds' song be the same. / And to do that to birds was why she came'. Frost, 'Never again would birds' song be the same' (1942), in *Poems*, 394.
87. Boyle, *Death*.
88. Good, 'Carrion', 157.
89. Ibid. 157.
90. Ibid. 157–8.
91. Kafka, 'The housefather's care', 160.
92. Good, 'Carrion', 158.
93. Stefan Zweig was a prominent Austrian Jewish novelist who committed suicide in America in 1942 after fleeing Nazi rule in Europe.
94. Jolas, 'Stefan Zweig and the malady of the uprooted', unpublished typescript, n.d. Box 62 Folder 1460, Jolas Papers.
95. Jolas to Blanche Matthias, 6 January 1941. Box 3, Folder 54, Jolas Papers.
96. Soupault, 'Souvenir de Gene Jolas', part of a 1958 Radio Strasbourg tribute. Translated by Kramer and Rumold and reproduced in Jolas, *Man from Babel*, xxx; quoted here from Box 26, Folder 499, Jolas Papers.
97. Deutsch, 'Pilot's confusion'.
98. Jolas, 'Rambles'.
99. Golding, 'Pound to Olson'.
100. Haughton, 'Sorry', 21; Jolas, *Man from Babel*, 87.
101. Jolas, *Man from Babel*, 273.

CONCLUSION

> The shattered hull of a rowboat stuck in the sand, a fire of driftwood, a bottle of black wine, black beetles, the weird cry of seagulls lost in the fog, the sound of the tide creeping in over the wet sands, the tombstone in the eel-grass behind the dunes.
> Harry Crosby, 'The end of Europe', 1929

> These are, as you say, evil days. It is hard keep going in the face of them.
> James Laughlin to Eugene Jolas, 1940[1]

On an otherwise blank sheet, near the centre of an issue in the middle of *transition*'s run, Harry Crosby's single paragraph 'The end of Europe' appears in bold type. In four short lines the author stands his reader on the edge of the sea, facing out towards the new continent. Creatures accompany the scene. A gull and a beetle adorn the prose, as if blown upwards and over the Atlantic in the wind. Crosby conjures a now familiar, even worn-out image of Europe as the tombstone of a lost and celebratory era. More a trope than an announcement by the independently wealthy, quintessential expatriate Crosby, the image produces a convenient set of juxtapositions whorled around the continent-dividing sea. With its oppositional symmetry and hyperbolic tendencies, Crosby's prose might be more properly approached through particular narratives of masculinity at the end of the 1920s than through *transition*'s modernist practice.[2] Yet Crosby wrote with an extraordinary energy that often appears on the pages of *transition* as anticipating many of its emergent figurations. After the author's premature death by suicide at 31 years old, a mere five months after the publication of 'The end of Europe', many of his fellow authors produced obituaries and elegies, which were printed in the June 1930 issue.[3] Crosby himself had secretly been sending Jolas a regular $100 to judge the best poet in each number and furnish him or her with an informal award. Jolas reveals this to his readers, acknowledging Crosby's formative support as having boosted the journal, and the memorials are a significant marker of one of *transition*'s most treasured contributors.[4] But beyond his historical and biographical significance for the *transition* circle, Crosby's writing often spoke for the journal more broadly, especially in its recurrent use of primordial animal imagery. The gull and the beetle are two silent onlookers of the old language, a mode Crosby links explicitly to Jolas's Revolution of the Word.

Earlier in the same issue one finds another of Crosby's brief summative statements, around which yet more primordial creatures eddy. Inserted amid a run of lexicological texts (Stuart Gilbert's 'Thesaurus minusculus', which is a comment on Joyce, that other, weightier centre of *transition*; a dictionary of neologisms called 'Slanguage'; and Jolas's essay 'Logos', in which the editor's fascination with the origin of language is aligned to the primitive reptilian brain), Crosby's short text 'The New Word' stands out.[5] The register of victory and vanquished enemies is distracting, as Crosby plays at a particular kind of masculinity. He anticipates many other red-blooded male American writers: Henry Miller, perhaps, or Norman Mailer. But here, less than a season before the Wall Street Crash, Crosby's unabashed hope for the language of the future is distinctly primordial:

> The New Word is the serpent who has sloughed off his old vocabulary [. . .]
>
> The New Word is a direct stimulant upon the senses, a freshness of vision, an inner sensation, the egg from which other words shall be produced, a herald of revolt.[6]

If Jolas was the executive producer of *transition*, Crosby was one of its leading actors. In these lines the reader encounters the journal's vision for a reconfigured Word, but also an example of its fantastical and off-key pronouncements. The fact that the 'New Word' does not exist hardly matters. From the serpent to the egg, the creative impulse to articulate regeneration and futurity in language using the most basic animals reveals two things: the 'New Word' is the power of much of the writing in this journal, and it is also its blind spot. More than any other contributor, Crosby embodies this quality. 'He was a mystic of the sun-mythos', Jolas writes in his eulogy for Crosby. 'This was not a literary caprice on his part, his very being was involved in it, he felt the planetary concussions, the fire-god was primordial in his soul.'[7]

A mere counting of creatures would not do this quality justice; it would simply be a game of bird-spotting, or metaphor-by-numbers. The written animality one finds in *transition* may appear as a series of amoeboid shapes, fish, reptilian brains and birds, but beyond such constellations, the 'low' animal brings new connections to light. The first chapter of this book explored the creative impulse towards abstraction in translated Surrealist verse, and in prose from American contributors engaged with Surrealism. With its caution and deep ambivalence about the urge towards the 'protoplasmic whole', Dorothy Boillotat's prose in particular suggests a hitherto overlooked Surrealist influence upon this generation of writers. As much as the 'amoebic silhouette' reflects the legacy of the cultural imperialism of Barr's schematisation of modern art at MoMA – a legacy to which *transition* contributed – the amoeba offers a way through this mass of material.

The amoeba is not alone, of course: *transition* has innumerable instances of writing devoted to the 'ancient ocean' of Lautréamont's calling. One could focus on the shell metaphor in Stuart Gilbert's translation of Antonin Artaud's 'The shell and the clergyman' – an iridescent receptacle of dark black liquid, and a new exploration of the powers of cinematic horror – as another major context.[8] The reader could also turn to *transition* regular Hart Crane, and the tarantulas and crabs and other oceanic contours of his verse. In a piece on Gertrude Stein and 'The new barbarism', Laura Riding valued Crane's verse as a vibrant reaction to modernity. He 'preserv[es] his vision from a theme', she writes, because 'his vision is reacting romantically against contemporary classicism.'[9] Riding quotes from Crane's 'For the marriage of Faustus and Helen', with an image that speaks to *transition* just as strongly as Crosby's primordial 'fire-gods':

> O, I have known metallic paradises
> Where cuckoos clucked to finches
> Above the deft catastrophes of drums.
> While titters hailed the groans of death
> Beneath gyrating awnings I have seen
> The incunabula of the divine grotesque.
> This music has a reassuring way.[10]

'The incunabula of the divine grotesque': the line evokes the ephemerality of early modern periodicals, and the logical space of the animal. The primordial life form is both beyond and beneath our language, looking back at us from the distance of an aeon of evolution. If *transition* itself could be said to be a modern incunabulum of a 'divine grotesque', my second chapter approached this idea via James Joyce's fishy evolutionary language. The 'Work in progress' was an agenda-setting presence, and the slither of that world of a book explored here has received a necessarily partial discussion. Shem's degeneracy is inscribed during an era of neo-Lamarckian evolutionary thought, best understood as late traces of a philosophical idealism with which Joyce was evidently engaged. The reactions against Darwinian selection theory during the first few decades of the twentieth century have yet to be sufficiently registered in critical approaches to literary history, especially with regard to magazine culture, but the fish – and its stink – is a start. Genetic and historical work needs to be done, not only in relation to Joyce – whose lifespan coincided almost exactly with what historians of science refer to as the 'eclipse of Darwinism' and the 'modern synthesis' – but also among the cultures of literary production, science journalism and modernist periodicals: a discursive space shared with popular biology. Shem, staring down the barrel of the 'unknown quarreller' with his 'purpose pattern', is a figure of the primordial animal that helps us navigate *transition*'s modernist culture. Again, Crosby's words ring true. At the end of 'The New Word' the voice calls up the importance of 'a Joyce', in 'defiance of the ages'.[11]

Gottfried Benn's quasi-scientific, totalised image of the reptilian 'small brain' is an awkward centre of gravity in *transition*, the 'darkness' of which formed the subject of the third chapter. By focusing on symbolic lizards and the magazine's many 'pineal eyes', the reader can better understand two important and interrelated lines of analysis. Benn's proto-fascist aesthetics and his idea of primal unity moved through the same prehistoric, reptilian and evolutionary imagery as did Jolas's fantastical notion of 'the man with the pineal eye'. The crucial difference between the two is that far from supporting the emergent ideology of right-wing nationalism, Jolas was simply unaware of or unwilling to accept the urgency with which artists needed to recognise the political landscape of 1930s Europe. His failure to grasp the implications of some of the material he was so keen to publish is, in the end, the limit point of his apolitical 'vertigralist' vision. As I hope to have shown, this was not restricted to Jolas. Henry Miller, William Carlos Williams and others were similarly drawn to the aura of 'the ganglia', to the visceral corporeality of the brain, and to the primordial animal metaphor in a variety of guises as part of a dubious strain of 1930s primitivist holism.

Much as Joyce's primitive fish is a site of textual proliferation, so Jolas's translated totemic birds offer an illuminative primordial animal in relation to *transition*'s modernist practice. It is too easy to read Jolas as simply rehearsing an older, principally Germanic romanticism in his creative and critical work, even if he saw modern writing as an 'offshoot' of that earlier formation.[12] The assuredness of Jolas's more robust manifesto and editorial content certainly suggests this. But, as the final chapter of this book indicates, when one reads the content of each issue as it was arranged, any such assurance disappears. Jolas's birds are linguistic components that offer a transporting gesture, and yet also stand in place of the imagined substance of the desired reconfiguration of the Word. From the bemused and cursory reception of the journal in early 1930s America to the invested francophone readings exemplified by Pelorson's elegiac (though troubling) appreciation, Jolas's editorial 'flights', like much of his work, are earnest literalisations of so many animal symbols of transcendence, so many birds as they flock from his mind, as André Masson perfectly captured in *Portrait d'Eugene Jolas* (1942) (see Figure 4.1 above). With *transition*'s final issues, we also see a distinctly American group of writers whose emblematic birds speak more to an exhausted or irrevocably broken symbolic framework. With the outbreak of war, even Jolas had to abandon his project, and after 1945 he set about the altogether more sobering work of the denazification of the German press – further celebration of which would greatly enrich the scholarly field.

Transition has an important connection to post-war American writing. The role of Jolas's imprimatur among the publishers and organisers of literary retrospectives in the 1940s is also in need of further study. James Johnson Sweeney, Frances Steloff and Davis Moss of the Gotham Book Mart, and James Laughlin of New Directions were all closely involved with the project, as readers, distributors, co-contributors and unofficial co-editors. Given the gaps in the Jolas papers, one should go to these archives in search of materials that might open up a substantiated 'bridge', not just between two continents as Jolas conceived it, but between two moments of literary production divided by the Second World War. The very first book that Laughlin produced – a 1936 collection of verse with a print run of 700 – featured a dedication to Jolas and his fellow *transition* editors, describing *transition* as 'the great international magazine' whose participants 'have begun successfully The Revolution of the Word'.[13] Such epithets sometimes tended to the animal, too, albeit in a jocular manner. Writing for *Twentieth Century Verse* in summer 1939, mere months before the war, George Barker offered some rather double-edged praise for Jolas's project in a statement that gestured towards its more esoteric elements: 'unless any poetry narrates it ceases to be poetry and becomes crossword puzzling such as [. . .] the school of abracadabra porpoises who ornament the alas discontinued course of the good ship Transition'.[14]

Similar lines of connection should be drawn between 'the good ship' *transition* and American novelists. Henry Miller's 'intoxication' with *transition* is but one example of the manner in which the magazine took on a fashionable status for avid readers and bibliophiles. Some post-1945 authors were compelled to mock it with faint nostalgia. Saul Bellow's *Humboldt's Gift* makes implicit mention of *transition*, for instance. Early on in the 1975 novel, Bellow's protagonist, the young Charlie Citrine, recounts how the older poet Von Humboldt Fleischer (a nod to Bellow's friend Delmore Schwartz) would break into reveries about Joyce:

> He had been on a *Finnegans Wake* kick for years. I remembered our many discussions of Joyce's view of language, of the poet's passion for charging speech with music and meaning, of the dangers that hover about

all the works of the mind, of beauty falling into abysses of oblivion like snow chasms of the Antarctic, of Blake and Vision versus Locke and the tabula rasa. As I saw the cops out I was remembering with sadness of heart the lovely conversations Humboldt and I used to have. Humanity divine incomprehensible!'[15]

In the announcement of poetic purpose, Jolas's presence here is strong. One wonders if the intertwined nature of the *Wake*, the 'Work in progress' and *transition* may have melded in Bellow's memory. The rhapsodic lines are tinged with the sadness of that lost belief in 'Vision' with a capital 'V', evocative of Blake's 'Damn braces! Bless relaxes!', which adorned *transition*'s most famous manifesto 'Proclamation'. Bellow's Citrine remembers Humboldt's Schwartz, but somewhere in the lineage lies an issue of *transition*. Easy prey to gentle mockery, perhaps, *transition* was one of the last formations of literary modernism to contain a genuine belief in the transformative power of language. If the magazine does mark the 'end of the happy avant-garde', as Rabaté puts it, its manifestations in post-war fiction might speak to a different kind of humour, a different kind of engagement with the idea of modernist experimentation.

In William Gaddis's 1955 novel *The Recognitions*, for example, such an impression of the magazine congeals into a signifier of little more than fashion and pretension itself, here on the stagey 'set' of a Montparnasse café:

> On the terrace of the Dome sat a person who looked like the young George Washington without his wig (at about the time he dared the Ohio country). She read, with silently moving lips, from a book before her. She was drinking a bilious-colored liquid from a globular goblet; and every twenty or so pages would call to the waiter, in perfect French, – Un Ricard . . . , and add one to the pile of one-franc saucers before her. – Voilà ma propre Sainte Chapelle, she would have said of that rising tower (the sentence prepared in her mind) if anyone had encouraged conversation by sitting down at her table. No one did. She read on. Anyone could have seen it was *transition* she was reading, if any had looked. None did. Finally an unshaven youth bowed slightly, as with pain, murmured something in American, and paused with a dirty hand on the back of a chair at her table. – J'vous en prie, she said, lucid, lowering *transition*, waiting for him to sit down before she went on. – Mursi, he muttered, and dragged the chair to another table.
>
> 'Paris lay by like a promise accomplished: age had not withered her, nor custom staled her infinite vulgarity.'[16]

Gaddis's physical copy of *transition* is an exacting form of satire. Later in the chapter, the sounds of 1920s Parisian tourism jangle with 'these transatlantic [American] visitors' who 'had learned to admire in this neatly parceled definition of civilization the tyrannous pretension of many founded upon the rebellious efforts of a few'.[17] The girl adopts the pose of a 'scene', for an absent audience. Gaddis chooses *transition* for her hands rather than any other little magazine because it best encapsulates that strange relationship between past and present, between the idea of a movement or moment of artistic creation and the inevitable staleness that results from such a goal.

A similar sense of the bygone avant-garde was perhaps on Lorine Niedecker's mind when she wrote her short (and first published) poem 'Transition'. Niedecker discovered the magazine via Louis Zukofsky and was drawn to its Surrealist works. The poem seems keenly aware of the magazine's various 'proclamations' of 'big change', and it invites comparison. In full:

> Colours of October
> wait with easy dignity
> for the big change –
> like gorgeous quill-pens
> in old inkwells
> almost dry.[18]

The autumnal fronds of a plush quill likened to fading autumn evinces an Imagist's economy of language. Is it possible that 'Transition' also refers to the magazine that failed to support her – an 'old inkwe[l] | almost dry'? Niedecker, after all, is curiously absent from *transition*. Jolas missed an opportunity to nurture her talent by omitting her submissions, but he included Zukofsky and other Objectivist poets.[19] Like Gaddis, Niedecker's text conveys an important quality in the history of *transition*. As with the primordial creature that reaches far back into the prehistoric, pre-human world as part of a modernist expression of the Word, this anachronistic quality is another legacy. Its animal part reveals many configurations that open up this quality – not as a reason to exclude *transition* from early twentieth-century Anglo-European literary history, but as a reason to reread it because of its strangeness. The primordial is merely one approach, but it speaks to an underlying pull in many of the magazine's writers towards logical extremes, binaries of culture that point to the constructedness of language and meaning. In the end, the primordial is another version of an old romantic ideal, refashioned in the garments of the new: the microscopic amoeba, the criminological language of degeneracy, the seductive pull of the endocrinological brain or the thinly veiled desire for religious experience. *Transition*'s primordial creatures mobilise a reading of the magazine on its own terms – in a language which is not artificial, as Jolas himself would later write, 'but one that has its roots in organic life itself'.[20] And finally, there is Eugene Jolas. It was the editor's energy that made *transition* such an important part of modernist culture. His commitment – his unfaltering faith in the power of the Word, however 'unmodernist' this might have been – was the essential ingredient, detectable as early as the dream of the scorpion with which I began. As his great friend Leon Edel wrote to Maria after Jolas's premature death in 1952, he was a force of nature. 'I remember how exciting it was in the old days, long ago, to see each successive issue of *transition*, and how one felt in it the pulse of life and vitality – it *was* Gene's pulse and Gene's vitality.'[21]

Notes

1. James Laughlin, postcard to Jolas, 5 June 1940. Box 3, Folder 47, Maria and Eugene Jolas Papers, Beinecke Rare Books and Manuscripts Library, Yale University. Subsequent references to this archive will be indicated by the Box and Folder numbers followed by an indication of the collection as the Jolas Papers.
2. See Crosby's 'Hail: death!', 170 and 'Suite', 21–4. For a complete list of Crosby's contributions to *transition*, see Silet, *transition*, 34–6.
3. Boyle, 'Homage'; Crane, 'Cloud juggler'; Gilbert, 'Harry Crosby'; Jolas, 'Harry Crosby'; MacLeish, 'Cinema'; Soupault, 'Harry Crosby'.
4. Jolas, 'Harry Crosby', 228.
5. Gilbert, 'Thesaurus minusculus'; Irwin, 'Slanguage', 32–4 (first published in *New York World*); Jolas, 'Logos'.
6. Crosby, 'New Word'.
7. Jolas, 'Harry Crosby', 229.
8. Artaud, 'Shell'.
9. Riding, 'New barbarism', 167.
10. Crane, 'For the marriage of Faustus and Helen', in *Collected Poems*, 97. Quoted in Riding, 'New barbarism', 168.
11. Crosby, 'New Word', 20.
12. Rabaté, '*Eugene Jolas*', 455.
13. Laughlin, *New Directions*, iii.
14. Barker, 'Note', 48.
15. Bellow, *Humboldt's Gift*, 52.
16. Gaddis, *Recognitions*, 63. Céline Mansanti was the first to make this connection. See her *La revue transition*, 303.
17. Gaddis, *Recognitions*, 65.
18. Niedecker, 'Transition', in *Collected Works*, 23.
19. According to Jenny Petherby, Jolas rejected some of Niedecker's submissions. Petherby, *Lorine Niedecker*, 17–27, 111 n.22. Many of the Objectivist poets gathered in the famous *Poetry* special issue (37:5, February 1931) had been published previously in *transition*. See C. H. Ford, 'Somewhat Monday' and 'Digressive announcements'; Rakosi, 'Dolce padre' and 'Founding'; Norman Macleod, 'Dreams'; Tyler, 'Elegy'; Richard Johns, 'Preparation'; W. C. Williams, 'Dead baby' and 'Winter'; Zukofsky, 'Untitled'.
20. Jolas, *Man from Babel*, 272.
21. Leon Edel, letter to M. Jolas, 30 May 1952, emphasis original. Box 30, Folder 584, Jolas Papers.

BIBLIOGRAPHY

Ackerley, Chris, 'Fatigue and disgust: the addenda to *Watt*', in Marius Buning and Lois Oppenheim (eds), *Beckett in the 1990s: Selected Papers from the Second International Beckett Symposium Held in The Hague, 8–12 April 1992* (Amsterdam and Atlanta: Rodopi, 1993), 175–88.
Adams, Raymond Delacy, and Webb Haymaker, *Histology and Histopathology of the Nervous System*, 2 vols (Springfield, IL: Thomas, 1982).
Adler, Vera Stadley, *The Findings of the Third Eye* (London: Rider, 1937).
Agamben, Giorgio, *The Open: Man and Animal* (Stanford: Stanford University Press, 2004).
Ahearn, Barry (ed.), *The Correspondence of William Carlos Williams and Louis Zukofsky* (Middletown: Wesleyan University Press, 2003).
Allbutt, Thomas Clifford (ed.), *A System of Medicine, by Many Writers*, 8 vols (London: Macmillan, 1896–9).
Anderson, Christiann, 'Henry Miller: born to be wild', *Bonjour Paris*, March 2004, at www.bonjourparis.com/story/henry-miller-born-to-be-wild/ (last accessed 9 July 2018).
Anonymous, 'Scribner publications', *The Dial*, LXV:773 (19 September 1918): 185.
Anonymous, 'Briefer mention', *The Dial*, LXXXVI:1 (January 1929): 525.
Anonymous, 'L'actualité littéraire à l'étranger', *Les nouvelles littéraires*, 2 July 1932, 5.

Anonymous, '*Transition* and its contemporaries', *transition*, 23 (July 1935): 202–5.

Anonymous, 'Review, *transition* 26', *New York Herald*, 28 June 1937, n. p.

Anonymous, *The Fish in Twentieth Century Art*, exhibition catalogue (London: Delance and Rowsey, 1953).

Antliff, Mark, *Inventing Bergson: Cultural Politics and the Parisian Avant-Garde* (Princeton: Princeton University Press, 1993).

Apollinaire, Guillaume, *Alcools*, 2nd edn, ed. and trans. Anne Hyde Greet (Berkeley and Los Angeles: University of California Press, 1974).

Ardis, Ann L., and Patrick Collier (eds), *Transatlantic Print Culture, 1880–1940: Emerging Media, Emerging Modernisms* (New York: Palgrave Macmillan, 2008).

Armstrong, Philip, *What Animals Mean in the Fiction of Modernity* (London: Routledge, 2008).

Armstrong, Tim, *Modernism: A Cultural History* (Cambridge and Malden, MA: Polity, 2005).

Armstrong, Tim, 'Biological tropes in interwar poetry', in John Holmes (ed.), *Science in Modern Poetry: New Directions* (Liverpool: Liverpool University Press, 2012), 101–15.

Arp, Hans, 'Arping', *transition*, 6 (September 1927): 113–14.

Arp, Hans, 'The light-shunning paradise (fragment)', *transition*, 7 (October 1927): 130–1.

Arp, Hans, 'Das Tages Gerippe', *transition*, 21 (March 1932): 150–2.

Arp, Hans, 'The skeleton of the day', *transition*, 26 (1937): 9–12.

Arp, Hans, Samuel Beckett, Carl Einstein, Eugene Jolas, Thomas McGreevy, Georges Pelorson, Theo Rutra, James J. Sweeney and Ronald Symond, 'Poetry is vertical', *transition*, 21 (March 1932): 148–9.

Artaud, Antonin, 'The shell and the clergyman: film scenario', trans. Stuart Gilbert, *transition*, 19/20 (June 1930): 63–9.

Auster, Paul (ed.), *The Random House Book of Twentieth Century French Poetry* (New York: Random House, 1982).

Ayo, Denise A., 'Mary Colum, modernism, and mass media: an Irish-inflected transatlantic print culture', *Journal of Modern Literature*, 35:4 (2012): 107–29.

B. K. H., 'The sideshow', *Providence, RI Journal*, 18 July 1935, n. p.

Baader, Franz von, *Schriften* (Leipzig: InselVerlag, 1921).

Bachelard, Gaston, *L'air et les songes: essai sur l'imagination du movement* (Paris: J. Corti, 1943).

Baker, Steve, *The Postmodern Animal* (London: Reaktion, 2000).

Balakian, Anna, *Surrealism: The Road to the Absolute* (London: University of Chicago Press, 1986).

Barkan, Elazar, and Ronald Bush (eds), *Prehistories of the Future: The Primitivist Project and the Culture of Modernism* (Stanford: Stanford University Press, 1995).
Barker, George, 'A note on narrative poetry', *Twentieth Century Verse*, 18 (June/July 1939: 48–9.
Barnett, Vivian Endicott, 'Kandinsky and science: the introduction of biological images in the Paris period', in Oliver A. I. Botar and Isabel Wünsche (eds), *Biocentrism and Modernism* (Farnham and Burlington, VT: Ashgate, 2011), 207–26.
Baron, Scarlett, 'Joyce, Darwin and literary evolution', in John Nash (ed.), *James Joyce and the Nineteenth Century* (New York: Cambridge University Press, 2013), 183–99.
Barr, Alfred H. Jnr, 'The LEF and Soviet art', *transition*, 14, (autumn 1928): 267–70.
Barr, Alfred H. Jnr, *Cubism and Abstract Art* (New York: Museum of Modern Art, 1936).
Barrell, Joseph, 'The influence of Silurian-Devonian climates on the rise of air-breathing vertebrates', *PNAS: Proceedings of the National Academy of Sciences of the United States*, 2 (1916): 499–504.
Bataille, Georges, 'The psychological structure of fascism', *La critique sociale*, 10 (November 1933): 159–65.
Bataille, Georges, *Prehistoric Painting: Lascaux, or, the Birth of Art*, trans. Austryn Wainhouse (Geneva: Skira, 1955).
Bataille, Georges, *Oeuvres complètes*, 2 vols (Paris: Gallimard, 1970).
Bataille, Georges, *Visions of Excess: Selected Writings, 1927–1939*, ed. and trans. Allan Stoekl (Minneapolis: University of Minnesota Press, 1985).
Bataille, Georges, *Story of the Eye, by Lord Auch*, 2nd edn, trans. Joachim Neugroschel (Harmondsworth: Penguin, 2001).
Beard, J., 'The parietal eye in fishes', *Nature*, 36 (1887): 246–8.
Beckett, Samuel, 'Dante ... Bruno. Vico ... Joyce', *transition*, 16/17 (June 1929): 242–53.
Beckett, Samuel, 'Dante ... Bruno. Vico ... Joyce', in Sylvia Beach (ed.), *Our Exagmination Round His Factification for Incamination of Work in Progress* (Paris: Shakespeare and Co., 1929), 3–22.
Beckett, Samuel, *The Theatrical Notebooks of Samuel Beckett*, ed. Dougald McMillan and James Knowlson (New York: Grove Press, 1994).
Beechold, Henry F., 'Finn MacCool and *Finnegans Wake*', *James Joyce Review*, 2 (1958): 3–12.
Begin, Paul, 'Entomology as anthropology in the films of Luis Buñuel', *Screen*, 48:4 (2007): 425–42.
Béguin, Albert, *L'âme romantique et le rêve* (Marseille: Cahiers du Sud, 1937).

Béguin, Albert, 'The night side of life', trans. Eugene Jolas and Stuart Gilbert, *transition*, 27 (April–May 1938): 197–218.
Bellow, Saul, *Humboldt's Gift*, rev. edn (New York: Penguin, 2008).
Benefiel, Andrea, and Molly Wheeler, *Guide to the Walter Lowenfels Papers, YCAL MSS 367* (New Haven, CT: Beinecke Rare Book and Manuscript Library, Yale University Library, 2010).
Benn, Gottfried, 'Gesänge', *Die Aktion*, 3:13 (March 1913): 269.
Benn, Gottfried, *Gehirne: Novellen* (Leipzig: K. Wolff, 1916).
Benn, Gottfried, 'The island', trans. Eugene Jolas, *transition*, 2 (May 1927): 64–73.
Benn, Gottfried, 'The birthday', trans. Eugene Jolas, *transition*, 5 (August 1927): 32–44.
Benn, Gottfried, 'Primal vision', trans. Malcolm Campbell, *transition*, 16/17 (June 1929): 302–9.
Benn, Gottfried, 'Der Aufbau der Persönlichkeit', *Die neue Rundschau*, 41:11 (1930): 693–705.
Benn, Gottfried, 'The structure of the personality (outline of the geology of the "I")', trans. Eugene Jolas, *transition*, 21 (March 1932): 195–205.
Benn, Gottfried, *Primal Vision: Selected Writings of Gottfried Benn*, ed. E. B. Ashton (London: Boyars, 1976).
Benn, Gottfried, *Impromptus: Selected Poems and Some Prose*, ed. and trans. Michael Hofmann (New York: Farrar, Straus and Giroux, 2013).
Benn, Gottfried, *Selected Poems and Prose*, ed. and trans. David Paisley (Manchester: Carcanet, 2013).
Benn, Gottfried, Eugene Jolas, Joë Bousquet, Marcel Brion, Henry S. Canby, Malcolm Cowley, Luc Durtain, Norman Foerster, Ivan Goll, Philippe Lamour, H. L. Mencken, Francis de Miomandre, Emanuel Mounier, Gorham Munson, C. K. Ogden, A. R. Orage, P. D. Ouspensky, Georges Pelorson, Armand Petitjean, Léon Pierre-Quint, Raja Rao, Theo Rutra, Jack Sanford, Camille Schuwer, Louis Untermeyer, Laurence Vail and Edmond Vandercammen, 'Inquiry about the malady of language', *transition*, 23 (July 1935): 144–74.
Bennett, David, 'Periodical fragments and organic culture: modernism, the avant-garde, and *The Little Magazine*', *Contemporary Literature*, 30:4 (1989): 480–502.
Bennett, Wendell, transcriber, 'A visit to the witch of darkness', *transition*, 26 (1937): 187–90.
Bernstein, Charles, 'Disfiguring abstraction', *Critical Inquiry*, 39:3 (2013): 486–97.
Blavatsky, H. P., *The Secret Doctrine: The Synthesis of Science, Religion, and Philosophy* (London: Theosophical Publishing Company, 1887–8).
Blinder, Caroline, *A Self-Made Surrealist: Ideology and Aesthetics in the Works of Henry Miller* (Columbia, SC: Random House, 2006).

Bodkin, Maud, *Archetypal Patterns in Poetry: Psychological Studies of Imagination* (London: Oxford University Press, 1934).
Boillotat, Dorothy, 'Escapes', *transition*, 18 (November 1929): 29–31.
Boillotat, Dorothy, 'Decaying', *transition*, 19/20 (June 1930): 48–52.
Boillotat, Dorothy, 'Heritage', *transition*, 21 (March 1932): 21–6.
Boillotat, Dorothy, 'Sensing', *transition*, 23 (July 1935): 11–15.
Boillotat, Dorothy, 'Dream of the end of time', *transition*, 27 (April–May 1938): 153–6.
Botar, Oliver A. I., 'Defining biocentrism', in Oliver A. I. Botar and Isabel Wünsche (eds), *Biocentrism and Modernism* (Farnham and Burlington, VT: Ashgate, 2011), 15–45.
Bousquet, Joë, 'Reine de mon silence', *transition*, 21 (March 1932): 153–6.
Bowers, Paul, '"Variability in every tongue": Joyce and the Darwinian narrative', *James Joyce Quarterly*, 36:4 (1999): 869–88.
Bowler, Peter J., *The Eclipse of Darwinism: Anti-Darwinian Evolution Theories in the Decades around 1900* (Baltimore: Johns Hopkins University Press, 1983).
Bowler, Peter J., 'Fins and limbs and fins into limbs: the historical context, 1840–1940', in Brian Keith Hall (ed.), *Fins into Limbs: Evolution, Development, and Transformation* (Chicago and London: University of Chicago Press, 2007), 7–14.
Bowler, Peter J., *Evolution: The History of an Idea*, 25th anniversary edn (Berkeley and London: University of California Press, 2009).
Bowles, Paul, 'Entity', *transition*, 13 (summer 1928): 219–20.
Boyle, Kay, 'Homage to Harry Crosby', *transition*, 19/20 (June 1930): 221–2.
Boyle, Kay, 'Glad day for L. V.', *transition*, 21 (March 1932): 157–8.
Boyle, Kay, *Death of a Man* (New York: Harcourt, Brace and Co., 1936).
Boyle, Kay, 'Your love song', *transition*, 27 (April–May 1938): 39–40.
Boyle, Kay, and Robert McAlmon, *Being Geniuses Together: An Autobiography* (London: Secker & Warburg, 1938).
Boyle, Robert H., '*Finnegans Wake*, page 185: an explication', *James Joyce Quarterly*, 4 (1966): 3–16.
Boyle, Robert H., 'You spigotty anglease?', *New York Times*, 23 July 2000, at www.nytimes.com/books/00/07/23/bookend/bookend.html?_r=1 (last accessed 9 July 2018).
Bracques, Georges, Eugene Jolas, Maria Jolas, Henri Matisse, André Salmon and Tristan Tzara, *Testimony Against Gertrude Stein* (The Hague: Servire Press, 1935).
Brennan, Marcia, 'The multiple masculinities of canonical modernism: James Johnson Sweeney and Alfred H. Barr Jr in the 1930s', in Anna Brzyski (ed.), *Partisan Canons* (Durham, NC: Duke University Press, 2007), 179–202.

Breton, André, 'Introduction au discours sur le peu de réalité', *Commerce*, 3 (winter 1924): 27–57.
Breton, André, *Introduction au discours sur le peu de réalité* (Paris: Gallimard, 1927).
Breton, André, 'Introduction to the discourse on the dearth of reality', trans. Eugene Jolas, *transition*, 5 (August 1927): 128–45.
Breton, André, *Nadja* (Paris: Gallimard, 1928).
Breton, André, '*Nadja* (opening chapter)', trans. Eugene Jolas, *transition*, 12 (March 1928): 28–50.
Breton, André, *Manifestoes of Surrealism*, trans. Richard Seaver and Helen R. Lane (Ann Arbor: University of Michigan Press, 1969).
Brooker, Peter, and Andrew Thacker (eds), *The Oxford Critical and Cultural History of Modernist Magazines*, 3 vols (Oxford: Oxford University Press, 2009–13).
Bryher, 'Different focus', *transition*, 3 (June 1927): 132–3.
Buren, Elizabeth Douglas Van, 'Fish offerings in ancient Mesopotamia', *Iraq*, 10 (1948): 101–21.
Burnett, Whit, 'Balls, or simple error', *transition*, 14 (autumn 1928): 121–5.
Burnett, Whit, 'Balkan journey', *transition*, 21 (March 1932): 37–41.
Burwick, Frederick, and Paul Douglass (eds), *The Crisis in Modernism: Bergson and the Vitalist Controversy* (New York: Cambridge University Press, 1992).
Caillois, Roger, 'Le Surréalisme comme univers de signes', in *Obliques* (Paris: Stock, 1975), 238–47.
Caillois, Roger, *The Edge of Surrealism: A Roger Caillois Reader*, ed. Claudine Frank with translations by Camille Naish (Durham, NC: Duke University Press, 2003).
Cain, Victoria, 'The art of authority: exhibits, exhibit-makers, and the contest for scientific status in the American Museum of Natural History, 1920–1940', *Science in Context*, 24:2 (2011): 215–38.
Calarco, Matthew, *Zoographies: The Question of the Animal from Heidegger to Derrida* (New York: Columbia University Press, 2008).
Cardinal, Roger, 'Tzara, Tristan', in Justin Wintle (ed.), *Makers of Modern Culture* (London: Routledge, 2002), 530.
Chenieux-Gendron, Jacqueline, 'The poetics of bricolage: André Breton's theoretical fables', trans. Georgiana M. M. Colvile, in Russell King and Bernard McGuirk (eds), *Reconceptions: Reading Modern French Poetry* (Nottingham: University of Nottingham, 1996), 65–80.
Cheung, Joyce, 'Mask, mimicry, metamorphosis: Roger Caillois, Walter Benjamin and Surrealism in the 1930s', *Modernism/Modernity*, 16:1 (2008): 61–86.
Childs, Donald J., *Modernism and Eugenics: Woolf, Eliot, Yeats, and the Culture of Degeneration* (Cambridge: Cambridge University Press, 2001).

Churchill, Suzanne W., and Adam McKible, *Little Magazines & Modernism: New Approaches* (Aldershot: Ashgate, 2007).
Colbert, Edwin H., 'William King Gregory, 1876–1970: a biographical memoir', *National Academy of Sciences*, 46 (1975): 90–133.
Cole, Lori, '"What is the avant-garde?" Questionnaires as communities in print' (unpublished doctoral thesis, New York University, 2012).
Coleman, Emily Holmes, 'The shepherd's vision' and 'The vision', *transition*, 21 (March 1932): 159–62.
Collier, Patrick, 'What is modern periodical studies?', *Journal of Modern Periodical Studies*, 6:2 (2015): 92–111.
Colum, Mary, 'Life and literature: the old and the new', *Forum and Century*, 102:4 (October 1939): 158–63.
Colum, Mary, *From These Roots: The Ideas That Have Made Modern Literature* (London and New York: Scribner's, 1937).
Colum, Mary, and Padraic Colum, *Our Friend James Joyce* (New York: Doubleday, 1958).
Connor, Steven, 'Thinking perhaps begins there: the question of the animal', *Textual Practice*, 21 (2007): 577–84.
Cope, Edward Drinker, 'The pineal eye in extinct vertebrates', *American Naturalist*, 22 (October 1888): 914–17.
Crane, Hart, 'To the cloud juggler – in memoriam: Harry Crosby', *transition*, 19/20 (June 1930): 223.
Crane, Hart, *The Collected Poems of Hart Crane* (New York: Liveright, 1946).
Crosby, Harry, 'Hail: death!', *transition*, 14 (autumn 1928): 169–70.
Crosby, Harry, 'Suite', *transition*, 15 (February 1929): 19–24.
Crosby, Harry, 'The New Word', *transition*, 16/17 (June 1929): 30.
Crosby, Harry, 'The end of Europe', *transition*, 16/17 (June 1929): 119.
Cumpiano, Marion W., 'The salmon and its leaps in *Finnegans Wake*', *James Joyce Quarterly*, 14 (1977): 255–73.
Cunningham, Valentine, *British Writers of the Thirties* (New York and Oxford: Oxford University Press, 1988).
Cuomo, Glenn R., 'Purging an "art-bolshevist": the persecution of Gottfried Benn in the years 1933–1938', *German Studies Review*, 9:1 (1986): 85–105.
Cushing, Harvey Williams, 'Partial hypophysectomy for acromegaly, with remarks on the function of the hypophysis', *Annals of Surgery*, 50 (1909): 1002–17.
Dacqué, Edgar, *Natur und Seele: Ein Beitrag zur Magischen Weltlehre* (Berlin: R. Oldenbourg, 1928).
Davies, Hugh Sykes, 'Biology and Surrealism', *International Bulletin of Surrealism*, 4 (September 1936): 13–15.

Deissler, Dirk, 'Introduction' to 'Part eight: across frontiers', in Klaus H. Kiefer and Rainer Rumold (eds), *Eugene Jolas: Critical Writings, 1924–1951* (Evanston: Northwestern University Press, 2009), 465–6.
Deleuze, Gilles, *Spinoza: Philosophie pratique* (Paris: Minuit, 1981).
Deleuze, Gilles, and Félix Guattari, *A Thousand Plateaus: Capitalism and Schizophrenia*, trans. Brian Massumi (London: Continuum, 2004).
Derrida, Jacques, 'The animal that therefore I am (more to follow)', trans. David Wills, *Critical Inquiry*, 28 (2002): 369–418.
Derrida, Jacques, 'And say the animal responded?', trans. David Wills, in Cary Wolfe (ed.), *Zoontologies: The Question of the Animal* (Minneapolis: University of Minnesota Press, 2003), 121–46.
Descartes, René, *Treatise of Man*, trans. Thomas Steele Hall (Cambridge, MA: Harvard University Press, 1972).
Descartes, René, *Selected Philosophical Writings*, ed. and trans. John Cottingham, Robert Stoothoff and Dugald Murdoch (Cambridge, New York and Melbourne: Cambridge University Press, 1988).
Desnos, Robert, 'The dove of the ark', trans. Eugene Jolas, *transition*, 1 (April 1927): 103.
Desnos, Robert, *La liberté ou l'amour!* (Paris: Simon Kra aux Éditions du Sagittaire, 1927).
Desnos, Robert, 'Liberty or love', trans. Elliot Paul, *transition*, 6 (September 1927): 107–12.
Desnos, Robert, 'The work of Man Ray', trans. Maria Jolas, *transition*, 15 (February 1929): 264–6.
Desoille, R., *Le rêve éveillé en psychothérapie: essai sur la fonction de régulation de l'inconscient collectif* (Paris: Presses Universitaires de France, 1943).
Deutsch, Babette, 'The pilot's confusion', *New York Herald Tribune*, 15 March 1942, n. p.
Donnelly, Dorothy, *The Golden Well: An Anatomy of Symbols* (London: Sheen and Ward, 1950).
Dugès, Antoine, 'Espèces indigènes du genre Lacerta,' *Annales des sciences naturelles*, 16 (1828): 337.
Eakin, Richard Marshall, *The Third Eye* (Berkeley: University of California Press, 1973).
Eco, Umberto, *The Aesthetics of Chaosmos* (Cambridge, MA: Harvard University Press, 1989).
Einstein, Carl, *Bebuquin oder Dilettanten des Wunders: Ein Roman* (Berlin: Die Aktion, 1912).
Einstein, Carl, 'Bebuquin', *transition*, 16/17 (June 1929): 298–301.
Eliot, T. S., 'Periodicals: English', *The Criterion*, 18:71 (January 1939): 395–400.
Éluard, Paul, *Les dessous d'une vie ou la pyramide humaine* (Marseille: Cahiers du Sud, 1926).

Éluard, Paul, 'Georges Braque', trans. Eugene Jolas, *transition*, 2 (May 1927): 116.
Éluard, Paul, 'In company (Surrealist text)', trans. Eugene Jolas, *transition*, 2 (May 1927): 112–13.
English, Daylanne K., *Unnatural Selections: Eugenics in American Modernism and the Harlem Renaissance* (Chapel Hill, NC and London: University of North Carolina Press, 2004).
Engstrom, Eric J., Matthias W. Weber, and Wolfgang Burgmair, 'Emil Wilhelm Magnus Georg Kraeplin, 1856—1926', *American Journal of Psychiatry*, 163:10 (October 2006): 1710.
Ernst, Max, *Une semaine de bonté: los collages originales* (Madrid: Fundacíon Mapfre, [1929] 2009).
Ernst, Max, *La femme 100 têtes/The Hundred Headless Woman*, trans. Dorothea Tanning (New York: Brazilier, [1929–30] 1981).
Ernst, Max, *Rêve d'une petite fille qui voulut entrer au carmel/A Little Girl Dreams of Taking the Veil*, trans. Dorothea Tanning (New York: Brazilier, [1930] 1982).
Fargue, Léon-Paul, 'Aeternae memorie patris', trans. Eugene Jolas, *transition*, 2 (May 1927): 149–50.
Fargue, Léon-Paul, 'Tumult', trans. Maria Jolas, *transition*, 11 (February 1928): 59–62.
Fargue, Léon-Paul, 'The drug', trans. Maria Jolas, *transition*, 8 (November 1928): 59–62.
Fargue, Léon-Paul, 'Plus je vais, et plus je vis . . .', *transition*, 16/17 (June 1929): 14.
Fargue, Léon-Paul, 'Exile', trans. Édouard Roditi, *transition*, 18 (November 1929): 106–8.
Fargue, Léon-Paul, 'The alchemist', trans. Eugene Jolas, *transition*, 23 (July 1935): 130–2.
Faÿ, Bernard, 'Travel and flight', trans. Maria Jolas, *transition*, 11 (February 1928): 141–50.
Faÿ, Bernard, 'Essay on poetry', trans. Maria Jolas, *transition*, 19/20 (June 1930): 241–7.
Ferber, Michael, *Romanticism: A Very Short Introduction* (Oxford: Oxford University Press, 2010).
Finney, Michael, 'Eugene Jolas, *transition*, and the Revolution of the Word', in David Hayman and Elliot Anderson (eds), *In the Wake of the Wake* (Madison: University of Wisconsin Press, 1978), 39–53.
Ford, Charles Henri, 'Somewhat Monday', *transition*, 18 (November 1929): 108.
Ford, Charles Henri, 'Digressive announcements of spring', *transition*, 19/20 (June 1930): 362.

Ford, Charles Henri, 'Spring', *transition*, 21 (March 1932): 163.
Ford, Hugh, 'Foreword', in Charles L. P. Silet, *transition: An Author Index* (New York: Whitston, 1980), vii–x.
Fordham, Finn, *Lots of Fun at Finnegans Wake: Unravelling Universals* (Oxford and New York: Oxford University Press, 2007).
Foster, Hal, *Compulsive Beauty* (Cambridge, MA: MIT Press, 1993).
Foster, Hal, 'At MoMA', *London Review of Books*, 35:2 (7 February 2013): 14–15.
Fox, Stephen A., 'The fish pond as symbolic center in *Between the Acts*', *Modern Fiction Studies*, 18 (1972): 467–73.
Frank, Joseph, *Responses to Modernity: Essays in the Politics of Culture* (New York: Fordham University Press, 2012).
Frisch, Karl Von, 'Beiträge zur Physiologie der Pigmentzellen in der Fischhaut', *Pflügers Archiv: European Journal of Physiology*, 138 (1911): 319–87.
Frost, Robert, *The Poems of Robert Frost* (New York: Random House, 1946).
Fry, Iris, *The Emergence of Life on Earth: A Historical and Scientific Overview* (New Brunswick, NJ: Rutgers University Press, 2000).
Fry, Iris, 'The origins of research into the origins of life', *Endeavour*, 30:1 (2006): 25–8.
Fuertes, Louis Agassiz, 'Impressions of the voices of tropical birds', *Bird-lore*, 17 (September–October 1914): 349.
Gaddis, William, *The Recognitions* (Urbana-Champaign: Dalkey, [1955] 2012).
Gilbert, Stuart, 'A prolegomena to "Work in progress"', *transition*, 13 (summer 1928): 65–70.
Gilbert, Stuart, 'Thesaurus minusculus: a short commentary on a paragraph of work in progress', *transition*, 16/17 (June 1929): 15–24.
Gilbert, Stuart, 'Harry Crosby: a personal note', *transition*, 19/20 (June 1930): 224–7.
Gilbert, Stuart, 'The subliminal tongue', *transition*, 26 (1937): 141–53.
Gilbert-Lecomte, Roger, 'La force des renoncements', *Le grand jeu*, 1 (summer 1928): 12–18.
Gilbert-Lecomte, Roger, 'The big game', trans. Eugene Jolas, *transition*, 14 (autumn 1928): 195–7.
Gilbert-Lecomte, Roger, 'L'horrible revelation . . . la seule', *Le grand jeu*, 3 (autumn 1930): 3–17.
Gilbert-Lecomte, Roger, 'The horrible revelation . . . the only one', in René Daumal and Roger Gilbert-Lecomte, *Theory of the Great Game* (London: Atlas Press, 2015), 122–35.
Gilbert-Lecomte, Roger, 'The power of renunciation', trans. Dennis Duncan, in René Daumal and Roger Gilbert-Lecomte, *Theory of the Great Game* (London: Atlas Press, 2015), 41–7.

Gilbert-Lecomte, Roger, Pierre Minet, René Daumal, Roger Vailland, René Maublanc, Véra Milanova and Jean Puyaubert, *Correspondance: Lettres adressées à René Daumal, Roger Vailland, René Maublanc, Pierre Minet, Véra Milanova, et Jean Puyaubert* (Paris: Gallimard, 1971).

Giroud, Vincent, 'Transition to Vichy: the case of Georges Pelorson', *Modernism/Modernity*, 7:2 (2000): 221–48.

Glasheen, Adaline, *Third Census of Finnegans Wake: An Index of the Characters and their Roles* (Evanston: Northwestern University Press, 1976).

Gold, Michael, '3 schools of U.S. writing', *New Masses*, 4:4 (September 1928): 13–14.

Golding, Alan, 'From Pound to Olson: the avant-garde poet as pedagogue', *Journal of Modern Literature*, 34 (2010): 86–106.

Goldman, Jane, *Modernism, 1910–1945: Image to Apocalypse* (Basingstoke and New York: Palgrave Macmillan, 2004).

Golffing, Francis, 'A note on Gottfried Benn', *Poetry*, 80:5 (August 1952): 271–5.

Golston, Michael, 'Petalbent devils: Louis Zukofsky, Lorine Niedecker, and the Surrealist praying mantis', *Modernism/Modernity*, 13:2 (2006): 325–47.

Good, Thomas, 'Carrion', *transition*, 27 (April–May 1938): 157–8.

Goodenough, Erwin Randall, *Jewish Symbols in the Greco-Roman World* (Pantheon: University of Virginia, 1968).

Gould, Stephen Jay, *Ever Since Darwin: Reflections in Natural History* (London and New York: W. W. Norton, 1977).

Graaf, Henri W. De, *Bijdrage tot de kennis van den bouw en de ontwikkeling der epiphyse bij amphibiën en reptiliën* (Leiden, 1886).

Grass, Delphine, 'The democratic languages of exile: reading Eugene Jolas and Yvan Goll's American poetry with Jacques Derrida and Hannah Arendt', *Nottingham French Studies*, 56:2 (2017): 227–44.

Gregory, William K., 'Two views on the origin of man', *Science*, 65:1695 (1927): 601–5.

Gregory, William K., 'The palaeomorphology of the human head: ten structural stages from fish to Man, part I: the skull in norma lateralis', *Quarterly Review of Biology*, 1 (June 1927): 267–79.

Gregory, William K., *Our Face from Fish to Man: A Portrait Gallery of Our Ancient Ancestors and Kinsfolk together with a Concise History of Our Best Features* (New York and London: G. P. Putnam's Sons, 1929).

Gregory, William K., 'The palaeomorphology of the human head: ten structural stages from fish to Man, part II: the skull in norma basalis', *Quarterly Review of Biology*, 4 (June 1929): 233–47.

Gregory, William K., 'The origin, rise, and decline of *Homo sapiens*', *Scientific Monthly*, 39:6 (December 1934): 481–96.

Griffin, Roger, *Modernism and Fascism* (Basingstoke: Palgrave Macmillan, 2007).
Grigson, Geoffrey, 'Comment on England', *Axis*, 1 (January 1935): 8.
Guattari, Félix, *Chaosmose* (Paris: Galilée, 1992).
Guest, Barbara, *Herself Defined: The Poet H. D. and Her World* (Garden City, NY: Doubleday, 1984).
Haeckel, Ernst, *Die Welträtsel* (Stuttgart: Kröner, 1894).
Haeckel, Ernst, *The Riddle of the Universe at the Close of the Nineteenth Century*, trans. Joseph McCabe (London: Watts, 1929).
Haldane, J. B. S., 'The origins of life', *The Rationalist Annual*, 148 (1929): 1–11.
Hamburger, Michael, *Reason and Energy: Studies in German Literature* (New York: Grove Press, 1957).
Hamburger, Michael, and Christopher Middleton (eds), *Modern German Poetry 1910–1960* (London: MacGibbon & Kee, 1962).
Hamilton, John Bowen, 'Hemingway and the Christian paradox', *Renascence*, 24 (1972): 141–54.
Hansen, J. T., and M. Karasek, 'Neuron or endocrine cell? The pinealocyte as an araneuron', in R. J. Reiter (ed.), *The Pineal and Its Hormones* (New York: Leiss, 1982), 1–9.
Hatch, David Allen, 'Beckett in *transition*: Three Dialogues, little magazines, and post-war Parisian avant-garde aesthetic debate', in Marius Buning, Matthijs Engelberts, Sjef Houppermans, Dirk Van Hulle and Danièle de Ruyter (eds), *Historicising Beckett: Issues of Performance* (Amsterdam and New York: Rodopi, 2005), 43–59.
Hatch, David Allen, 'Eclectic/subversive period: Eugene Jolas and the modernist laboratory of *transition*', *Journal of Modern Periodical Studies*, 7, 1–2 (2016): 48–73.
Haughton, Hugh, 'Sorry to be so vague', *London Review of Books*, 21:15 (29 July 1999): 18–21.
Hayes, C., *The Historical Evolution of Modern Nationalism* (New York: Macmillan, 1931).
Hayes, Edward Cary, 'The "social forces" error', *American Journal of Sociology*, 16 (March 1911): 613–25.
Hays, H. R., 'Surrealist influence in contemporary poetry', *Poetry*, 54:4 (July 1939): 202–9.
Hemingway, Ernest, *The Old Man and the Sea* (New York: Scribner's, 1952).
Hermans, Theo, *The Structure of Modernist Poetry* (London: Croom Helm, 1982).
Hoffman, Frederick J., Charles Allen and Carolyn F. Ulrich, *The Little Magazine: A History and a Bibliography*, 2nd edn (Princeton: Princeton University Press, 1947).
Hoffman, Leigh, 'Anamnesis', *transition*, 11 (February 1928): 65–70.

Hoffman, Leigh, 'Catastrophe', *transition*, 13 (summer 1928): 76–81.
Hofmann, Michael, 'Notorious ever after: a note on Benn', *Poetry*, 186 (2006): 39–42.
Hogan, William, '*Transition*'s tenth anniversary', *San Francisco Chronicle*, 26 June 1938, n. p.
Hölderlin, Friedrich, 'Hoelderlin's poems of madness' ('Homeland', 'To Heinse', 'As birds . . .', 'Greece', 'To know little', 'The eagle', 'Yet from self-inflicted wounds . . .', 'New world', 'To the Madonna', 'Fate', 'On fallow leaf', 'Vineyard and bees', 'Klopstock' and 'From the abyss'), trans. Eugene Jolas, *transition*, 21 (March 1932): 166–70.
Holme, H. Christopher, 'Art and revolution', *transition*, 18 (November 1929): 162–5.
Holz, Arno, 'From Phantasus', trans. Eugene Jolas, *transition*, 2 (May 1927): 145–8.
Hooke, S. H., 'Fish symbolism', *Folklore*, 72 (September 1961): 535–8.
Hortega, Pío del Río, and Wilder Penfield, *Cytology and Cellular Pathology of the Nervous System* (New York: Hoeber, 1932).
Huebner, Friedrich Marcus, 'The road through the word', trans. Eugene Jolas, *transition*, 22 (February 1933): 110–13.
Huebner, Friedrich Marcus, 'Possession', *transition*, 23 (July 1935): 56–9.
Hulle, Dirk Van, 'Growth and the grid: organic vs constructivist conceptions of poetry', *Neophilologus*, 90 (2006): 491–507.
Huxley, Julian S., *Evolution: The Modern Synthesis – The Definitive Edition* (London and Cambridge, MA: MIT Press, [1942] 2010).
Huxley, Julian S., and A. C. Haddon, *We Europeans: A Survey of 'Racial Problems'* (London: Jonathan Cape, 1935).
Irwin, Theodore D., 'Slanguage: 1929', *transition*, 16/17 (June 1929): 32–4.
Jabre, Ferris, 'How brainless slime molds redefine intelligence', *Scientific American*, 7 November 2012, at www.nature.com/news/how-brainless-slime-molds-redefine-intelligence-1.11811 (last accessed 25 June 2018).
Jay, Martin, *Downcast Eyes: The Denigration of Vision in Twentieth-Century French Thought* (Berkeley, Los Angeles and London: University of California Press, 1993).
Jeffers, Robinson, *Hungerfield and Other Poems* (New York: Random House, 1954).
Jewell, Edward Alden, 'Whichness of the what: concerning the revived "transition" and various thorny problems of the day', *New York Times*, 12 July 1936, 7.
Johns, Richard, 'Preparation for arrival', *transition*, 19/20 (June 1930): 299–302.
Jolas, Eugene, 'Poems by Eugene Jolas', *Rhythmus: A Magazine of the Poetry of the Arts*, 2:2 (May–June 1924): 16–64.
Jolas, Eugene, 'Rambles through literary Paris', *Chicago Tribune*, Paris edition, 27 July 1924, 2.

Jolas, Eugene, 'Rambles through literary Paris', *Chicago Tribune*, Paris edition, 5 July 1925, 5.
Jolas, Eugene, 'From "Landscapes"', *transition*, 4 (July 1927): 134–6.
Jolas, Eugene, 'From "Nocturnes"', *transition*, 4 (July 1927): 132–3.
Jolas, Eugene, 'Gottfried Benn', *transition*, 5 (August 1927): 146–9.
Jolas, Eugene, 'Monologue', *transition*, 6 (September 1927): 133–6.
Jolas, Eugene, 'Enter the imagination', *transition*, 7 (October 1927): 157–60.
Jolas, Eugene, 'On the quest', *transition*, 9 (December 1927): 191–6.
Jolas, Eugene, 'The revolution of language and James Joyce', *transition*, 11 (February 1928): 109–16.
Jolas, Eugene, 'Almanach', *transition*, 13 (summer 1928): 71–5.
Jolas, Eugene, 'Daily graphic', *transition*, 13 (summer 1928): 174–5.
Jolas, Eugene, *Secession in Astropolis* (Paris: Black Sun Press, 1929).
Jolas, Eugene, 'Construction of the enigma', *transition*, 15 (February 1929): 56–62.
Jolas, Eugene, 'The new vocabulary', *transition*, 15 (February 1929): 171–4.
Jolas, Eugene, 'Pablo Picasso: quelques tableaux de 1928', *Documents* 1:1 (April 1929): 35–8.
Jolas, Eugene, 'Logos', *transition*, 16/17 (June 1929): 25–30.
Jolas, Eugene, 'Harry Crosby and *transition*', *transition*, 19/20 (June 1930): 228–9.
Jolas, Eugene, 'Literature and the new man', *transition*, 19/20 (June 1930): 13–19.
Jolas, Eugene, '*Transition*: an epilogue', *American Mercury*, 23:90 (June 1931): 185–8.
Jolas, Eugene, *Epivocables of 3* (Paris: René Riff, 1932).
Jolas, Eugene, *The Language of Night* (The Hague: Servire Press, 1932).
Jolas, Eugene, 'Night through night', *transition*, 21 (March 1932): 171–7.
Jolas, Eugene, *Mots-déluge: hypnologues* (Paris: Éditions des Cahiers Libres, 1933).
Jolas, Eugene, 'Confession about grammar', *transition*, 22 (February 1933): 124.
Jolas, Eugene, 'Intrialogue', *transition*, 22 (February 1933): 21.
Jolas, Eugene, 'Lillitoo's voyage', *transition*, 22 (February 1933): 18–20.
Jolas, Eugene, 'Night is 3', *transition*, 22 (February 1933): 20.
Jolas, Eugene, 'The primal personality', *transition*, 22 (February 1933): 78–83.
Jolas, Eugene, 'Twilight of the horizontal age', *transition*, 22 (February 1933): 6.
Jolas, Eugene, 'Verbirrupta of the mountainmen', *transition*, 22 (February 1933): 22–3.
Jolas, Eugene, 'What is the revolution of language', *transition*, 22 (February 1933): 125–6.
Jolas, Eugene, 'Malady of language', *transition*, 23 (July 1935): 175–80.

Jolas, Eugene, 'Paramyths', *transition*, 23 (July 1935): 7.
Jolas, Eugene, 'Paramyths from a dreambook: musique de la syntaxe endormie', *transition*, 23 (July 1935): 15–25.
Jolas, Eugene, 'Transmutation vertigraliste', *transition*, 23 (July 1935): 107.
Jolas, Eugene, 'Workshop', *transition*, 23 (July 1935): 97–106.
Jolas, Eugene, 'Dreamers of the world unite', *transition*, 24 (June 1936): 113.
Jolas, Eugene, 'Ergriffenheit', *transition*, 24 (July 1936): 17–19.
Jolas, Eugene, 'Notes for a lexicon of night', *transition*, 24 (June 1936): 113–14.
Jolas, Eugene, 'The third eye: ascension to the tremendum', *transition*, 26 (1937): 154–8.
Jolas, Eugene, 'Frontier-poem', *transition*, 27 (April–May 1938): 219–24.
Jolas, Eugene, 'Homage to the mythmaker', *transition*, 27 (April–May 1938): 169–75.
Jolas, Eugene, 'Vertigral', *transition*, 27 (April–May 1938): 159.
Jolas, Eugene, *I Have Seen Monsters and Angels* (Paris: Transition Press, 1938).
Jolas, Eugene, *Vertigralist Pamphlet* (Paris: Transition Press, 1938).
Jolas, Eugene, 'Surrealism: ave atque vale', *Fantasy: A Literary Quarterly with an Emphasis on Poetry*, 7:1 (1941): 23–30.
Jolas, Eugene (ed.), *Vertical: A Year-Book for Romantic-Mystic Ascensions* (New York: Gotham Bookmart, 1941).
Jolas, Eugene, *Words from the Deluge* (New York: Poets' Messages, 1941).
Jolas, Eugene, *Wanderpoem, or Angelic Mythamorphosis of the City of London* (Paris: Transition Press, 1946).
Jolas, Eugene (ed.), *Transition Workshop* (New York: Vanguard, 1949).
Jolas, Eugene, 'Across frontiers', *New York Herald Tribune*, European edition, 11 April 1950, n. p.
Jolas, Eugene, 'Georg Trakl: *Die Dichtungen*', *Critique*, 49 (June 1951): 553–5.
Jolas, Eugene, *Man from Babel*, ed. Andreas Kramer and Rainer Rumold (London and New Haven, CT: Yale University Press, 1998).
Jolas, Eugene, *Critical Writings, 1924–1951*, ed. Klaus H. Kiefer and Rainer Rumold (Evanston: Northwestern University Press, 2009).
Jolas, Eugene, 'Romanticism and metapolitics', in Klaus H. Kiefer and Rainer Rumold (eds), *Eugene Jolas: Critical Writings, 1924–1951* (Evanston: Northwestern University Press, 2009), 214–18.
Jolas, Eugene, and Elliot Paul, 'Suggestions for a new magic', *transition*, 3 (June 1927): 178–9.
Jolas, Eugene, and Elliot Paul, 'A review', *transition*, 12 (March 1928): 139–47.
Jolas, Eugene, and Robert Sage (eds), *Transition Stories: Twenty-Three Stories from 'Transition'* (New York: Walter V. McKee, 1929).
Jolas, Eugene, Hans Arp, Samuel Beckett, Carl Einstein, Thomas McGreevy, Georges Pelorson, Theo Rutra, James J. Sweeney and Ronald Symond, 'Poetry is vertical', *transition*, 21 (March 1932): 148–9.

Jolas, Eugene, Gabriel Audiosio, Gottfried Benn, Martin Buber, Whit Burnett, Leo Frobenius, Stuart Gilbert, Richard Huelsenbeck, C. G. Jung, H. L. Mencken, Georges Ribemont-Dessaignes, Camille Schuwer, David Alfaro Siqueiros, Philippe Soupault, Gertrude Stein, Ronald Symond, Roger Vitrac and Ewald Wasmuth, 'Crisis of Man', trans. Eugene Jolas, Maria Jolas, and Ronald Symond, *transition*, 21 (March 1932): 106–45.

Jolas, Eugene, Gottfried Benn, Joë Bousquet, Marcel Brion, Henry S. Canby, Malcolm Cowley, Luc Durtain, Norman Foerster, Ivan Goll, Philippe Lamour, H. L. Mencken, Francis de Miomandre, Emanuel Mounier, Gorham Munson, C. K. Ogden, A. R. Orage, P. D. Ouspensky, Georges Pelorson, Armand Petitjean, Léon Pierre-Quint, Raja Rao, Theo Rutra, Jack Sanford, Camille Schuwer, Louis Untermeyer, Laurence Vail and Edmond Vandercammen, 'Inquiry about the malady of language', *transition*, 23 (July 1935): 144–74.

Jolas, Eugene, Gottfried Benn, Georges Ribemont-Dessaignes, Benjamin Péret, André Gaillard, Marcel Brion, Tristan Tzara, W. Mayr, Pierre Macorlan, Jules Romaines, Leon Bazalgette, Ivan Goll, Max Rychner, Theo Van Dœsburg, Bernard Faÿ, Luc Durtain, M. Seuphor, Philippe Soupault, René Lalou, Georges Hugnet, Joseph Deltheil, Jean-George Auriol, Henry Poulaille, Ferdand Divoire and Regis Michaud, 'Inquiry among European writers into the spirit of America', *transition*, 13 (summer 1928): 248–70.

Jolas, Eugene, Kay Boyle, Whit Burnet, Hart Crane, Caresse Crosby, Harry Crosby, Martha Foley, Stuart Gilbert, A. L. Gillespie, Leigh Hoffman, Elliot Paul, Douglas Rigby, Theo Rutra, Robert Sage, Harold J. Salemson and Laurence Vail, 'Proclamation' and 'The Revolution of the Word, PROCLAMATION', *transition*, 16/17 (July 1929): frontispiece, 13.

Jolas, Maria, *Maria Jolas, A Woman of Action: A Memoir and Other Writings*, ed. Mary Ann Caws (Columbia: University of South Carolina Press, 2004).

Joyce, James, 'Continuation of a work in progress', *transition*, 7 (October 1927): 34–56.

Joyce, James, *Finnegans Wake* (London: Faber, 1939).

Joyce, James, *Letters of James Joyce*, 3 vols, ed. Stuart Gilbert (New York: Viking, 1957–66).

Joyce, James, *Finnegans Wake* (London and New York: Penguin, 2000).

Joyce, James, *The Finnegans Wake Notebooks at Buffalo, Notebook VI. B. 1*, ed. Vincent Deane, Daniel Ferrer and Geert Lernout (Turnhout: Brepols, 2003).

Joyce, James, *Ulysses* (Oxford and New York: Oxford University Press, 2008).

Jung, C. G., 'Instinct and the unconscious', *British Journal of Psychology*, 10:1 (November 1919): 15–23.

Jung, C. G., *Psychological types* (1921), trans. Gerhard Adler and R. F. C. Hull, in Gerhard Adler and R. F. C. Hull (eds), *Collected Works of C. G. Jung*, vol. 6 (Princeton: Princeton University Press, 1971).

Jung, C. G., 'Psychology and poetry', trans. Eugene Jolas, *transition*, 19/20 (June 1930): 23–45.
Jung, C. G., 'Psychology and literature', in *The Spirit in Man, Art and Literature*, trans. R. F. C. Hull (London: Routledge, 1967), 84–105.
Kafka, Franz, *Die Verwandlung* (Leipzig: K. Wolff, 1917).
Kafka, Franz, 'Metamorphosis', trans. Eugene Jolas, *transition*, 25 (autumn 1936): 27–38.
Kafka, Franz, 'Metamorphosis', trans. Eugene Jolas, *transition*, 26 (1937): 53–76.
Kafka, Franz, 'The housefather's care', trans. Eugene Jolas and Stuart Gilbert, *transition*, 27 (April–May 1938): 160–1.
Kafka, Franz, 'Metamorphosis (conclusion)', trans. Eugene Jolas, *transition*, 27 (April–May 1938): 79–103.
Kandinsky, Wassily, 'Composition, 1937', *transition*, 27 (April–May 1938): 271.
Kantor, Sybil Gordon, *Alfred H. Barr, Jr and the Intellectual Origins of the Museum of Modern Art* (Cambridge, MA and London: MIT Press, 2002).
Kappers, J. Ariëns, 'Evolution of pineal concepts', in A. Oksche and P. Pévet (eds), *The Pineal Organ: Photobiology – Biochronometry – Endocrinology* (Amsterdam, New York and Oxford: Elsevier/North-Holland Biomedical Press, 1981), 3–23.
Katz, Daniel, *American Modernism's Expatriate Scene* (Edinburgh: Edinburgh University Press, 2007).
Keats, John, *Complete Poems* (Harmondsworth and New York: Penguin, 1988).
Kelbert, Eugenia, 'Eugene Jolas: a poet of multilingualism', *L2 Journal*, 7:1 (2015): 49–67.
Keller, Lyn, 'Green reading: modern and contemporary American poetry and environmental criticism', in Cary Nelson (ed.), *The Oxford Handbook of Modern and Contemporary Poetry* (Oxford: Oxford University Press, 2012), 602–23.
Kiefer, Klaus H., and Rainer Rumold (eds), *Eugene Jolas: Critical Writings, 1924–1951* (Evanston: Northwestern University Press, 2009).
Kindley, Evan, 'Ismism', *London Review of Books*, 36:2 (23 January 2014): 33–5.
Klee, Paul, 'Fish-man; man-eater' (1920), *transition*, 18 (November 1929), opposite p. 65.
Knight, William F. Jackson, *Cumaean Gates: A Reference of the Sixth Aeneid to the Initiation Pattern* (Oxford: Blackwell, 1936).
Kohn, Hans, *The Idea of Nationalism: A Study in Its Origins and Background* (New York: Macmillan, 1944).
Koloctroni, Vassiliki, 'Minotaur in Manhattan: Nicolas Calas and the fortunes of Surrealism', *Modernist Cultures*, 4 (2009): 84–102.
Kraus, Rosalind E., *The Originality of the Avant-Garde and Other Modernist Myths* (Cambridge, MA and London: MIT Press, 1985).

Krell, David Farrell, 'Paradoxes of the pineal: from Descartes to Georges Bataille', *Royal Institute of Philosophy Lecture Series*, 21 (1987): 215–28.

Kuberski, Philip, *Chaosmos* (Albany: State University of New York Press, 1994).

Kudo, R. R., '*Pelomyxa* and related organisms', *Annals of the New York Academy of Sciences*, 78:2 (1959): 474–86.

Lacoue-Labarthe, Philippe, and Jean-Luc Nancy, *The Literary Absolute: The Theory of Literature in German Romanticism*, trans. Philip Barnard and Cheryl Lester (Albany: State University of New York Press, 1988).

Lamarck, Jean-Baptiste, *Philosophie zoologique, ou, exposition des considerations relative à l'histoire naturelle des animaux* (Paris: Chez Dentu et L'Auteur, 1809).

Lamy, Thomas Josephus, *Commentarium in librum genesos* (Mechelen: H. Dessain, 1883).

Landuyt, Ingeborg, 'Tale told of Shem: some elements at the inception of FW 1.7', in Wim Van Mierlo and Sam Slote (eds), *Genitricksling Joyce* (Amsterdam and Atlanta: Rodopi, 1999), 115–34.

Landuyt, Ingeborg, 'Cain – Ham – (Shem) – Esau – Jim the Penman: Chapter 1.7', in Luca Crispi and Sam Slote (eds), *How Joyce Wrote Finnegans Wake* (Madison: University of Wisconsin Press, 2007), 142–62.

Lankester, E. Ray, 'Parasitic amœbæ and disease', *Nature*, 2615:104 (11 December 1919): 369–70.

Larson, Edward J., 'Biology and the emergence of the Anglo-American eugenics movement', in Denis R. Alexander and Ronald L. Numbers (eds), *Biology and Ideology from Descartes to Dawkins* (Chicago and London: University of Chicago Press, 2010), 165–91.

Lasker-Schüler, Else, 'A song', trans. Eugene Jolas, *transition*, 1 (April 1927): 123.

Laughlin, James (ed.), *New Directions in Prose and Poetry* (Norfolk, CT: New Directions, 1936).

Lautréamont, Comte de (Isidore Ducasse), 'From the lay of Maldoror: canto I', trans. John Rodker, *transition*, 7 (October 1927): 105–14.

Leeder, Karen, 'Nihilismus und Musik: Gottfried Benn (1886–1956), the unlikely Expressionist', *Oxford German Studies*, 42:1 (2013): 23–37.

Leidy, Joseph, 'Amoeba proteus', *American Naturalist*, 12:4 (April 1878): 235–8.

Lerner, Aaron B., J. D. Chase, Y. Takahashi, T. H. Lee and N. Mori, 'Isolation of melatonin, pineal factor that lightens melanocytes', *Journal of the American Chemical Society*, 80 (1958): 2587–9.

Levie, Sophie, *Commerce, 1924–1932, une revue international moderniste* (Rome: Fondazione Camilo Caetani, 1989).

Levin, Harry, *James Joyce: A Critical Introduction* (Norfolk, CT: New Directions, [1941] 1960).

Levy, Joseph, 'Studies on Reproduction in *Amoeba Proteus*', *Genetics*, 9:2 (March 1924): 124–50.
Lévy-Bruhl, Lucien, *La mentalité primitive* (Paris: Librairie Felix Alcan, 1922).
Lewis, Wyndham, 'The diabolical principle,' *The Enemy*, 1:3 (January 1929): 9–83.
Leydig, Franz, *Die in Deutschland lebenden Arten der Saurier* (Tübingen: H. Laupp, 1872).
Lhote, André, 'L'inconscient dans l'art', *Gazette des Beaux-Arts*, 78:6 (July–August 1936): 113–23.
Lhote, André, 'The unconscious in art', trans. Eugene Jolas, *transition*, 26 (1937): 82–96.
Lomas, David, 'André Breton's "Subject" (1917): simulation and the origins of automatic writing', *Papers of Surrealism*, 8 (2010): 2–8.
Loving, Pierre, 'Praying insects', *transition*, 16/17 (June 1929): 192–4.
Lowenfels, Walter, 'Solstice', *transition*, 13 (summer 1928): 59.
Lutwack, Leonard, *Birds in Literature* (Gainesville: University Press of Florida, 1994).
MacLeish, Archibald, 'Vernissage', 'Birth of eventually Venus', 'Poem', 'Project for an aesthetic sub-title: moonlight of a man', and 'Poem dedicated to the advancement of aviation', *transition*, 6 (September 1927): 115–19.
MacLeish, Archibald, 'Cinema of a man – in memoriam: Harry Crosby', *transition*, 19/20 (June 1930): 230–1.
MacLeish, Archibald, 'Five lost poems', *Poetry*, 137:2 (November 1980): 63–5.
MacLeish, Archibald, *Collected Poems 1917–1982* (Boston: Houghton Mifflin, 1985).
Macleod, Glen (ed.), *William Carlos Williams Review: Special Edition – Williams and Surrealism*, 22:1 (1996).
Macleod, Glen, 'The visual arts', in Michael Levenson (ed.), *The Cambridge Companion to Modernism* (Cambridge: Cambridge University Press, 1998), 194–216.
Macleod, Norman, 'Dreams: twelve knives; revenge of three brothers; cacked', *transition*, 19/20 (June 1930): 59–60.
Mansanti, Céline, 'William Carlos Williams' *A Novelette*: an American counterproposal to French Surrealism', *Journal of Surrealism of the Americas*, 1 (2007): 30–43.
Mansanti, Céline, *La revue transition, 1927–1938, le modernisme historique en devenir* (Rennes: Presses Universitaires de Rennes, 2009).
Mansanti, Céline, 'Between modernisms: *transition* (1927–38)', in Peter Brooker and Andrew Thacker (eds), *The Oxford Critical and Cultural History of Modernist Magazines*, vol. 2 (Oxford: Oxford University Press, 2009–13), 718–36.

Marquis, Alice Goldfarb, *Alfred H. Barr Jr: Missionary for the Modern* (Chicago and New York: Contemporary Books, 1989).
Masson, André, 'Combat de poissons', *transition*, 3 (June 1927): opposite p. 113.
Masson, André, 'Le coquillage', *transition*, 15 (February 1929): following p. 256.
Masson, André, 'Le piège et l'oiseau', *transition*, 15 (February 1929): following p. 256.
Masson, André, 'Animal pris au piège', *transition*, 19/20 (June 1930): opposite p. 274.
Matthias, Blanche, 'The altar stone', *transition*, 5 (August 1927): 126.
Matthias, Blanche, 'The formless ones on Carmel Point', *transition*, 5 (August 1927): 123.
Matthias, Blanche, *The Wish to Sing* (San Francisco: Blanche Matthias, 1978).
McCord, Carey Pratt, and Floyd P. Allen, 'Evidences associating pineal gland function with alterations in pigmentation', *Journal of Experimental Zoology*, 23 (1917): 207–24.
McGreevy, Thomas, 'Treason of Saint Laurence O'Toole' and 'Elsa', *transition*, 21 (March 1932): 178–80.
McHugh, Roland, *The Sigla of Finnegans Wake* (London: E. Arnold, 1976).
McHugh, Roland, *Annotations to Finnegans Wake*, 3rd edn (Baltimore: Johns Hopkins University Press, 2006).
McMillan, Dougald, *Transition: The History of a Literary Era, 1927–1938* (London: Caldar and Boyars, 1975).
Mead, G. R. S., *Pistis Sophia: A Gnostic Miscellany* (London: John M. Watkins, 1921).
Mendelsohn, J. Andrew, 'Lives of the cell', *Journal of the History of Biology*, 36:1 (2003): 1–37.
Mercanton, Jacques, 'Le X-ème anniversaire de la review *transition* (de notre rédaction de Paris)', *Le moment, journal de Bucarest: quotidien illustré d'informations politiques, économiques et sociales*, 988 (11 June 1938): n. p.
Miller, Henry, 'The cosmological eye', *transition*, 27 (1938): 322–31.
Miller, Henry, and Michael Fraenkel, *The Michael Fraenkel–Henry Miller Correspondence, Called Hamlet* (London: Carrefour, 1962).
Miller, Tyrus, 'Poetic contagion: Surrealism and Williams's *A Novelette*', *William Carlos Williams Review*, 22:1 (1996): 17–27.
Miller, Tyrus, *Late Modernism: Politics, Fiction, and the Arts Between the World Wars* (Berkeley: University of California Press, 1999).
Milne-Edwards, M. H., 'Recherches zoologiques pour servir à l'histoire des lézards, extraites d'une monographie de ce genre', *Annales des sciences naturelles*, 16 (1828): 50–89.
Milner, Catherine, 'The eeriest couple in art', *The Telegraph*, 24 January 1998, at www.telegraph.co.uk/culture/4711679/The-eeriest-couple-in-art.html (last accessed 18 June 2018).

Minet, Pierre, 'Poem', *transition*, 7 (October 1927): 123.
Miró, Joan, 'Drawing', *transition*, 6 (September 1927): 113–14.
Mitchell, Peter Chalmers, 'Evolution', *Encyclopaedia Britannica*, 11th edn, vol. X (New York: Encyclopaedia Britannica Co., 1910–11), 22–37.
Mitchell, Peter Chalmers, 'Variation and selection', *Encyclopaedia Britannica*, 11th edn, vol. XXIX (New York: Encyclopaedia Britannica Co., 1910–11), 906–12.
Mitchell, W. J. T., '*Ut pictura theoria*: abstract painting and the repression of language', *Critical Inquiry*, 15:2 (1989): 348–71.
Mitchell, W. J. T., *Picture Theory: Essays on Verbal and Visual Representation* (London and Chicago: University of Chicago Press, 1994).
Monk, Craig, 'Modernism in *transition*: the expatriate American magazine in Europe between the wars', *Miscelánea: A Journal of English and American Studies*, 20 (1999): 55–72.
Monk, Craig, *Writing the Lost Generation: Expatriate Autobiography and American Modernism* (Iowa City: University of Iowa Press, 2008).
Morley, Patricia, 'Fish symbolism in chapter seven of *Finnegans Wake*', *James Joyce Quarterly*, 6 (1969): 267–70.
Morrisson, Mark, *The Public Face of Modernism: Little Magazines, Audiences, and Reception, 1905–1920* (Madison: University of Wisconsin Press, 2001).
Mundan, Lothar, 'Vertigral poetry: the third eye', *transition*, 23 (July 1935): 60–1.
Mundy, Jennifer, 'The naming of biomorphism', in Oliver A. I. Botar and Isabel Wünsche (eds), *Biocentrism and Modernism* (Farnham and Burlington, VT: Ashgate, 2011), 61–75.
Needham, Joseph, 'Organicism in biology', *Journal of Philosophical Studies*, 3 (January 1928): 29–40.
Niedecker, Lorine, 'Transition', *Will-o-the-Wisp: A Magazine of Verse*, 3 (1928): 12.
Niedecker, Lorine, *Collected Works* (Berkeley and London: University of California Press, 2002).
Noll, Marcel, 'Two poems: she; sabres', trans. Eugene Jolas, *transition*, 1 (April 1927): 126.
Noll, Marcel, 'From a notebook', trans. Elliot Paul, *transition*, 5 (August 1927): 50–6.
Noll, Marcel, 'From a note book', trans. Maria Jolas, *transition*, 12 (March 1928): 63–9.
Noll, Richard, *The Jung Cult: Origins of a Charismatic Movement* (London: Fontana, 1996).
Nordau, Max Simon, *Degeneration* (Lincoln: University of Nebraska Press, [1895, 2nd edn] 1993).

Norris, Margot, *Beasts of the Modern Imagination: Darwin, Nietzsche, Kafka, Ernst, & Lawrence* (Baltimore and London: Johns Hopkins University Press, 1985).

North, Michael, 'Words in motion: the movies, the readies, and the "Revolution of the Word"', *Modernism/Modernity*, 9 (2002): 205–23.

North, Michael, *Camera Works: Photography and the Twentieth-Century Word* (Oxford and New York: Oxford University Press, 2005).

Oparin, Alexander I., 'The origin of life' (1924), trans. A. Synge, in John Desmond Bernal, *The Origin of Life* (London: Wiedenfeld & Nicolson, 1967), 199–234.

Oparin, Alexander I., *The Origin of Life*, trans. Sergius Morgulis (New York: Macmillan, 1938).

Orwell, George, *Inside the Whale and Other Essays* (Harmondsworth: Penguin, [1940] 1979).

Osborn, Henry Fairfield, *Men of the Old Stone Age: Their Environment, Life and Art* (New York: Scribner's, 1915).

Özkirimli, Umut, *Theories of Nationalism: A Critical Introduction*, 2nd edn (Basingstoke and New York: Palgrave Macmillan, 2010).

Padian, Kevin, '*The Bone Sharp: The Life of Edward Drinker Cope* by Jane Pierce Davidson (review)', *Journal of Vertebrate Paleontology*, 18 (10 April 1998): 243–6.

Pailthorpe, Grace, *Ancestors II, 1935*, *transition*, 26 (1937): opposite p. 82.

Pailthorpe, Grace, and Reuben Mednikoff, *Sluice Gates of the Mind: The Collaborative Work of Dr Grace W. Pailthorpe and Reuben Mednikoff*, ed. Nigel Walsh and Andrew Wilson (Leeds: Leeds Museums and Galleries, 1998).

Panofsky, Erwin, 'Style and medium in the moving pictures', *transition*, 26 (1937): 121–33.

Panofsky, Erwin, *Idea: A Concept in Art History*, trans. Joseph J. S. Peake (Columbia: University of South Carolina Press, [1924] 1968).

Parks, Jason, '"A kind of higher journalism": Eugene Jolas, the new mythos and *transition* (1927–1938)' (unpublished doctoral thesis, Ball State University, Muncie, 2016).

Paul, Elliot, 'The new nihilism', *transition*, 2 (May 1927): 164–8.

Pawlitt, Joanna, 'Surrealism, Beat literature, and the San Francisco renaissance', *Literature Compass*, 10:2 (2013): 97–110.

Pelorson, Georges, 'Isocele' and 'Plans', *transition*, 21 (March 1932): 181–3.

Pelorson, Georges, 'À Eugene Jolas', *transition*, 22 (February 1933): 24–30.

Péret, Benjamin, 'In a clinch', trans. Elliot Paul, *transition*, 12 (March 1928): 54–61.

Péret, Benjamin, *Death to the Pigs: Selected Writings of Benjamin Péret*, trans. Rachel Stella (London: Atlas, 1988).

Perlès, Alfred, *My Friend Henry Miller* (London: Neville Spearman, 1955).

Perloff, Marjorie, '"Logocinéma of the frontiersman": Eugene Jolas's multilingual poetics and its legacies', Marjorie Perloff homepage at http://marjorieperloff.com/essays/jolas-multilingual/ (last accessed 11 June 2018).

Petherby, Jenny, *Lorine Niedecker and the Correspondence with Louis Zukofsky, 1931–1970* (Cambridge: Cambridge University Press, 1993).

Platt, Len, *Joyce, Race, and Finnegans Wake* (Cambridge: Cambridge University Press, 2007).

Platt, Len, '"Unfallable encyclicing": *Finnegans Wake* and the *Encyclopedia Britannica*', *James Joyce Quarterly*, 47 (2009): 107–18.

Pollock, Griselda, 'Moments and temporalities of the avant-garde "in, of, and from the feminine"', *New Literary History*, 41:4 (2010): 795–820.

Pound, Ezra, 'Dr Williams' position', *The Dial*, LXXXV:5 (November 1928): 395–404.

Price, Katy, 'Finite but unbounded: *Experiment* magazine, Cambridge, England, 1928–31', *Jacket*, 20, 2002, at http://jacketmagazine.com/20/price-expe.html (last accessed 20 June 2018).

Putnam, Samuel, 'If Dada comes to America', *Contempo*, 2 (25 July 1932): 5.

Putnam, Samuel, *Paris Was Our Mistress: Memoirs of a Lost and Found Generation* (New York: Viking, 1947).

Rabaté, Jean-Michel, 'Joyce and Jolas: late modernism and early Babelism', *Journal of Modern Literature*, 22:2 (1998-9): 245–52.

Rabaté, Jean-Michel, '*Eugene Jolas: Critical Writings, 1924–1951* (review)', *Modernism/Modernity*, 18 (2011): 455–8.

Rahv, Philip, 'The literary class war', *New Masses*, 8 (August 1932): 7–10.

Rainey, Lawrence, *Institutions of Modernism: Literary Elites and Public Culture* (New Haven, CT: Yale University Press, 1998).

Rainger, Ronald, *An Agenda for Antiquity: Henry Fairfield Osborn and Vertebrate Paleontology at the American Museum of Natural History* (Tuscaloosa: University of Alabama, 1991).

Rakosi, Carl, 'Dolce padre and Ephebus' and 'The founding of New Hampshire', *transition*, 12 (March 1928): 123–4.

Ray, Man, 'Section of film', *transition*, 6 (September 1927): 113–14.

Ray, Susan, *Beyond Nihilism: Gottfried Benn's Postmodernist Poetics* (Oxford: Peter Lang, 2003).

Read, Herbert, 'Beyond realism', *The Listener*, 3:66 (16 April 1930): 679.

Read, Herbert (ed.), *Surrealism* (London: Faber, 1936).

Read, Herbert, 'Myth, dream, and poem', *transition*, 27 (April–May 1938): 176–92.

Recht, Charles, 'Fire fanfare', *transition*, 6 (September 1927): 147–53.

Reid, Christopher, 'Introduction' to 'From romanticism to the avant-garde', in Klaus H. Kiefer and Rainer Rumold (eds), *Eugene Jolas: Critical Writings, 1924–1951* (Evanston: Northwestern University Press, 2009), 203–4.

Reverdy, Pierre, 'Inn', trans. Eugene Jolas, *transition*, 7 (October 1927): 127.

Reynolds, Andrew, 'Amoebae as exemplary cells: the protean nature of an elementary organism', *Journal of the History of Biology*, 41:2 (2008): 307–37.

Ribemont-Dessaignes, Georges, untitled text, trans. Eugene Jolas, *transition*, 3 (June 1927): 147.

Richards, David, 'At other times: modernism and the "primitive"', in Vincent Sherry (ed.), *The Cambridge History of Modernism* (Cambridge: Cambridge University Press), 64–82.

Riding, Laura, 'The new barbarism, and Gertrude Stein', *transition*, 3 (June 1927): 153–68.

Rilke, Rainer Maria, *The Duino Elegies, A Bilingual Edition*, trans. Stephen Cohn (Evanston: Northwestern University Press, 1989).

Ritchie, J. M., *Gottfried Benn: The Unreconstructed Expressionist* (London: Oswald Wolff, 1972).

Robertson, Alexander W., *Surrealism in Britain in the Thirties: Angels of Anarchy and Machines for Making Clouds* (Leeds: City Art Galleries, 1986).

Rochelle, Pierre Drieu La, 'The young European', trans. Elliot Paul, *transition*, 2 (May 1927): 9–18.

Roditi, Édouard, 'Mirages', *transition*, 21 (March 1932): 95–7.

Rodriguez, Michael Angelo, '"Everywhere stone is gaining": the struggle for the sacred in Samuel Beckett's *Ill Seen Ill Said*', *Samuel Beckett Today/Aujourd'hui*, 14 (2004): 105–16.

Rohman, Carrie, *Stalking the Subject: Modernism and the Animal* (Chichester and New York: Columbia University Press, 2009).

Romer, Alfred Sherwood, *Vertebrate Paleontology* (Chicago: Chicago University Press, 1933).

Rosenbaum, Susan, 'Exquisite corpse: Surrealist influence on the American poetry scene, 1920–1960', in Cary Nelson (ed.), *The Oxford Handbook of Modern and Contemporary Poetry* (Oxford: Oxford University Press, 2012), 268–300.

Rumold, Rainer, *Gottfried Benn und der Expressionismus: Provokation des Lesers – absolute Dichtung* (Königstein: Scriptor-Verlag, 1982).

Rumold, Rainer, 'Archeo-logies of modernity in *transition* and *Documents* 1929/30', *Comparative Literature Studies*, 37 (2000): 45–67.

Rumold, Rainer, *The Janus Face of the German Avant-Garde: From Expressionism to Postmodernism* (Evanston: Northwestern University Press, 2002).

Rumold, Rainer, *Archaeologies of Modernity: Avant-Garde Bildung* (Evanston: Northwestern University Press, 2015).

Rumold, Rainer, and Andreas Kramer (eds), *Eugene Jolas: Man from Babel* (London and New Haven, CT: Yale University Press, 1998).

Rumrich, Diana, 'Introduction' to 'Part three: the language of night', in Klaus H. Kiefer and Rainer Rumold (eds), *Eugene Jolas: Critical Writings, 1924–1951* (Evanston: Northwestern University Press, 2009), 129–30.
Ruse, Michael, *Monad to Man: The Concept of Progress in Evolutionary Biology* (Cambridge, MA: Harvard University Press, 1996).
Sachs, Arieh, 'Religious despair in mediaeval literature and art', *Mediaeval Studies*, 26 (1964): 231–56.
Sage, Robert, 'The young European', *transition*, 5 (August 1927): 150–4.
Salisbury, Laura, 'Linguistic trepanation: brain damage, penetrative seeing and a revolution of the word', in Deidre Coleman and Hilary Fraser (eds), *Minds, Bodies, Machines, 1770–1930* (Basingstoke: Palgrave Macmillan, 2011), 179–208.
Salisbury, Laura, and Andrew Shail (eds), *Neurology and Modernity: A Cultural History of Nervous Systems, 1800–1950* (Basingstoke: Palgrave Macmillan, 2010).
Schaeffer, Asa A., 'Taxonomy of the amebas [*sic*], with descriptions of thirty-nine new marine and freshwater species', *Papers of the Tortugas Laboratory, Carnegie Institution of Washington*, 24 (1926): 1–116.
Schapiro, Meyer, 'The nature of modern art' (1937), in Neil Jumonville (ed.), *The New York Intellectuals Reader* (New York and London: Routledge, 2007), 123–42.
Scheerbart, Paul, 'Gesang der Walfische', *transition*, 21 (March 1932): 184–7.
Schiller, Francis, 'Pineal gland, perennial puzzle', *Journal of the History of the Neurosciences*, 4 (1995): 155–65.
Schmidt, Peter, *William Carlos Williams, the Arts, and Literary Tradition* (Baton Rouge: Louisiana State University Press, 1988).
Scholes, Robert, and Clifford Wulfman, *Modernism in the Magazines: An Introduction* (New Haven, CT: Yale University Press, 2010).
Schulze, Robin G., *The Degenerate Muse: American Nature, Modernist Poetry, and the Problem of Cultural Hygiene* (Oxford and New York: Oxford University Press, 2013).
Schwab, I. R., and G. A. O'Connor, 'The lonely eye', *British Journal of Ophthalmology*, 89:3 (2005): 256.
Schwartzburg, Molly, Elspeth Healey, Kelsey Harmon, Anna Chen, Jessica Meyerson, Chelsea Weathers and Bethany Johnsen, 'Pierre Loving', *The Greenwich Village Bookshop Door: A Portal to Bohemia 1920–1925*, Harry Ransom Center Web Exhibition, at http://norman.hrc.utexas.edu/bookshopdoor/signature.cfm?item=202#1 (last accessed 25 June 2018).
Schwitters, Kurt, 'priimiitittiii', trans. Eugene Jolas, *transition*, 3 (June 1927): 143.
Setz, Cathryn, '"Transocean": *transition*'s anachronistic zeitgeists', *Modernist Cultures*, 11:1 (2016): 65–85.

Setz, Cathryn, 'Nietzsche's spider: forging and furnishing the Revolution of the Word', *Affirmations: Of the Modern*, 5:1 (2017): 126–53.

Shideler, W. H., 'Paleontology and evolution', *Ohio Journal of Science*, 52 (July 1952): 177–86.

Shils, Edward, 'Primordial, personal, sacred and civil ties', *British Journal of Sociology*, 8:2 (1957): 130–45.

Shipman, Evan, 'Premonition (to André Masson)', *transition*, 12 (March 1928): 135.

Silet, Charles L. P., *Transition: An Author Index* (New York: Whitston, 1980).

Smith, Andrew D., *Theories of Nationalism*, 2nd edn (London: Duckworth, 1983).

Solveen, Henri, 'Psalm', *transition*, 7 (October 1927): 126.

Sorenson, Lee, 'James Johnson Sweeney', *Dictionary of Art Historians* (Durham, NC: Duke University Libraries, 1996), at http://arthistorians.info/sweeneyj (last accessed 25 June 2018).

Soupault, Philippe, 'Harry Crosby', *transition*, 19/20 (June 1930): 232.

Soupault, Philippe, 'Mots-déluge', *Europe*, 15 June 1954, 295–6.

Spiteri, Raymond, 'Surrealism and its discontents: Georges Bataille, Georges Ribemont-Dessaignes, and the 1929 crisis of Surrealism', *French History and Civilization: Papers from the George Rudé Seminar*, 4 (2011): 145–56, at https://h-france.net/rude/wp-content/uploads/2017/08/SpiteriVol4.pdf (last accessed 9 July 2018).

Stark, Bruce P., *Guide to the Blanche Matthias Papers, the Beinecke Rare Book and Manuscript Library* (New Haven, CT: Yale University Library, 1990).

Stein, Gertrude, *The Autobiography of Alice B. Toklas* (London: John Lane, 1933).

Stein, Gertrude, Hilaire Hiler, Robert McAlmon, Leigh Hoffman, George Antheil, Kay Boyle, Abraham Lincoln Gillespie Jnr, Walter Lowenfels, Pierre Loving, Emily Homes Coleman, Berenice Abbott, Lansing Warren, Ivan Beede, Harry Crosby, Harold J. Salemson, Kathleen Cannell, H. Wolf Kaufman, and the editors, 'Why do Americans live in Europe?', *transition*, 14 (autumn 1928): 97–119.

Stillmark, Alexander, 'Problems and principles in translating Trakl', in *Von Eierschwammerlhöhen zur D. H. Lawrence-Ranch* (Berlin and New York: Peter Lang, 2010), 183–92.

Stinchcombe, J., 'Trakl's "Elis" Poems and E. T. A. Hoffmann's "Die Bergwerke zu Falun"', *Modern Language Review*, 59 (1964): 609–15.

Stravinsky, Igor, and Robert Craft, *Dialogues and a Diary* (Garden City, NY: Doubleday, 1963).

Studnička, F. K., 'Die Parietalorgane', in A. Oppel (ed.), *Lehrbuch der vergleicherden mikroskopischen Anatomie der Wirbeltiere*, vol. 5 (Jena: Gustav Fischer, 1905), 1–254.

Studnička, F. K., 'Schematization of the pineal region in Sphenodon' (1905). Reproduced in Frederick Tilney and Luther Fiske Warren, *The Morphology and Evolutionary Significance of the Pineal Body* (Philadelphia: Wistar Institute of Anatomy and Biology, 1919), 34.
Surya, Michael, *Georges Bataille: An Intellectual Biography* (London: Verso, 2002).
Sweeney, James Johnson, 'Mole', *transition*, 21 (March 1932): 188.
Sweeney, James Johnson, *African Negro Art* (New York: MoMA, 1935).
Tanguy, Yves, 'Landscape', *transition*, 6 (September 1927): 113–14.
Tanguy, Yves, 'Painting', *transition*, 11 (February 1928): opposite p. 93.
Tashjian, Dickran, *Skyscraper Primitives: Dada and the American Avant-Garde, 1900–1925* (Middletown, CT: Wesleyan University Press, 1975).
Tashjian, Dickran, *A Boatload of Madmen: Surrealism and the American Avant-Garde* (New York: Thames & Hudson, 1995).
Taylor-Batty, Juliette, *Multilingualism in Modernist Fiction* (Basingstoke and New York: Palgrave Macmillan, 2013).
Thayer, Scofield, 'James Joyce', *The Dial*, LXV:773 (19 September 1918): 201–3.
Thomas, Dylan, 'The mouse and the woman', *transition*, 25 (autumn 1936): 45–58.
Thomas, Dylan, 'Poem', *transition*, 25 (autumn 1936): 20–1.
Thomas, Dylan, *Collected Poems, 1934–1952* (London: J. M. Dent & Sons, 1952).
Thomas, Dylan, *Poet in the Making: The Notebooks of Dylan Thomas*, ed. Ralph Maud (London: J. M. Dent & Sons, 1968).
Tilney, Frederick, and Luther Fiske Warren, *The Morphology and Evolutional Significance of the Pineal Body* (Philadelphia: Wistar Institute of Anatomy and Biology, 1919).
Tindall, William York, *A Reader's Guide to Finnegans Wake* (London: Thames & Hudson, 1969).
Trakl, Georg, 'To the lad, Elis', trans. Eugene Jolas, *transition*, 3 (June 1927): 146.
Trakl, Georg, *Poems and Prose: A Bilingual Edition*, trans. Alexander Stillmark (London: Libris, 2001).
Trakl, Georg, *The Poems of Georg Trakl*, trans. Margitt Lehbert (London: Anvil Poetry, 2007).
Travers, Martin, *The Poetry of Gottfried Benn: Text and Selfhood* (Oxford and New York: Peter Lang, 2007).
Turda, Marius, *Modernism and Eugenics* (New York: Palgrave Macmillan, 2010).
Turda, Marius, 'Race, science, and eugenics in the twentieth century', in Alison Bashford and Philippa Levine (eds), *The Oxford Handbook of the History of Eugenics* (Oxford and New York: Oxford University Press, 2010), 62–79.

Turnell, G. M., 'Malady of language', *Catholic Herald London*, 24 August 1935, n. p.

Tyler, Parker, 'Elegy for a dead idol of the screen (for Carlyle Blackwell)', *transition*, 19/20 (June 1930): 360–1.

Tzara, Tristan, 'The approximate man', trans. Eugene Jolas, *transition*, 19/20 (June 1930): 325–9.

Tzara, Tristan *L'homme approximatif* (Paris: Éditions Fourcade, 1931).

Tzara, Tristan, *Seven Dada Manifestos and Lampistries* (London: John Caldar, 1981).

Tzara, Tristan, Jean Arp, Alberto Magnelli and Pierre-André Benoit, *De nos oiseaux: poèmes* (Paris: Kra, 1925).

Vailland, Roger, 'Arthur Rimbaud ou guerre à l'homme!', *Grand jeu*, 2 (spring 1929): 18–25.

Vailland, Roger, 'Arthur Rimbaud or war on man!', trans. Stuart Gilbert, *transition*, 18 (November 1929): 66–71.

Verene, Donald Phillip, *Vico and Joyce* (Albany: State University of New York Press, 1987).

Vickery, John B., '*Finnegans Wake* and sexual metamorphosis', *Contemporary Literature*, 13 (1972): 213–42.

Vulliet, Andre, 'Americans on the continent', *The Washington Post*, 10 March 1935, 7.

Wallace, David Rains, *Beasts of Eden: Walking Whales, Dawn Horses, and Other Enigmas of Mammal Evolution* (London, Berkeley and Los Angeles: University of California Press, 2004).

Walsh, Denis, 'Teleology', in Michael Ruse (ed.), *The Oxford Handbook of the Philosophy of Biology* (Oxford and New York: Oxford University Press, 2008), 113–37.

Watson, James D., and Francis Crick, 'A structure for deoxyribose nucleic acid', *Nature*, 171:4356 (1953): 737–8.

Webster, Harvey C., 'Review, *transition* 26', *Louisville KY Times*, 15 May 1937, n. p.

Werness, Hope B., *The Continuum Encyclopedia of Animal Symbolism in Art* (London and New York: Continuum, 2004).

White, Eric B., *Transatlantic Avant-Gardes: Little Magazines and Localist Modernism* (Edinburgh: Edinburgh University Press, 2013).

Whitworth, Michael, 'Late modernism', in Michael Whitworth (ed.), *Modernism* (Oxford: Blackwell, 2007), 272–96.

Wickes, George, 'Henry Miller, the art of fiction, no. 28' (1961), interview, *Paris Review*, at www.theparisreview.org/interviews/4597/the-art-of-fiction-no-28-henry-miller (last accessed 31 May 2018).

Wilde, Alan, *Horizons of Assent* (Baltimore and London: Johns Hopkins University Press, 1981).

Williams, Rhys W., 'Primitivism in the works of Carl Einstein, Carl Sternheim and Gottfried Benn', *Journal of European Studies*, 13 (1983): 247–67.

Williams, Rhys W., 'Prosaic intensities: the short prose of German Expressionism', in Neil H. Donahue (ed.), *A Companion to the Literature of German Expressionism* (Woodbridge and New York: Camden House, 2005), 89–110.

Williams, Wendy, and Linda Wheeler, 'Editorial, special issue: the animals turn', *New Formations*, 76 (2012): 5–7.

Williams, William Carlos, 'The dead baby', *transition*, 2 (May 1927): 118.

Williams, William Carlos, 'A voyage to Pagany', excerpt, *transition*, 7 (October 1927): 9–17.

Williams, William Carlos, 'A note on the recent work of James Joyce', *transition*, 8 (November 1927): 149–54.

Williams, William Carlos, 'Winter', *transition*, 9 (December 1927): 129.

Williams, William Carlos, 'Letter to the editor', *transition*, 10 (January 1928): 145–6.

Williams, William Carlos, 'Theessentialroar', *transition*, 10 (January 1928): 49–50.

Williams, William Carlos, 'George Antheil and the cantilene critics: a note on the first performance of Antheil's music in New York City (April 10, 1927', *transition*, 13 (summer 1928): 237–40.

Williams, William Carlos, 'Improvisations', *transition*, 13 (summer 1928): 55–8.

Williams, William Carlos, 'A point for American criticism', *transition*, 15 (February 1929): 157–66.

Williams, William Carlos, 'The somnambulists', *transition*, 18 (November 1929): 147–51.

Williams, William Carlos, 'The simplicity of disorder', *transition*, 19/20 (June 1930): 279–86.

Williams, William Carlos, 'How to write', in James Laughlin (ed.), *New Directions in Prose and Poetry* (Norfolk, CT: New Directions, 1936), 45–8.

Wilson, Leigh, *Modernism and Magic: Experiments with Spiritualism, Theosophy and the Occult* (Edinburgh: Edinburgh University Press, 2013).

Witemeyer, Hugh (ed.), *William Carlos Williams and James Laughlin: Selected Letters* (New York: W. W. Norton, 1989).

Woolf, Virginia, *Between the Acts* (London: Vintage, 1941).

Young, Timothy G., 'Guide to the Eugene and Maria Jolas Papers: GEN MSS 108', Yale University Library, April 1993, rev. 2 February 2010, at http://drs.library.yale.edu:8083/fedora/get/beinecke:jolas/PDF (last accessed 18 June 2018).

Ziska, Helen, 'Our face from fish to man'. Frontispiece to William K. Gregory, *Our Face from Fish to Man: A Portrait Gallery of Our Ancient Ancestors and Kinsfolk together with a Concise History of Our Best Features* (New York and London: G. P. Putnam's Sons, 1929).

Ziska, Helen, 'Man's debt to the lower vertebrates', in William K. Gregory, 'The origin, rise, and decline of *Homo sapiens*', *Scientific Monthly*, 39:6 (December 1934): 481–96.

Zukofsky, Louis, 'Untitled', *transition*, 15 (February 1929): 125.

INDEX

abstraction, 26, 29, 34, 41, 44–5, 47–50
  biomorphic, 25, 27–8, 30–1, 43, 51n8
  geometric, 24–5
Acéphale, 112
affect, 96
Agamben, Giorgio, 15
Allbutt, Thomas Clifford, 109
Allen, Floyd P., 110–11
All's Well, 45
Ambrosino, Georges, 112
American Museum of Natural History, 65–7, 70
American Quarterly, 149
American Surrealist Review, 16
Anderson, Margaret, 3, 26
animal studies, 14–15
animals
  amoeba: amoebic mode, 36, 43, 47, 50; as artistic atrophy, 28, 31; as an optic, 25–6, 50; and plasticity, 29–30; public imagination of, 27; scientific knowledge of, 28–9
  anemone, 13
  animalcule, 39–40
  ape, 13, 98–9, 113
  bird: and augury, 137; as modernist, 143, 147–8, 160, 171; as omen, 131, 138; as totemic, 130–2, 134, 156–8; as 'uprush', 132–3, 141, 145, 148; 'bird body', 9; blackbird, 131, 135–7, 140, 142, 145–6; crow, 139; cuckoo, 158, 169; dove, 135, 138, 142; duck, 86; eagle, 130; finch, 169; goldfinch, 131; gull, 167–8; hawk, 124; lapwing, 159; motmot, 130; owl, 139, 148–9; parrot, 139, 143; peacock, 157–8; petrel, 161; sparrow, 140–1; swallow, 142; vulture, 124, 158
  canine, 13
  crab, 34, 169
  crocodile, 94
  cuttlefish, 76
  dinosaur, 44–5, 95, 98, 99, 109
  elk, 64
  fish: and artistry, 55–6, 59, 75, 77, 84–5; cultural history of, 56–8, 88n22; evolution of, 66–7; and filth, 62, 78–9; hybrid forms of, 60, 62; and racial othering, 60, 62; barbel, 59; herring, 84; minnow, 110, salmon, 59–60, 78, 81, 87n22; shark, 92; tuna, 92
  fly, 37, 40, 138, 151
  frog, 92
  giraffe, 63
  insect, 139, 155: beetle, 167–8
  lamprey, 92
  larvae, 119
  lizard, 35, 105, 109, 113–14, 118–20, 124: chameleon, 9–10; 'monsterlizard', 116–17; tuatara, 110, 115–16
  marsupial, 98
  mole, 40
  octopus, 34

205

INDEX

animals (cont.)
  pig, 40
  porcupine, 40
  porpoise, 171
  rat, 40, 124
  sabre-toothed tiger, 64
  salamander, 92
  'sardine butterfly', 40
  'saurian', the, 107, 118–19
  scorpion, 1–3, 19, 174
  sloth, 94
  snake, 159, 168
  tadpole, 111
  tarantula, 169
  toad, 124
  Ungerziefer, 7–8
  worm, 48, 124
anthropocentrism, 9, 14, 16, 39–40, 73, 105
  anti-anthropocentrism, 14–15
anthropology, 11, 12, 30, 31, 62, 85, 86, 94, 112, 114, 119
anthropomorphism, 14, 39
anti-Semitism, 15, 93, 97, 123
Apollinaire, Guillaume, 143
Arendt, Hannah, 6
Aristotle, 79
Armstrong, Philip, 15
Armstrong, Tim, 16, 27
Arp, Hans, 141, 146, 147–8
Arson, 153
Artaud, Antonin, 3, 169
Ashton, E. B., 94
astrology, 2
avant-gardes
  Anglo-European, 93, 155
  European, 6
  Franco-American, 37
  'happy avant-garde', the, 134, 172
  parodies of, 29

Baader, Franz von, 104
Bachelard, Gaston, 150
Baker, Steve, 15
Balakian, Anna, 34
Ball, Hugo, 123
Barkan, Elazer, 94
Barker, George, 171
Barnes, Djuna, 3
Baron, Scarlett, 56, 71, 74
Barr, Alfred H., 23–4, 25, 26, 43, 50, 169
  cultural imperialism of, 27
  pedagogy of, 31
Barrell, Joseph, 66
Barthes, Roland, 113
Bataille, Georges, 26, 31, 94, 159
  biological discourse of, 112
  'expenditure', 113, 131
  pineal writings of, 111–13

Bataille, Sylvia, 26
Baudelaire, Charles, 41
Bayonet, The, 2
Beach, Sylvia, 26
Beard, J., 109
Beckett, Samuel, 3, 57, 85, 86, 87n8, 120, 146
Beckett, Sylvia, 26
Béguin, Albert, 150
Bellow, Saul, 171–2
Benn, Gottfried, 16, 17–18, 92–3, 100, 170
  'After nihilism', 102
  and animal metaphors, 98–9
  biologism of, 95–6
  as deemed 'degenerate', 103
  'Diesterweg', 98
  'Eugenics I', 102
  'Expressionism', 102
  fascism of, 102–3
  Gehirne (Brains), 99
  influence of, 120–3
  Lyric Self, 101
  lyricism of, 97
  'Mind and body of future generations', 102
  'Monologue', 123–4
  placement in *transition*, 104
  'Poems', 124
  'Primal vision', 101
  pseudo-anthropological language of, 94, 98
  repudiation of literary establishment, 102
  'Songs', 99
  'The birthday', 100
  'The island', 99–100
  'The people and the writer', 102
  'The structure of the personality', 92, 94–5, 98, 100, 101–2, 103, 112, 120
  'Writing needs inner latitude', 102
Bennett, David, 16
Bennett, Wendell, 118
Bergson, Henri, 11, 27
Bernstein, Charles, 28
Bible
  Genesis, 43, 58
  Isaiah, 57, 84
  John, 56
  Luke, 2, 84
  Peter, 135
biocentrism, 14–15
biologism, 15, 17, 27, 31, 94, 125
biology
  ichthyology, 66–7
  'modern synthesis', the, 64
  palaeontology, 64–5
Birnbaum, Karl, 95, 96
Black Sun Press, 74
Blake, William, 172
BLAST, 5, 131
Blavatsky, Madame, 94

Bodkin, Maud, 149
Boillotat, Dorothy, 13, 47–50, 169
Borel, Petrus, 41
Bosch, Hieronymus, 30
Botar, Oliver A. I., 15
Botticelli, Sandro, 39
Bouguereau, William-Adolfe, 39
Bousquet, Joë, 146
Bowers, Paul, 56, 71
Bowler, Peter J., 63, 65
Bowles, Paul, 48
Boyle, Kay, 3, 146, 148, 156–8
Boyle, Robert H., 75, 78, 87
brains, 35, 37, 92–3, 99–100, 102, 124
    cranial theory, 96
    depth model, 97, 104, 122
    'middle', 115, 120, 121
    'reptilian', 95, 168
Brâncuşi, Constantin, 25, 26, 143
Braque, Georges, 136
Breton, André, 16, 25–6, 31, 33, 35, 38, 40, 41–3, 111
Breysig, Kurt, 95
Brion, Marcel, 100
Brooker, Peter, 5
Broom, 5
Bryher, Winifred, 44–5
Buñuel, Luis, 112
Burckhardt, Jacob Christoph, 11
Burnett, Whit, 29–30, 117–18
Bush, Ronald, 94

Cabanel, Alexandre, 39
Cable, Chester H., 149
Caetani di Bassiano, Princess Marguerite, 42
Caillois, Roger, 31, 50
Calarco, Matthew, 15
Campbell, Malcolm, 101
Camus, Albert, 26
capitalism, 10, 12
Carrefour Press, 41
Caws, Mary Ann, 5
Césaire, Aimé, 26
Chicago Evening Post, 45
Chicago Herald, 45
Chicago Tribune, 41, 42, 45, 151
Christianity, 1–2, 7, 10
    'Anti-Christ', 95
    Catholicism, 2
    Eucharist, 43
    Holy Trinity, 131
    ichthus, 56
    Jesus Christ, 135
    Lucifer, 150
    Missale Romanum, 10
    Noah's ark, 135
    transubstantiation, 79
    see also Bible

Cole, Lori, 6
Coleman, Emily Holmes, 41, 146
Colum, Mary, 17, 150
Commerce, 3, 42, 54n85
Connor, Steve, 15
Contact: An American Quarterly Review, 38
Cope, Edward Drinker, 64–5, 73
Crane, Hart, 3, 169
Cravan, Arthur, 26
Criterion, The, 6
Crosby, Caresse, 26, 74
Crosby, Harry, 26, 74, 167–8, 170
Cubism, 24–5
Cushing, Harvey, 111
Cuvier, Georges, 66

Dacqué, Edgar, 95, 103–4
Dada, 8, 16, 25, 26, 36, 113
Daily Worker, 42
Dalí, Salvador, 112
Darwin, Charles, 14, 63–4, 71, 84, 170
Darwinism
    'eclipse' of, 64
    post-Darwinism, 14
    social Darwinism, 12, 17, 63, 80, 97
    'survival of the fittest', 74
Daumal, René, 113
Davies, Hugh Sykes, 27
Deleuze, Gilles, 15, 113
Delteil, Joseph, 100
Dementia Praecox, 1–2
denazification, 156, 171
Derrida, Jacques, 6, 15
Descartes, René, 37, 92, 99, 112
Desnos, Robert, 39, 46–7, 135, 139
Desoille, Robert, 150
Deutsch, Babette, 152, 161
Dial, The, 3, 18, 72
Die Aktion, 99
Die neue Rundschau, 92
Die Wandlung, 156
Dilthey, Wilhelm, 96
Döblin, Alfred, 3, 101
Documents, 3, 6, 31, 111, 114, 131
Driesch, Hans, 95
Duchamp, Marcel, 26
Dugès, Antoine, 109
Duthuit, Georges, 111

Edel, Leon, 174
Egyptian mythology, 57
Einstein, Carl, 6, 9–10, 100, 111
Eliot, T. S., 3, 6, 12, 93, 95, 133
Éluard, Paul, 8–9, 10, 136, 139–40, 154
Emminghaus, Herman, 97
Encyclopaedia Britannica, 71, 72–3
endocrinology, 27, 96, 109–10, 173; *see also* pineal cytology

INDEX

Ernst, Max, 3, 14, 131, 146
ethnographic writing, 12, 118
eugenics, 17, 62–3, 70, 97
evolution theory
    adaptation, 63, 80
    natural selection, 64, 79–80, 81
    racialised, 70, 71
    variation, 73, 80
    see also Darwinism; orthogenesis
Examiner, The, 45
Expressionism, 10, 25, 92, 98, 101, 123, 136–7

fable, 16, 48, 86, 94–5, 115, 142
Fargue, Léon-Paul, 16, 36–7, 52n55, 53n60
fascism, 11–12, 22n64, 99, 102, 115, 117, 123, 151, 154, 155, 170
    anti-fascism, 6, 95, 125
    proto-fascism, 17, 93, 104, 105
Fauvism, 25
Fäy, Bernard, 18, 22n64, 93
Fechner, G. T., 150
Ferber, Michael, 132, 133
Finney, Michael, 7
First World War, 1, 11, 27, 93, 112, 139
Ford, Charles Henri, 38, 146
Ford, Ford Madox, 3, 161
Ford, Hugh, 37
Fordham, Finn, 79, 80, 81
Forum and Century, 17, 45
Foster, Hal, 33–4
Foucault, Michel, 113
Fraenkel, Michael, 41, 123
Frank, Claudine, 113
Frazer, James, 31
Freud, Sigmund, 11, 31, 95, 97
Frisch, Karl Von, 110
Frobenius, Leo, 12
Frost, Robert, 158, 166n86
Fry, Roger, 12
Fuertes, Louis Agassiz, 130
Futurism, 16

Gabo, Naum, 25
Gaddis, William, 172–3
Galton, Francis, 62, 64, 76
Galton Society, 70
Garlin, Sender, 38
Gaugin, Paul, 25
Gazette des Beau-Arts, 30
gender, 157, 167–8
geological periods
    Jurassic, 44
    Mesozoic, 18, 96, 99, 108
    Palaeozoic, 13, 120
    Precambrian, 43, 82
    Quaternary, 98–9

germplasm, 76
Giacometti, Alberto, 26
Giedon-Welcker, Carola, 12
Gilbert, Stuart, 3, 33, 132–3, 168, 169
Gilbert-Lecomte, Roger, 94, 113–14
Goethe, Johann Wolfgang von, 25, 98
Gold, Michael, 7
Goldman, Jane, 7
Golffing, Francis, 102
Goll, Ivan, 100, 104
Good, Thomas, 158–60
Gotham Book Mart, 27
Gould, Stephen Jay, 55, 64
Grass, Delphine, 6
Greco, El, 30
Gregory, William K., 65–7, 70, 71, 73
Griffin, Roger, 11–12
Grünewald, Matthias, 30
Guattari, Félix, 15
Guest, Barbara, 18–19

Haddon, Alfred C., 62
Haeckel, Ernst, 56, 95
Haldane, J. B. S., 13, 27, 72
Hamburger, Michael, 95
Harper's Bazaar, 26
Hatch, David Allen, 6
Haughton, Hugh, 93, 161
Hayes, C., 11
Hayes, Edward, 73
Heap, Jane, 3
Heidegger, Martin, 103
Hemingway, Ernest, 58
Heym, Georg, 101
Hinduism, 13
Hitler, 88, 102, 103, 113, 123, 124, 153
Hoffman, Leigh, 42–3
Hofmann, Michael, 103
Hogan, William, 26
Hölderlin, Friedrich, 146
Holme, H. Christopher, 49
Holz, Arno, 100, 137
Hooker, Joseph Dalton, 84
Hortega, Pío del Río, 110
Huebner, F. M., 118–19
Huebner, Friedrich Marcus, 13
Hull, R. F. C., 11
Hulle, Dirk Van, 25
human sovereignty, 15
humanism, 105, 151
    anti-humanism, 16
Hutt, G. A., 93, 104
Huxley, Aldous, 18
Huxley, Julian S., 62, 64, 74

Icke, David, 95
Impressionism, 24
International Congress of Eugenics, 70

International Surrealist Bulletin, 27
involution, 108–9
Isherwood, Christopher, 85

Jack, Peter Monro, 145
Jackson, John Hughlings, 97
Janet, Pierre, 97
Jaspers, Karl, 119
Jay, Martin, 112
jazz, 29, 100
Jeffers, Robinson, 46
Jennings, H. S., 27
Jewell, Edward Alden, 17
Johannsen, Wilhelm, 95
Jolas, Eugene
  anti-fascism of, 6, 95, 124–5
  'Babelism' of, 5
  break with Gottfried Benn, 124
  break with Surrealism, 16, 152
  and faith, 2, 160–1
  idealism of, 6–7, 18, 102, 105, 131, 134, 141, 151, 171
  multilingualism of, 2–3, 6
  post-war work of, 156
  romanticism of, 18–19
  WORKS
  'Across Frontiers', 149; 'Almanach', 141–2; 'Construction of the enigma', 142–3; 'Crisis of Man', 102; 'Daily graphic', 142; 'Document', 145; 'Egriffenheit', 119; 'Epivocables of 3', 133; 'Frontier-poem', 132, 143; 'Inquiry about the malady of language', 104; 'Inquiry among European writers into the spirit of America', 100–1; 'Landscapes', 139; 'Literature and the new man', 16; 'Logos', 46; *Man from Babel*, 2, 5, 103, 162; 'Migration 1', 144–5; 'Migration', 143; 'Monologue', 140–1; 'Nocturnes', 139; 'On the quest', 1, 141; 'Paramyths from a dreambook', 116; 'Prolegomenon', 150; *Secession in Astropolis*, 105; 'Suggestions for a new magic', 1; *The Language of Night*, 104–5, 153; 'The primal personality', 103–4; 'The third eye: ascension to the tremendum', 108, 114; 'Transmutation vertigraliste', 107–8; 'Twilight of the horizontal age', 105; *Vertigralist Pamphlet*, 149; 'White romanticism', 138; 'Why do Americans live in Europe?', 41; *Vertical: A Year-Book for Romantic Mystic Ascensions*, 124
Jolas, Eugene et al., 'Poetry is vertical', 146
Jolas, Maria, 3, 5, 29, 37, 46, 48, 103, 174
Joyce, James, 3, 5, 16, 120, 130, 169
  Dubliners, 78
  elucidations of, 119
  and evolution theory, 79
  excremental aesthetics of, 77–9, 81
  and filth, 75–7
  Finnegans Wake, 17, 55, 58–9, 71–2, 75, 83, 171–2
  genetic approaches to, 80
  and Irish mythology, 59
  notebooks of, 71–2
  and racialised language, 82–3
  as responsive to critics, 55
  sigla, 58–59
  and social Darwinism, 83
  Ulysses, 71, 74, 75, 78
  'Work in Progress', 17, 55, 74, 85–7, 169–70
  and the writing scene, 82
Jung, Carl Gustav, 7, 10, 11, 13, 96

Kafka, Franz, 3, 7, 14, 16, 159
Kandinsky, Wassily, 25, 27, 50
Kant, Immanuel, 96, 140
Kantor, Sybil, 27
Kelbert, Eugenia, 6
Kenmore, Dallas, 149
Kiefer, Klaus H., 6
Kindley, Evan, 7
Klages, Ludwig, 15, 103
Klee, Paul, 27, 57, 60–2
Kling, Joseph, 5
Klossowski, Pierre, 112
Knight, William F. Jackson, 149
Kohn, Hans, 11
Kolocotroni, Vassiliki, 37
Kraeplin, Emil, 97
Kramer, Andreas, 5, 18, 93, 104, 151, 156
Kraus, Friedrich, 96
Krell, David, 109
Kretshmer, Ernst, 95
Kreymborg, Alfred, 5
Kristeva, Julia, 113
Kronfeld, Arthur, 95

Lacan, Jacques, 26
Lacoue-Labarthe, Philippe, 132
Lamarck, Jean-Baptiste, 15
  neo-Lamarckism, 63, 72–3, 170; *see also* orthogenesis
Landuyt, Ingeborg, 58, 62
language, 'malady' of, 5, 7, 94, 104
Larbaud, Valery, 26
Larson, Edward, 70
Lasker-Schüler, Else, 95, 135, 139
Latimer, Margaret, 45
Laughlin, James, 120, 167, 171
Lautréamont, Comte de, 33–5, 121, 169
Lawrence, D. H., 14
Lazarus, Moritz, 97
Le grand jeu, 113–14

INDEX

Le moment, 152
Lehbert, Margaret, 137
Leidy, Joseph, 28
Leiris, Michel, 12, 26, 111
Lerner, Aaron, 111
Les Nouvelles littéraires, 153
Lévi-Strauss, Claude, 114
Levin, Harry, 59
Lévy-Bruhl, Lucien, 11, 12, 103, 114
Lewis, Wyndham, 5, 34, 55
Lhote, André, 30–1, 33, 47
Linnaeus, Carolus, 29
Linnean Society, 73
Listener, The, 5
Little Review, The, 3, 37
Loeb, Harold, 5
Logos, 56, 76, 93, 103, 107, 108, 125, 135, 140, 146, 161
Lombroso, Cesare, 62
Louisville KY Times, 151
Loving, Pierre, 41
Lowenfels, Walter, 41–2

McAlmon, Robert, 41
McCord, Carey Pratt, 110–11
McGreevy, Thomas, 147
McHugh, Roland, 58, 59, 77, 78, 79, 81, 83, 84
MacLeish, Archibald, 39–40, 43
Macleod, Glen, 25
McMillan, Dougald, 5, 6, 92, 103, 124, 156
Mailer, Norman, 168
Malevich, Kazimir, 25
Malraux, André, 26
Mann, Klaus, 103
Mansanti, Céline, 6, 7, 12, 19
Mantell, Gideon, 96
Marinetti, F. T., 103; *see also* Futurism
Marquis, Alice Goldfarb, 26
Marxism, 113, 117
Masson, André, 7, 25, 26, 30, 161–2, 171
Masson, Rose, 26
Matisse, Henri, 25
Matthew, William Diller, 73
Matthias, Blanche, 45–6
melatonin, 111
Mendel, Gregor, 62, 80
mental ill health, 2, 97, 150
Mercanton, Jacques, 152–3
Merleau-Ponty, Maurice, 26
microbiology, 27, 28
Middleton, Christopher, 95, 124
Miller, Henry, 13, 95, 115, 121–3, 154, 161, 168, 170, 171
Miller, Tyrus, 7, 26, 85–6
Milne-Edwards, H. M., 109
Minet, Pierre, 141

Minotaure, 38
Miró, Jean, 25, 27
Mitchell, Peter Chalmers, 72–3
modernism
  and animal studies, 14–16
  and canonicity, 131
  'the "dark" side of', 114, 125
  high modernism, 3
  late modernism, 85–6, 161
  and multiculturalism, 107–8
  museumification of, 23–7
  transatlantic, 2–3, 8, 93, 173
modernist magazines studies, 5–7
modernity
  bourgeois, 43, 94, 111, 113
  corruption of, 31, 104–5
Mondrian, Piet, 24
Monk, Craig, 6
Monnier, Adrienne, 26
Moore, Marianne, 3
Morley, Patricia, 59
Moss, David, 171
Mundan, Lothar, 95, 115, 117
Munson, Gorham, 104
Museum of Modern Art, 17, 23, 25, 26, 43, 169
mythos, 12, 119, 131, 141, 146, 156, 168

Nancy, Jean-Luc, 113, 132
Nation, The, 41
National Socialism *see* Nazi Germany
nationalism, 11–12, 16–17, 93, 100, 115, 170
Natural History, 66
Nazi book burning, 124
Nazi Germany, 70, 93, 102, 105, 123, 158, 159
Nazi ideology, 11, 14, 18, 99, 122, 153; *see also* fascism
Nazi 'paganism', 93
Needham, Joseph, 27
New Directions, 171
New Left Review, 93
New Masses, 6, 7, 151
New Republic, 148
New York Herald, 41, 151
New York Herald Tribune, 149, 152
New York Times, 41, 145
Niedecker, Lorine, 173, 174n19
Nietzsche, Friedrich, 11, 14, 15, 97, 98, 100, 102
Noll, Marcel, 48
nomos, 11–12
Norris, Margot, 14–15
North, Michael, 6
Nouvelle revue française, 30
Novalis (Georg Philipp Friedrich von Hardenberg), 138, 150

INDEX

O'Keefe Georgia, 45
Objectivism, 173, 174n19
Ogden, C. K., 74, 104
Olson, Charles, 161
Oparin, Alexander, 13, 44
orthogenesis, 64–5, 67, 70, 72–3, 81, 86;
see also evolution theory
Orwell, George, 122
Osborn, Henry Fairfield, 64–5, 67, 70, 72, 73, 75
Ovid, 77

Pagan, The, 5
Pagany, 45
Pailthorpe, Grace, 13–14
Paris Review, 122
Parks, Jason, 6
Partisan Review, 6, 38
Paul, Elliot, 1, 3, 8, 29, 48, 100
Pearson, Karl, 62
Pearson, Norman Holmes, 149–50
Pelorson, Georges, 18, 147, 153–6, 161, 170–1
Penfield, Wilder, 110
Péret, Benjamin, 40–1
Perlès, Alfred, 122
Perloff, Marjorie, 6, 131
personality, 95–6
Pevsner, Antoine, 24
Phillips, William, 38
Picabia, Francis, 26
Picasso, Pablo, 12, 111
pineal cytology, 108–11
pineal eye
   creative uses of, 114, 115–16
   history of, 92–3, 103
   visual art of, 121–2; see also third eye
pineal gland, 93, 96–9, 109–11, 113
Platt, Len, 56, 63, 72, 80
Poe, Edgar Allan, 150
Poetry, 45
Pound, Ezra, 3, 6, 93
Prairie, 45
preformation, 40
prehistoric man, 71–2
primitivism, 10, 12, 13, 94–5, 104, 114–15, 117–18, 124, 153, 170
primordial gesture, the, 17
primordial image, 11
'primordial rhythms', 31, 33
primordial sea, 34–5, 93, 169
primordial soup, 13, 44
'primordialist' nationalism, 11–12
protoplasm, 13, 31, 44, 50, 122, 124, 169
protozoic, the, 16, 25, 50, 82
   protozoic ooze, 144

Providence RI Journal, 151
Putnam, Samuel, 26

Queneau, Raymond, 154

Rabaté, Jean-Michel, 6, 131, 133, 134, 172
racial slurs, 82–3
Rahv, Philip, 7, 38, 151–2
Rainger, Ronald, 66
Rao, Raja, 13
Ray, Man, 26, 47
Ray, Susan, 100
Read, Herbert, 33
Recht, Charles, 13
Redon, Odilon, 25
Reichel, Hans, 121–2
Reid, Christopher, 133
Remy, Michael, 13
Reverdy, Pierre, 26, 38–9, 42
Revolution of the Word, the, 3–4, 7, 16, 18–19, 33, 37, 49, 93, 103, 131, 151, 168, 171; see also transition
Ribemont-Dessaignes, Georges, 138, 163n29
Ribot, Théodule-Armand, 97
Richards, David, 12
Riding, Laura, 169
Rimbaud, Arthur, 16, 33
Rochelle, Pierre Drieu La, 18, 22n64
Roditi, Édouard, 95, 118
Rodker, John, 34
Rohman, Carrie, 15–16
romanticism, 131, 142, 146–7
   as exhausted, 157–8, 159–60, 161
   German romanticism, 133, 136, 138, 170
   Jena romantics, 132
   Romantic movement, 41
Romer, Alfred, 71
Root, Waverly, 151
Roselhof, August Johann Rösel, 28
Rosenbaum, Susan, 26
Rottenberg, Johanna Gertrude, 94
Rudin, Ernst, 97
Rumold, Rainer, 5, 6, 7, 11, 12, 18, 93, 104, 107, 111, 124–5, 151, 156
Rumrich, Diana, 105
Ruse, Michael, 64, 70
Rychner, Max, 100

Sage, Robert, 3, 18
Sartre, Jean-Paul, 26
Schaeffer, Asa A., 28
Schapiro, Meyer, 27–8, 33
Scheerbart, Paul, 147
Schilder, Paul, 95
Schiller, Francis, 111
schizo-affective disorder, 1
Schuwer, Camille, 154
Schwartz, Delmore, 171–2

INDEX

Schwitters, Kurt, 8, 10, 123
Scientific Monthly, 66
Second World War, 19, 26, 158, 171
Shakespeare, William, 123
shell shock, 139
Shipman, Evan, 23, 30
Simmel, Georg, 15
Skira, Albert, 38
Smith, Andrew D., 11
Solveen, Henri, 3, 141
Sontag, Susan, 113
Soupault, Philippe, 161
spirituality, 9, 41, 100, 131, 141, 143–4, 148, 150, 152
Stein, Gertrude, 3, 16, 25, 120, 169
Steloff, Frances, 27, 171
Stillmark, Alexander, 137
Storch, Alfred, 95
Story, 29
Stravinsky, Igor, 18
Studnička, F. K., 110
subjectivity, 85–6
Sullivan, J. W. N., 74
Surrealism, 12, 16, 25–6, 136, 138, 148
    American suspicion of, 41
    anglophone, 33, 37, 39, 49
    automatic writing, 30, 33, 40, 151–2
    Bretonian influence of, 42
    dissident, 31, 111–14
    influence on American literature, 37–44
    London exhibition of, 27
    second movement of, 38
Surrealist image, the, 38–9, 42–3
Sweeney, James Johnson, 3, 19, 26, 147, 171
Symbolism, 150

Tanguy, Yves, 3, 31–2, 50
Tashjian, Dickran, 25–6, 38
Taylor-Batty, Juliette, 6
teleology, 65, 66, 74, 82, 85
Thacker, Andrew, 5
Thayer, Scofield, 3, 72
third eye, 94, 98, 103, 104, 105, 107, 108, 113–15, 119, 123; *see also* pineal eye
This Quarter, 45, 58
Thomas, Dylan, 120
Tindall, William York, 59
totalitarianism, 113, 114, 119–20, 124, 160
totemism, 1, 15, 59, 86, 95, 132, 134, 142, 148, 156, 170
Trakl, Georg, 137–8, 139

transition
    anachronism of, 173
    as apolitical, 156
    conservatism of, 6, 128n79
    distribution of, 27
    ethnographic content of, 12
    Jungian bent of, 11, 16
    mockery of, 1, 7, 17–18, 93
    obscurity of, 3
    patronage of, 168
    reception of, 151–3
    sales of, 51n19
    scholarship, 6–7
    'vertigralism', 105, 107–8, 115, 133, 149, 152, 170
    see also Revolution of the Word, the
Twentieth Century Verse, 171
Tyler, Parker, 38
Tzara, Tristan, 35–7, 100

Untermeyer, Louis, 2

Vail, Laurence, 104
Vailland, Roger, 33, 35, 113
View, 38, 153
Virchow, Rudolf, 96
vitalism, 27, 73, 75, 76, 81, 95, 102, 108
Vogel, Lucien, 26
Vogue, 26
Volontés, 154

Wahl, Jean, 26, 112
Walsh, Denis, 82
Warren, Lansing, 41
Weaver, Harriet, 75, 80
Webster, Harvey C., 151
Weldon, W. F. R., 62
Wheeler, Linda, 13
Whitman, Walt, 122, 150
Whitworth, Michael, 85
Wilde, Alan, 85
Wilde, Oscar, 157
Williams, Wendy, 13
Williams, William Carlos, 7, 38, 40, 120–1, 170
Wilson, Leigh, 6
Wolfe, Cary, 15
Woolf, Virginia, 58
Wright, Richard, 26

Yeats, W. B., 133

Zukofsky, Louis, 121, 173
Zweig, Stefan, 160, 166n93

EU representative:
Easy Access System Europe
Mustamäe tee 50, 10621 Tallinn, Estonia
Gpsr.requests@easproject.com

www.ingramcontent.com/pod-product-compliance
Lightning Source LLC
Chambersburg PA
CBHW070353240426
43671CB00013BA/2484